# THE LAST OUTFITTING STATION ON THE MISSOURI RIVER

# PRAISE FOR THE LAST OUTFITTING STATION ON THE MISSOURI RIVER

"For those interested in American Western Migration Trail History, *The Last Outfitting Station on the Missouri River* is a compelling must-read! Insightfully preserved resourceful information; heartfelt diary quotations bring together a much neglected study of the Mormon Trail system during the years of 1864 and 1866 which saw many of the faithful enjoy and suffer from much of the same conditions of other trails, including the Brigham Young led Vanguard Company of 1847. I heartily endorse this book and the years of dedicated research of Erick Wadsworth."

— GARY HARLO CLAYTON (GREAT-GREAT GRANDSON OF WILLIAM CLAYTON) DONIPHAN, NE. SEMI-RETIRED SALES CAREER. FOREVER A STUDENT OF THE TRAILS

"Wadsworth brings a solidly documented clarity and understanding to the 1864-66 period when pious Mormons shared the Nebraska City-Fort Kearny Cut-Off with Russell, Majors, and Waddell's profane bullwhackers. This book clearly belongs on the shelf of every trails historian for its perspective on this little studied period of westward migration."

— HARLAN SEYFER-TRAIL BOSS, NEBRASKA CHAPTER OF THE OREGON-CALIFORNIA TRAILS ASSOCIATION

"In 1997 newspaper and television accounts created interest for the sesquicentennial celebration of the North Platte route of the original Mormon Trail. I led a team that created color maps of the original Trail, and a grade school packet entitled "Walk through Nebraska," which was presented to over 1,400 students. As we researched this initial trail, it became apparent that other trail sites within Nebraska were gaining interest. Ancestry, town development and western lore, were driving desire for site specific trail marking and preservation.

Other than a few books written concerning freighting across the Mid-West, Erick Wadsworth stands virtually alone in this visually and meticulously written reference work. It is arguably the most romantic and less known of the trails, waiting to be discovered by Trail-Rut enthusiasts and serious historic researchers. As I read *The Last Outfitting Station on the Missouri River*, I traveled it!"

— R. VAL RASMUSSEN, NEBRASKA MORMON TRAILS ASSOCIATION (NMTA) EDUCATIONAL CHAIRMAN, CACHE JCT. UTAH

# THE LAST OUTFITTING STATION ON THE MISSOURI RIVER

1864 TO 1866 WYOMING, NT & THE NEBRASKA CITY CUT-OFF TRAIL

## ERICK WADSWORTH

Trail Publishing

Copyright © 2019 by Erick Wadsworth

Cover Copyright © 2019

Cover Design by Shandy Vogt

Front and Back cover photos courtesy of the Church History Library, Salt Lake City, UT.

Editing and Formatting: Stacey Smekofske EditsByStacey.com

Special permissions have been granted for the photos and maps contained within this book.

All rights reserved.

No part of this book may be reproduced in any form or by any electronic or mechanical means, including information storage and retrieval systems, without written permission from the author, except for the use of brief quotations in a book review.

ISBN: 978-1-7334717-0-1

Published by Trail Publishing

*I dedicate this book to my wife Marilyn and our family.
These pages are an expression of my love for you.*

# CONTENTS

| | |
|---|---|
| *Maps of the Nebraska City Cut-off Trail* | xiii |
| *Preface* | xv |
| 1. The Gathering Begins | 1 |
| 2. Winter Quarters, Growth, Troubles, Down and Back Trains | 19 |
| 3. Wyoming, Nebraska Territory selected as an Outfitting Station 1864 | 38 |
| 4. The Nebraska City Cut-off Trail | 51 |
| 5. The First Wagon Trains of 1864 | 65 |
| 6. Additional Wagon Trains Head West During 1864 | 80 |
| 7. Migration to Zion 1865 | 99 |
| 8. Formation of the 1866 Down and Back Church Trains | 119 |
| 9. The Journey East | 127 |
| 10. Leaving the Homeland Behind | 132 |
| 11. The Thousand Mile trek to the Great Basin Begins | 142 |
| 12. Travels Across Nebraska, Wyoming and on to Zion | 149 |
| 13. The Cholera Train from Sanpete County | 157 |
| 14. Arza Hinckley and the Rescue Train of 1866 | 168 |
| 15. Wrapping Up | 177 |
| *Acknowledgments* | 189 |
| *Appendix* | 191 |
| *Notes* | 203 |
| *Bibliography* | 233 |
| *Index* | 263 |
| *About the Author* | 287 |

"Years from now your grandchildren will tell with amazement stories of your choices, which changed their lives. You will be called their pioneers."

— Bonnie D. Parkin, April 1997, General Young Women Meeting, "Finding Faith in Every Footstep"

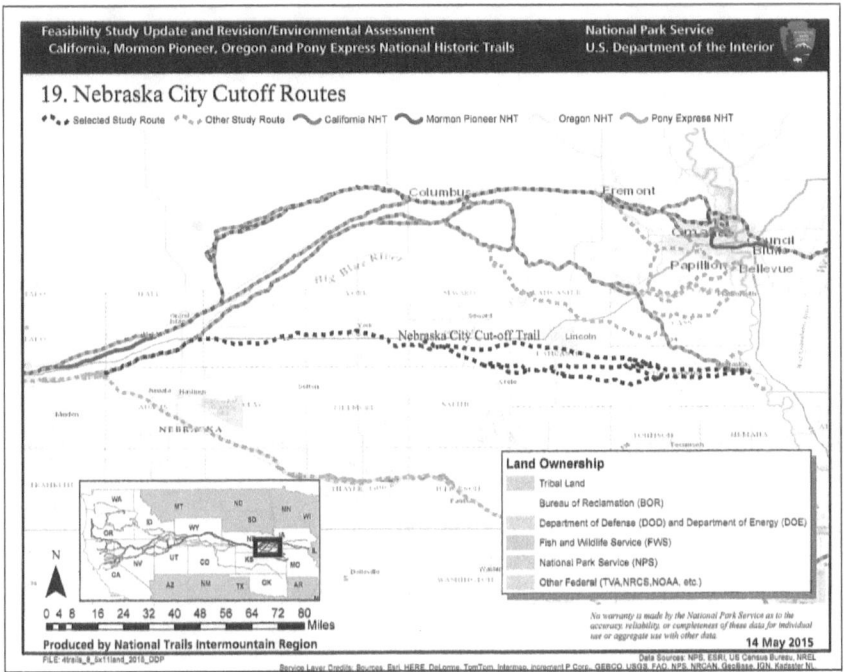

Courtesy of the National Park Service. This map is a draft indicating possible routes of the Nebraska City Cut-off Trail from Nebraska City, Nebraska Territory to the merging point with the Oxbow Trail. The blending of the two trails occurs near the current site of Beaver Crossing, Nebraska. Author is responsible for labeling the Cut-off Trail on the map.

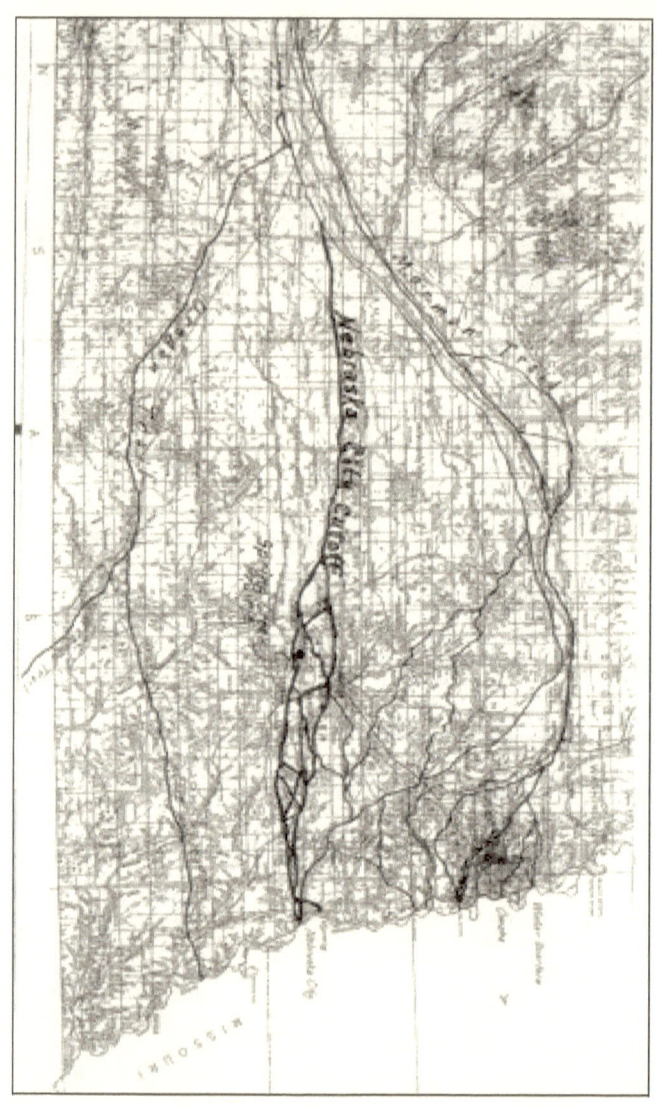

Courtesy of David Murphy of the Nebraska State Historical Society. Mr. Murphy shows in additional detail the evolving alignments of the Trail. A possible route from Wyoming, Nebraska Territory to the Cut-off Trail is indicated on this particular map. Reference should be made to "D. Murphy files, Nebraska Historical Society".

# PREFACE

The gathering of members of The Church of Jesus Christ of Latter-day Saints to a specific geographic location began in 1830 and continued until the end of the nineteenth century. By the late 1800s, situations slowed and ultimately halted the foreign immigration for the church. Multiple books and numerous articles have been written about the early migrations—particularly from the vanguard wagon train of 1847 to the tragic Martin-Willie handcart companies. Their decision to travel to Utah Territory late in the 1856 immigration year proved fateful. However, following the 1856 immigration, little has been written. Yet, those who traveled during the later migration years experienced similar joy, heartache, and sadly death just like their predecessors. The migration years of the 1860s are rich with stories that help us gain a better understanding of our own history.

Because many of the migrating pioneers began their journey in Europe, details of their ocean voyage, rail and river boat journey from New York City to Wyoming, Nebraska Territory (NT) are shared. The walking migrations in this book began in the sleepy village of Wyoming, NT. A gentleman named Jacob Dawson founded the town during the mid-1850s, but like so many other early settlements on the western frontier vanished into oblivion. In early 1864, Joseph A. Young, son of Brigham Young, and Joseph W. Young, nephew of Brigham, traveled to eastern NT to determine if the church's outfitting station should remain in Florence (near Omaha) or move further south to take advantage of the Nebraska City Cut-off Trail. This Trail shortened the distance to Fort Kearny over the other overland trails and saved the immigrants from several hazardous river crossings.

The stories contained in this book are meant to honor the thousands of courageous men, women and children who left families, home and friends to gather to their hoped for Zion in the west. The gathering, called for by leaders of The Church of Jesus Christ of Latter-day Saints, brought approximately 60 thousand members of the church to Utah Territory during the years between 1847 and 1868. In the years 1864 to 1866, over 7,000 immigrants passed through Wyoming, NT and took the Nebraska City Cut-off Trail to Fort Kearny before continuing their long journey to Salt Lake City. The three years of emigration in this book represent over ten percent of the total overall migration for the church. Since this was a religious gathering, the first chapter provides background information about the church itself, and how the early gathering locations did not work as planned. Next, the slaying of Joseph Smith, the difficulty of succession in the fledgling church and the expulsion of citizens from Nauvoo are detailed, followed by the establishment of Winter Quarters, the western migration, and early years in Utah. Wyoming, NT, and the Nebraska City Cut-off Trail are discussed in detail. The next chapters offer remarkable stories from the lives of those who followed the directive to gather to Utah Territory.

One can experience sailing across the Atlantic Ocean through the diaries and remembrances of these amazing immigrants. The difficulties faced during the train ride from the east coast to the central portion of our country are sensed through the stories contained herein. Through their accounts, the trek across the plains and mountains of this country come alive. Every human emotion imaginable was experienced during the days, weeks, and months on the trail. Life on the trail during the 1860s comprised birth, marriage, prayer, music, death, burial, arguments, gunfights, and battles with a group of Native Americans. After arriving in Utah Territory some settlers experienced disappointment with polygamy, Brigham Young, or the shortcomings of others and left for different parts of the country. However, the vast majority remained and faced the challenges of living in an unwelcoming geographic area with different cultural norms and a new religion. What follows is their story.

1
---

## THE GATHERING BEGINS

Religious, secular, and forced migrations have been a part of the world's history since time began. Moses led the Children of Israel out of Egypt. The Huguenots fled France during a series of religious persecutions. Between 1629 and 1640, thousands of Puritans left England for what would later become the United States. Multitudes of Native Americans were removed by force from their ancestral lands to make room for settlers. During the years of slavery, between 9.4 and 12 million Africans were forcibly removed from their homes and brought to the Americas. To fully appreciate the religious migration of those who belonged to The Church of Jesus Christ of Latter-day Saints from 1864 to 1866, one should understand the beginnings of this American religion. Almost three hundred years after the Reformation first began in Europe, an individual was born in New England who profoundly impacted Christianity—first in the United States and later throughout the world. Joseph Smith was born 23 December 1805 at Sharon, Windsor County, Vermont. Joseph was the fourth of ten children born to Joseph Smith Sr. and Lucy Mack Smith.[1] Three consecutive years of crop failure and a poor business choice caused the Smith family to move several times during Joseph's early years.[2] Eventually the family arrived near Palmyra, New York which is a small town located in western New York State. At the time of the move to the Palmyra area, Joseph was ten years old, placing the Smith family in western New York sometime in 1815 or early 1816.[3]

During the early part of the nineteenth century, certain regions in the United States were consumed by revival fever. The religious intensity caused such an upheaval that historians later coined the name "Burned-over District" to describe the passion with which different denominations and preachers sought converts.[4] Camp meetings offered opportunities for preachers to gain adherents, pitting preacher against preacher battling for new converts. This religious renaissance, or Second Great Awakening, was strong in western New York from Lake Ontario to the Adirondack Mountains.[5] As noted earlier, Joseph Smith and his family lived in Palmyra at the time, and the religious revivalism was extremely strong in the region. In writing about the situation later in life, Smith declared he became confused by the intensity of fighting among the different religious movements. The core question confronting Smith during this tumultuous time was, "Who of all these parties are right; or, are they wrong together?"[6]

As Joseph struggled with his religious impasse, he came across a passage of scripture, in the Book of James, found in the New Testament, which directed him to seek God in prayer. For all the confusion in Joseph's mind, he had yet to pray vocally. He concluded prayer was his next step, so he retired to a grove of trees near the Smith family home. Once he found himself alone, he began to earnestly pray to God.[7] The year was 1820, and Joseph Smith was fourteen years of age. Young Smith stated his prayer brought a vision of God and Jesus Christ.[8] Smith wrote the following about his experience, "When the light rested upon me I saw two personages, whose brightness and glory defy all description, standing above me in the air." Joseph asked the personages which church he should join. The reply was to join none of the existing churches.[9] As can be expected, when young Mr. Smith related his encounter to others, he experienced a great deal of prejudice and persecution. He was astonished that a young man, who was poor by worldly standards and unacquainted with the world, could experience such negative responses from men of high moral standing in his community.[10]

## The Book of Mormon

For the next three years, Joseph stated he went about his daily activities and experienced no further heavenly visitations. In writing about his early life experiences, Joseph wrote that on 21 September 1823 he experienced a visit from an angel. Joseph had retired for the night to his bed, and he prayed to God for forgiveness of his "sins and follies." During his prayer a light began appearing in his room and grew in intensity until it was "lighter than at noonday." A personage appeared and introduced himself as Moroni. Smith's account continues with the angelic visitor telling Joseph that, "God had a great work for me to do; and that my name should be had for good and evil among all nations, kindreds, and tongues . . ."[11] The heavenly guest visited Joseph on three occasions during the night and one time the next day. Each time the angel delivered the same message. First, he told Mr. Smith a set of gold plates were deposited in a nearby hill that gave an account of some former inhabitants of the Americas. Next, the visitor quoted scripture from several books of the Bible. In conclusion, the messenger told Joseph that when the time came for him to retrieve the gold plates from the hill, he was not to show the plates to any person. Joseph related his experience to his father the next day and sought direction on how to proceed. His father told Joseph that this occurrence was from God and to proceed as directed by the angel.[12]

Once a year until 22 September 1827, Smith visited the hill where the plates were stored, when the same heavenly messenger, who had appeared to him in 1823, gave the plates to Joseph with a stern warning to guard the plates with vigilance. Smith quickly learned the reason for the firm warning to protect the plates. Regarding the efforts people would employee to steal the plates Joseph wrote:

---

I soon found out the reason why I had received such strict charges to

> keep them safe and why it was that the messenger had said that when I had done what was required at my hand, he would call for them. For no sooner was it known that I had them, that the most strenuous exertions were used to get them from me. Every stratagem that could be invented was resorted to for that purpose.[13]

Over the next several years, Joseph Smith protected the plates and kept them out of the hands of those who sought to steal them. As noted earlier, Smith was warned to show the plates to no other people. In due time, he was granted permission to show the plates to a total of eleven other men. In late June 1829, three men were shown the plates by Moroni, the same angelic messenger who appeared to Smith in 1823. In addition, eight other men saw and handled the plates near the Smith home in Palmyra Township.[14] Following the visitation of the angel to the first three witnesses, Joseph returned home. Regarding the others who verified the existence of the plates, Joseph's mother wrote the following words of her son: "Father, mother, you do not know how happy I am: for the Lord has now caused the plates to be shown to three more besides myself... I feel as if I was relieved of a burden which was almost too heavy for me to bear."[15] The Book of Mormon was first published in 1830.

**Organization of The Church of Jesus Christ of Latter-day Saints**

On 6 April 1830, Joseph Smith, along with six other men, organized The Church of Jesus Christ of Latter-day Saints at Fayette, Seneca, New York. The organizational meeting took place in the home of Peter Whitmer Senior, an early leader in the Church.[16] According to David Whitmer, approximately 50 members and six elders were present at this first official meeting of the new church.[17] During this semi-formal meeting, the six men who were involved in the actual organization were baptized, even though these men had been previously baptized. Smith recounted that before the church was officially organized, Joseph Smith and Oliver Cowdery had received a heavenly visitor while working on the translation of the gold plates. John the Baptist appeared to both Smith and Cowdery in May 1829, and he gave the two men the authority to baptize themselves and others. Accordingly, they baptized each other immediately following the visitation.[18] Shortly thereafter, Peter, James, and John, Apostles of the Savior in ancient times, appeared to Joseph and Oliver and conferred the authority to give the Gift of the Holy Ghost following baptism.[19] As the gathering on 6 April continued, those attending partook of the bread and wine for the sacrament and various individuals were ordained to specific responsibilities within the church.[20] Evidence indicates the organization of the church on 6 April was not necessarily formal, but was possibly organized as an unincorporated religious society—a "voluntary association of individuals or families . . . united for the purpose of having a common place of worship, and to provide a proper teacher to instruct them . . . and to administer the ordinances of the church"—not as a religious corporation.[21] The church was now organized, and the gathering began swiftly.

## Gathering to Kirtland, Ohio

Shortly after the establishment of the new church, Joseph Smith declared he received a revelation from God to travel to Ohio. Thus, in January 1831, just nine months following the organization of the church, Joseph Smith, his wife, and other friends began the journey to a small village named Kirtland, Lake, Ohio.[22] The call to migrate to Ohio came in December 1830. "Behold, I say unto you that it is not expedient in me that ye should translate any more until ye shall go to the Ohio, and this because of the enemy and for your sakes."[23] This directive to gather to Ohio was also meant for all members who were living in New York. Like Joseph Smith and Sidney Rigdon, the direction to gather was issued "unto the church," which meant every individual should move to Ohio.[24] One month later, members of the church received a revelation that told them about "a land of promise, a land flowing with milk and honey, upon which there shall be no curse when the Lord cometh." Concerning the land of promise, the revelation went on to state, "I will give it unto you for the land of your inheritance, if you seek it with all your hearts. And this shall be my covenant with you, you shall have it for the land of your inheritance, and for the inheritance of your children."[25] In June 1831, Joseph Smith and several key members of the church traveled to Jackson County, Missouri for the purpose of establishing Zion.[26] By August 1831, Zion, located twelve miles west of Independence, Missouri was dedicated for the gathering of the Saints.[27] The fledgling church, just over one year old, now had two centers of operation, Kirtland, Ohio and Jackson County, Missouri. Early members of the church believed the directive to migrate to specific locations was an edict from God and refusal to move could indicate a lack of faith.

Although Missouri was designated as Zion, Kirtland was the organizational center of the new church. Kirtland was a crucial location of the Church of Jesus Christ of Latter-day Saints from 1830 to 1838. Individuals and families flocked to Kirtland and surrounding areas. Many important divine manifestations were received in Kirtland. The ecclesiastical organization of the church began during the eight years Kirtland was utilized as a gathering place. Extensive missionary efforts were initiated in Kirtland, a temple was built, and a bank (which later failed) was established. Kirtland, Ohio was a critical component of the early church, and many positive results came from the Saints settling in the area. What began in 1830 as a place of refuge for early church members, bowed under the pressure of defection by church members, desertion by friends, a bank failure, and relentless lawsuits to force the abandonment of Kirtland as a gathering place.[28]

## Joseph Smith and Sidney Rigdon Escape Kirtland

By 1838, some of Joseph Smith's closest friends and confidants became dissatisfied with his leadership. The banking failure led some members to reject Joseph Smith as their religious leader. Nearly one-third of church leadership and over ten percent of the local church membership questioned Joseph's ability to lead. Some attempted to establish a church of their own and take over the Kirtland Temple. Oliver Cowdery, one of the three witnesses to the gold plates, was overwhelmed with devastating personal financial losses, which led him to privately disparage Joseph Smith. In addition, other residents of Kirtland continued to threaten and harass Smith and other Latter-day Saints.[29] To escape the threat of arrest and violence, Joseph Smith and Sidney Rigdon fled Kirtland on the night of 12 January 1838. The two rode for sixty miles before stopping to rest. The failed bank, abandonment of trusted friends, and an unremitting buildup of lawsuits seemed to leave little choice for the prophet. He decided that he must leave Kirtland to its own destiny.[30] Missouri was the next place to gather for members of the church. However, the prophet and his followers would find themselves as unwelcome guests.

**Gathering to Missouri**

Mentioned previously, the instruction to gather to Missouri was received after the church had been organized for only a few months. At the time, members of the church were counseled to move west. Missouri was on the borders of the United States. Independence, Missouri, where the Saints were directed to settle, was established in 1827. Originally the town bordered the Missouri River, and the site appeared excellent for landing river boats. Rather quickly, a number of merchants began supplying goods to the traders and farmers moving into the area. A one-story log courthouse was built, and the town began to grow. Only four years after the town was founded, in the early months of 1831, four men representing the newly organized church appeared on the "ungraded, ungraveled streets of the thriving frontier town."[31] A few months later, Joseph Smith and other church leaders traveled to Independence to build the first house in Kaw Township, which lay a few miles west of Independence. A site for a temple was dedicated, and hundreds of Saints began gathering to Jackson County, much to the displeasure of existing settlers. Church members brought a form of religious communitarianism, or consecration and stewardship, to the area. The new arrivals set up a mercantile business to dispose of excess products produced by the group. A printing press was established to print a religious periodical for the local members and also to print textbooks for the free school established by the community.[32]

. . .

## Friction Develops Between Members of the Church and Current Residents

In a rather short time, these new colonizers were expelled from Jackson County, but they found temporary refuge in Clay County. However, the citizens in Clay County and the LDS settlers both believed church members would be allowed back into Jackson County. When it became apparent that that the Saints would be remaining in Clay County, the citizens there held a mass meeting 29 June 1836 with the intent of requesting church members find another area to settle. Although the petition was more civilized than the one presented three years earlier by the angry group in Jackson County, the intent was the same. Members of this newly organized religion were not welcome to remain in Clay County long term. Suggestions were made about suitable locations to settle, and justifications were given for wanting the Saints to relocate. The request from the Clay County residents was made to church leaders, and three days later these demands were accepted. Church members also thanked the people of Clay County for their hospitality during the two-and-a-half-year stay.[33] Several church leaders sought out locations for the displaced Saints to settle. They found an area and filed claims for twenty eighty-acre parcels in an area northeast of Clay County.[34] John Corrill and John Murdock asked for permission from Ray County residents to migrate to the area—even though the settlement was in a non-county location. The local citizenry consented after the promise was made to create no settlements closer than six or eight miles of the northern boundary of Ray County.[35] When the Missouri legislature established Caldwell County, exclusively for LDS settlements, a six mile buffer zone was created between it and Ray County.[36] For a brief period it appeared as though church members would have a place to live.

The end of the church experience in Missouri came quickly. On 5 November 1838, General John B. Clark assembled all men, who were members of the church, at Far West and ordered them to form a line. Clark then called out the names of 56 men for arrest. The next day General Clark delivered a written statement to the settlers of Far West alleging that their leaders had entered into a treaty requiring them (church members) to sign over their property to pay for the "war" and expenses incurred.[37] February 1839 brought about the first large-scale evacuation of the Saints from Missouri to Illinois. Lucy Mack Smith, mother of Joseph Smith described the scene as the migration to Illinois was about to begin.

> The brethren were all driven in from the country. There was an acre of ground in front of our house, completely covered with beds, lying in the open sun, where families were compelled to sleep, exposed to all kinds of weather; these were the last who came into the city, and, as the houses were all full, they could not find a shelter. It was enough to make the heart ache to see the children, sick with colds, and crying around their mothers for food, whilst their parents were destitute of the means of making them comfortable.[38]

Church members were forced out of Missouri during the time their prophet was imprisoned in Liberty Jail. In addition, the evacuation took place during the inclement weather of winter. The exact number of church members who were driven from Missouri is unknown. Some approximations range as high as twelve to 15 thousand. Other estimates place the number of those displaced at about eight thousand.[39] Whatever the precise number, thousands of Latter-day Saints were heading east for Illinois. The gathering in Missouri, which began with so much promise, was now ending with a forced expulsion. In less than nine years, many Saints who had left their original homes and gathered to both Kirtland, Ohio and Missouri, were now driven to a new gathering place. The future of the church appeared bleak. Multiple moves in less than nine years, losing key leadership, inaction by the government, and the imprisonment of their prophet-leader created a somber atmosphere for many of these early Saints. Yet, like the mythological phoenix, the thousands who were stranded across Missouri and their imprisoned prophet leader would be reborn through the furnace of affliction.

. . .

**Nauvoo, Illinois: the City Beautiful**

The expulsion from Missouri, the imprisonment of Joseph Smith, and a host of other matters created a short lapse in the principle of gathering. A realization that the religious gathering to communities was creating antagonism among local citizenry became a reality for members of the Church. On 16 January 1839, Joseph Smith advised Brigham Young and Heber C. Kimball that for the present, "the gathering of necessity [is] stopt [sic]."[40] At the time of Joseph's directive to Young and Kimball, he was incarcerated in a jail cell in Missouri. However, shortly after Joseph's escape from prison and his arrival in Quincy, Illinois, he again began teaching that a gathered community of believers was essential for building a house of the Lord.[41] The principle of gathering that began immediately after the church was organized continued. Even though members were forced out of Kirtland, Ohio and the state of Missouri, the divine mandate to go on with the gathering would continue moving forward in Illinois. The exodus of the displaced refugees eventually began arriving at Quincy, Illinois, where they received a warm welcome by the citizens of that town. One can only imagine the gratitude felt by the weary travelers as they were kindly greeted by the residents of this village on the banks of the Mississippi River.[42]

During the month of April 1839, Joseph Smith purchased 135 acres of land from Hugh White, and he purchased another farm west of the White acreage for $9,000. These two properties were located within a village known as Commerce, Illinois. This is the site where the city of Nauvoo was established. Joseph Smith moved his family to a small cabin on White's land on 10 May 1839. The land was covered with trees, brush, and wilderness. In addition, the land near the river drained poorly, which caused problems. However, the Mississippi River makes a half circle around the location where Nauvoo was established, giving the town three fronts to the river. The city of Nauvoo lay about 190 miles upriver from St. Louis, Missouri, and about the same distance from Chicago, Illinois.[43] Because of the swampy lowlands and malarial fevers, sickness constantly plagued the inhabitants during their seven-year stay in the city.[44] From its beginning, Nauvoo rapidly grew. The highly transitory nature of Nauvoo's population from 1839 to 1846 made calculating the population very difficult. Sources are available that cite the growth experienced by Nauvoo. In 1839, approximately 100 people lived in Nauvoo. A census conducted by church leadership in 1842 recorded roughly 4,000 residents. In 1844, estimates showed about 12 thousand people living in Nauvoo, and the number stood at around 11 thousand in 1845.[45] Although other tracts of land were purchased across the Mississippi River in Iowa, Nauvoo became the center point for gathering. Because of its ideal location between St. Louis and Chicago, Nauvoo became a river town. Upwards of ten steamers a week passed Nauvoo during the mid-1840s, and by 1843 four or five steamboats a day stopped at the town.[46] For a brief period, Nauvoo stood as an important city in Illinois and a crucial river town for the expanding traffic on the Mississippi.

**Polygamy**

One challenging component of LDS doctrine that was brought to light during the Nauvoo period was the introduction of polygamy. As early as summer 1831, Joseph Smith told some people living in Kirtland that in time plural marriage would become part of the doctrine and practice of the church. However, this practice was not advanced to certain church members until the Nauvoo period. Joseph Smith first taught the concept of plural marriage to a select few who were living in Nauvoo, but the doctrine was publicly disavowed at Nauvoo. The renunciation remained in effect for six years following the western migration. Many prominent men and women living in Nauvoo had entered into plural marriage before starting the trek west. The practice of plural marriage was not made public until 1852.[47] Polygamy caused a strong negative reaction by many outside the church, and it eventually led to the church being disenfranchised by the federal government.[48] Ecclesiastical units began forming during the Nauvoo period with the concept of wards and bishoprics. The wards were specific geographic areas, and bishoprics were appointed to lead the various wards. The main purpose of forming wards was to coordinate church economics and help the poor.[49] The Nauvoo period witnessed much doctrinal development for the young church.

**The Beginning of the End**

For several years, the city of Nauvoo boomed and Joseph's dream of a gathering place for the body of believers seemed possible. After failing in both Kirtland and Missouri, the prospect of a city with a temple (where church members could assemble for sacred ordinances) and a body of believers in one geographic location was moving forward. The temple was under construction, and thousands of believers were gathering to Nauvoo and surrounding areas. However, the constant barrage of legal issues, dissidents from within, new doctrines that met with negative public opinion, the continued relocation of church members, and the struggles of creating a city on the western frontier caused Joseph Smith to struggle under the strain. Shortly before his death, during a visit to the home of his friend Benjamin Franklin Johnson, Joseph fell into a chair and acknowledged:

---

Oh! I am so tired—so tired that I often feel too long for my day of rest. For what has there been in this life but tribulation for me? From a boy I have been persecuted by my enemies, and now even my friends are beginning to join with them, to hate and persecute me! Why should I not wish for my time of rest?[50]

---

Events would unfold from June 1844 to July 1847 that would change the face of gathering for the church and its members, and Joseph would find his opportunity to rest. Residents, who initially welcomed the Mormons in 1839, were now determined to remove those who were living in Nauvoo. For the third time in fourteen years, members of the church would again be required to relocate. The search for a gathering place would eventually lead to the valleys of present day Utah.

## Martyrdom of Joseph Smith

As Nauvoo grew in political and military power, local residents grew alarmed at the seemingly uncontested expansion of the church. Joseph Smith's ability to evade extradition to Missouri caused angst among the citizenry in Illinois. Eventually neighbors were convinced the only solution to the problem was to force the Saints out of Nauvoo. Joseph Smith also faced increased dissention within the church. The doctrine that impacted some members the most was the introduction of polygamy. Evidence indicates Joseph Smith began taking additional wives in April 1841. By June 1844, when the Prophet was murdered, over 150 men and women had received temple related ordinances which included the sanctioned but secret practice of plural marriage. For a brief period, William Law, Nauvoo Stake President William Marks, and Hyrum Smith sought to bring the matter of plural marriage before the Saints living in Nauvoo.[51] However, Hyrum Smith eventually became convinced polygamy had been divinely revealed to Joseph Smith, which then estranged Law from both Joseph and Hyrum regarding the practice of plural marriage. Several attempts were made to convince Law that plural marriage was divinely directed, but none were successful. Eventually, Law legally charged Joseph Smith with adultery in May and June 1844, and he published Smith's teachings about polygamy on the pages of a newspaper known as the *Nauvoo Expositor*. Law misjudged the response of the LDS population who supported Joseph Smith as the Lord's mouthpiece. His open attack on the church leader estranged himself completely from the church, and he was labeled an enemy.[52] Law's publication of the *Nauvoo Expositor* led to swift action by the Nauvoo City Council, which declared the establishment and paper as a nuisance and ordered the destruction of the press. Thus, the Nauvoo city marshal took the press, materials, and paper into the street and scorched them.[53]

As events surrounding the destruction of the *Nauvoo Expositor* intensified, the split between church leadership, the dissenters within the church, and the residents living in surrounding communities widened into an impassable chasm. William Law and others who were excommunicated from the church held meetings and put together plans to take the prophet's life. In addition, the excommunicated members sought to organize a new church by actively attempting to gain church member converts.[54] Neighbors in surrounding areas began seeking the arrest of Joseph and Hyrum. Joseph Smith sent correspondence to the governor of Illinois seeking assistance, but to no avail. Local communities were raising a militia for protection and offensive maneuvers—even to the extent of destroying and exterminating the Mormons.[55] Joseph, Hyrum, and a few close friends began the journey to Carthage 24 June 1844. While journeying to Carthage the company was presented with an order for all state munitions in possession of the Nauvoo Legion to be turned over to the state. Joseph countersigned the order and returned to Nauvoo to assist in the disarming of the legion.[56]

Joseph Smith and the other prisoners surrendered to the constable 25 June 1844 at Carthage, Illinois. Joseph and Hyrum were arrested for treason against the state of Illinois.[57] Joseph Smith, Hyrum Smith, John Taylor, and Willard Richards were incarcerated at the Carthage jail. During the night of 26 June 1844, John S. Fullmer, Stephen Markham, and Dan Jones were permitted to spend the evening with the prisoners. That night Joseph explained to John S. Fullmer he felt he was going to die. Joseph also stated, "I would like to see my family again. I would to God that I could preach to the Saints in Nauvoo once more."[58] Shortly after 8:00 a.m. on the morning of the martyrdom, 27 June 1844 Joseph penned a letter to Emma. He concluded his letter with these poignant words, "P.S.—Dear Emma, I am very much resigned to my lot, knowing I am justified, and have done the best that could be done. Give my love to the children and my friends."[59] Nine hours later, shortly after 5:00 p.m., a mob estimated at over 100 men rushed the prison and Joseph and Hyrum Smith were killed. John Taylor received serious wounds, while Willard Richards escaped virtually unharmed. The entire assault lasted only about two minutes.[60] Those who murdered Joseph and his brother were made up primarily of Carthage and Warsaw militiamen, who with blackened faces completed their loathsome deed. Moreover, Governor Thomas Ford had given his personal guarantee of safety—a promise he did not keep.[61]

## Leadership Crisis

The deaths of Joseph Smith and his brother Hyrum brought about a crisis of leadership for the church. The new religion had been formally organized for just over fourteen years, and there was no succession plan in place. Upon hearing of the death of Joseph Smith, Sidney Rigdon, who had served with Smith as one of the early leaders of the new church, returned to Nauvoo, Illinois and laid his claim as the next head of the church. Concurrent with Rigdon's return to Nauvoo, Brigham Young and other members of the Quorum of the Twelve Apostles, the highest-ranking authority in the religious organization under Joseph Smith, also hastily returned to the town of Nauvoo. Mr. Rigdon returned to Nauvoo desiring to assume leadership of the church as its guardian, even though Joseph Smith sought to replace Rigdon in his church leadership position as early as 1841.[62] Brigham Young affirmed that the leadership of the church rightfully fell to the Apostles. Young stated that Joseph Smith himself had committed the leadership to the Quorum of the Twelve Apostles.[63] On 8 August 1844, just over one month following the death of Joseph Smith and his brother Hyrum, a special meeting was held at Nauvoo to determine leadership succession. During the meeting, the majority of those in attendance voted to sustain the apostles as the rightfully chosen leadership.[64] For the next three years the LDS Church was led by those known as the Quorum of the Twelve Apostles, and any decisions relative to the overall church was made under their authority.

Not everyone accepted the new leadership. Sidney Rigdon returned to Pittsburgh and tried to start his own church. However, followers began deserting him when his prophecies failed and he introduced a form of polygamy.[65] Other off-shoots included one founded by William E. McLellin and David Whitmer, two prominent early leaders of the Church. Another splinter group, headed by Lyman Wight, migrated to Texas. A gentleman named James Strang gathered a sizable group and structured his own organization. During the 1850s, several former members of the LDS Church, along with four other gentlemen, were instrumental in founding the Reorganized Church of Jesus Christ of Latter-day Saints (RLDS), which became the most successful faction of the original church. Emma Smith remained in Nauvoo for the rest of her life, and refused to follow the group, led by Brigham Young.[66] Joseph Smith's son, Joseph Smith III, served as the first president of the RLDS church beginning in 1860.[67] The transition to apostolic leadership caused many to leave the church during the adjustment.[68] However, the fact that the majority of members living in and around Nauvoo followed the Quorum of the Twelve Apostles was a watershed point in time during early Church history.

**Forced Expulsion**

After a few short years in Illinois, the Saints were forced to gather to another location. This move would not seek sanctuary in another state. Ohio, Missouri, and Illinois had all turned their backs on the church members, so the directive now was to turn west. In less than seven years, members had fled Kirtland, Ohio, the state of Missouri, and now Nauvoo, Illinois. The resulting moves in such a short span of time created poverty among many who were obedient to their leader's constant call to relocate. However, the call to resettle was endorsed by those who believed in divine leadership of the Quorum of the Twelve, and approximately fifteen thousand members of the church fled Nauvoo and the surrounding areas. The decision to vacate Nauvoo by the spring of 1846 was made public September 1845. The monumental task of preparing thousands of people to travel into a wilderness began. Brigham Young began appointing captains of companies on 11 October 1845, and each captain recruited people for his company. Thousands of wagons were under construction, food rations for the journey were compiled, and residents began doing their all to prepare for the spring departures.[69] On 2 February 1846, church leaders decided that the Saints should leave the city. The first group crossed the Mississippi River to Iowa two days later. Over the next several days, several hundred

Saints left Nauvoo for temporary quarters.[70] Historian William Hartley notes three distinct stages are represented during the evacuation. The first stage comprised the winter removal of Brigham Young and about two thousand Saints. It lasted from 1 March to 13 June 1846, concluding on the western banks of the Missouri River. The largest group, totaling almost twelve thousand members, spread out across Iowa as they worked their way west. The third stage took place in the fall of 1846 and was mostly at gunpoint. By October 1846, virtually all members of The Church of Jesus Christ of Latter-day Saints had fled the city and surrounding areas.[71]

The first to flee Nauvoo began their journey in the winter, and the actual trip to the Missouri River took months as rain and terrible mud afflicted their travels. This traveling camp utilized about 100 individuals moving ahead of the larger group to improve roads, to build bridges, and to find camping spots and obtain firewood.[72] William Hartley writes the second group contained no large wagon trains and most companies comprised a dozen or fewer wagons. Because this group left later, the immigrants experienced better road conditions, and the trip to the Missouri River took about one month instead of the three-and-a-half months it took Brigham Young's group. [73] The final group to leave Nauvoo included the poorest of the Saints. This band signed a formal surrender to the mobs encompassing Nauvoo and was forced to ferry across the Mississippi River at gunpoint. Several rescue trains were sent to carry the poorest Saints across Iowa to the relative safety of the main camps.[74] It is estimated that seventeen thousand Mormons lived in and around Nauvoo in 1845. Of that number, about two thousand decided against moving west. Some were waiting for the Saints to find a permanent location while others returned to their families in other parts of the country. By the end of 1846, Nauvoo stood virtually empty of church members and looked much like a ghost town.[75]

Brigham Young initially desired to send a company of men, without their families, west to plant crops for the benefit of those who followed. He continued to focus to that end as late as June 1846.[76] Young felt so strongly about sending an advance group that he warned a group as follows: "Remember, I have told you, how, when, and where to gather and if you do not go now, remember and bear witness in the day-of-judgment."[77] However, President Young soon realized the enormous amount of planning needed to transport several thousand people on a thousand-mile journey. One situation that stopped Young from sending an advance group west was the formation of the Mormon Battalion. While the Saints prepared to move west, the United States initiated the Mexican American War, and troops were needed. The immigrants were short on cash, stranded across the state of Iowa, and needed a location to rest. Captain James Allen was dispatched to meet with Brigham Young and obtain his support to enlist a group of men to march to California. These Saints became known as the Mormon Battalion and created the only religious military unit in United States history. As one historian notes, "The Mormon men enlisted not for patriotic reasons, but to fulfill a defined program and mission of the church."[78] On 16 July 1846, some 500 men took the oath of allegiance to the United States and began the long grueling march to California.[79] Evidence indicates that this journey was the longest march in military history, beginning in Council Bluffs, Iowa Territory and concluding in San Diego, California.[80]

In addition to the needed cash to help the stranded Saints move west, Brigham Young obtained permission to reside for a time on the western side of the Missouri River on Potawatomi lands. Although Captain Allen did not have the authority to make such a commitment for the federal government, Brigham Young took Allen's promise at face value and established what is later referred to as Winter Quarters.[81] Some accomplishments of the Mormon Battalion include participating in the discovery of gold in California leading to the migration of thousands of people seeking to find gold in the west. The Battalion opened a wagon route to current day Southern California, known as Cooke's Wagon Road. The former soldiers who were involved with the discovery of gold created the Mormon-Carson Emigrant Trail, which became the "preferred route to Gold-Rush California in 1849 and 1850."[82] The Saints were stalled on the banks of the Missouri River and across Nebraska. Five hundred of their most hearty men were now involved in protecting the United States government in a war to obtain more land. The gathering would need to wait for a short period.

## 2

# WINTER QUARTERS, GROWTH, TROUBLES, DOWN AND BACK TRAINS

After the Saints were driven out of Nauvoo, the main body of the church was stranded across the state of Iowa. Brigham Young and several hundred others stopped on the east banks of the Missouri River, locating for a time at Council Bluffs across the river from present day Omaha, Nebraska. The arrival of this forward company took place on 14 June 1846. The travel from Nauvoo to Mount Pisgah had taken four months, and the distance traveled was about one hundred seventy-five miles. The final 90 miles from Mount Pisgah, Iowa, to the Missouri River took about 12 days.[1] As the Saints who had been spread out across Iowa arrived on the Iowa side of the Missouri River, new settlements were formed. Estimates place the number of new villages as high as ninety. Council Bluffs lay on the east side of the Missouri River. A new village named Winter Quarters was formed on the western side of the river.[2] About 30 minutes after 10:00 a.m. on Friday, 11 September 1846, Brigham Young, Heber C. Kimball, Orson Pratt, Willard Richards, Wilford Woodruff, George Albert Smith, and Amasa Lyman left the small village of Cutler's Park, walked north, and selected the site for the town of Winter Quarters.[3] Following dinner that evening, Young, accompanied by others, walked back to the site of Winter Quarters and began laying out and surveying the village. In the evening, twenty-five men and women were selected to travel back to Nauvoo, "or intermediate points" to bring back those left behind.[4] For the next two years, Winter Quarters would become the headquarters and the beginning point for the western migration. At the time Winter Quarters was established, the final destination for the Saints was still being debated.

Winter Quarters, one of the first cities in Nebraska, was divided into five-acre blocks, with each block measuring 380 feet by 660 feet. The city plat called for 41 blocks, 16 named streets, and a total of 594 lots. The lots measured 72 feet in width by 165 feet deep. Each full-size block could accommodate 20 houses, and a population of between 150 to 300 people.[5] Winter Quarters boasted 538 log cabins, 83 sod houses, and 3,483 settlers during the first year. By 1847, the population grew to 4,000 inhabitants. During the winter of 1846-47, roughly 7,000 church members lived either in Winter Quarters or across the Missouri River in Council Bluffs.[6] Because of the lateness of arrival, the first order of business for the evicted Saints was to break ground for spring crops, fence off fields, and perform other critical tasks to provide food for the beleaguered outcasts. Those who lived in Winter Quarters banded together to support each other. Winter was about to set in. Most provisions were depleted; many were sick or completely exhausted. Despite their best efforts, death began taking a toll on the besieged Saints. Estimates indicate a minimum of 723 died between June 1846 and May 1847—on both sides of the Missouri River and along the trail in Iowa. Sadly, infants two years and younger accounted for almost half the recorded deaths.[7] Yet, with all the sorrows faced by those living in Winter Quarters, schools opened up, singing and dancing schools began, and concerts with musical performances were often presented.[8]

Women played a significant role during the time the Saints resided in Winter Quarters. The Relief Society, which had been founded during the Nauvoo years, was discontinued following the expulsion, confining women even more to the home and family. Women devised spontaneous and informal gatherings to meet their social needs and to "provide an outlet for service, spiritual creativity, and social camaraderie."[9] Several women organized visits for those who were pregnant or sick, held prayer circles, and led healing sessions with the laying on of hands.[10] Isolation and separation from home and family created a critical need for women to strengthen each other. Concerning the vital need for female visits, Maureen Beecher wrote, "Women bonding to each other, drawing support from each other, was essential to survival in Mormon Winter Quarters and later to the creation of Mormonism's Utah Society."[11] Mary Haskin Parker Richards' diary describes her visits on Sunday, 6 December 1846. She portrays the weather as being so cold, that the Sunday meeting was cancelled. She first visited with the Van Cott family to see how his wife and mother were feeling. She spent about an hour with the two and ate some bread, butter, honey, and cheese. Next Mary visited with a Sister Noons and spent a few minutes with her. She then called on Ellen Wilding and spent an hour with her alone in her wagon. Next, she stopped by to see Uncle Levis and Aunt Rhoda at the wagon. After seeing them, her next visit was to Uncle Willard's house, where she met with both the Bullock and Rushton families. Her final visit was to see Sister Jane. She found her suffering with an illness, so Mary spent the evening and night with her.[12]

**Western Movement Debated**

One of the most important aspects of life in Winter Quarters was the discussion about where they Saints would ultimately gather. The spirit of gathering, which was initiated by Joseph Smith, was still a powerful motivating force for the displaced Saints. Although settlement in the Great Salt Lake or Bear River Valley seemed to be the focus for a destination, the actual location and the method of travel were still being debated. Historian Richard Bennett maintains there were several subtly distinguishable stages of development. The precise time for departure, the number of people, the trails to follow, and who is in authority were debated among the leaders at Winter Quarters.[13] The original plan called for a group of able-bodied men to cross the mountains to the Great Basin or Bear River Valley. These men would plant crops, make improvements to the area, and after one or two years bring as many people as possible to settle.[14] A group known as the Council of Fifty, which had been organized during the latter part of the Nauvoo period, had other plans. A core component of their plan was the establishment of a large farm or way station, in Yellowstone country north of Fort Laramie. The Council believed this plan was safer than sending a group over the mountains. Fewer men would be needed, and the bulk of the church could move west in the spring of 1848. Several meetings were held by the Council of Fifty, and letters were sent out describing the benefits of the proposal. Even though he had reservations, Brigham Young gave his tentative agreement to the plan put forward by the Council of Fifty.[15]

**Brigham Young Takes Responsibility**

Brigham Young offered tentative approval, but he never completely agreed with the proposal. He felt a way station away from the main line was risky. He also believed that the Native Americans living in the area would make passage through their lands difficult. In addition, the soil surrounding the Yellowstone area was described as poor and not suitable for raising crops. Finally, Brigham wanted to dispel any doubts that the Quorum of the Twelve were in command—not the Council of Fifty. Several of the Winter Quarter's pioneers believed the Council of Fifty were directing the migration west. Thus, Brigham felt a forceful declaration was needed to remove any control of the trek west from the Council of Fifty. On 14 January 1847, Brigham Young presented a canonized revelation to the church.[16] The declaration begins with "The Word and Will of the Lord concerning the Camp of Israel in their journeyings to the West."[17] In the revelation, the western migration was to be under the direction of the Twelve Apostles.[18] How the companies were to be organized was spelled out. Saints were told to use their influence to "remove this people to the place where the Lord shall locate a stake of Zion." [19] The divine manifestation was accepted by the general membership of the church on 19 January 1847.[20] The struggles and debates of the previous months had given way to a revelation that placed the Quorum of the Twelve in charge of the migration. From that point forward Brigham Young, assumed ownership of the move west.

Even though the location had still not been finalized, the entire church was firmly under the direction of Brigham Young and the Quorum of the Twelve Apostles.

**The Vanguard Trek West**

The vanguard wagon train of 1847, which concluded its journey in the current state of Utah, began near present-day Florence, Nebraska known as Winter Quarters. This initial train traveled along the north bank of the Platte River for 504 miles to the current Wyoming state line.[21] Evidence indicates the pioneers in 1847 possessed maps of the west (which detailed some existing trails).[22] However, in several cases they fashioned their own road, as noted by William Clayton after the group had forded the Loup Fork River. "There is no road here, consequently, President Young, Kimball, and some others went ahead on horseback to hunt out the best track."[23] Camping spots were located as the group traveled along the Platte River. At times, wells were dug to obtain drinking water for both the pioneers and their livestock.[24]

As the pioneer group continued their western march into Wyoming Territory, the rise in elevation became apparent. The nights became cold, and the hot days were replaced by cooler ones. Sunday morning, 27 June 1847, three years after the martyrdom of the Prophet Joseph Smith, the vanguard group of pioneers crossed a landmark known as South Pass. This pass was the continental divide for the Atlantic and Pacific Oceans. South Pass made the Oregon and Mormon Trail possible by providing a route over the mountains that otherwise would be almost impassable. Historian Will Bagley notes the South Pass will be "remembered for its critical role in the lives of the half-million Americans who crossed it between 1840 and 1869 on their way to new homes in the West."[25] However, on this day, three years after the murder of their prophet-leader, South Pass opened the way to the Salt Lake Valley and a refuge in the desert. Orson Pratt, one of the members of the vanguard group, and their best scientist, was sent to locate the highest point before the trail descended toward the Pacific. He described the path as some 15 to 20 miles in length and breadth, and the highest point covering a basin of 15 or 20 acres, destitute of wild sage but containing good grass. Pratt calculated the elevation at 7,085 feet above sea level.[26]

Shortly after crossing South Pass, Samuel Brannan who had sailed on the ship *Brooklyn* in February 1846, met Brigham Young and the vanguard group on the trail. Brannan and his group of 238 church members had arrived at Yerba Buena (San Francisco Bay) on 29 July 1846. Their journey had taken them around Cape Horn and included ten days in the Hawaiian Islands. Brannan had left San Francisco on 4 April 1847, determined to convince Brigham Young the Saints should settle in California. Young listened to Brannan's report concerning the value of settling in California, but he was not convinced California was the best location to settle.[27] As the weary travelers continued their journey in the higher elevations, many members began experiencing occurrences of mountain fever. Some men were unable to drive their teams as they experienced extreme headaches, severe lower back pain, and high fever. Orson Pratt determined the rash of illnesses spreading through the camp was "probably occasioned by the suffocating clouds of dust which rise from the sandy road and envelop the whole camp when in motion, and also by the sudden change in temperature."[28] Erastus Snow recorded on 3 July that about one-half of the company had been afflicted with the illness. He also described the pain as almost insufferable. The remedy included drinking warm drinks such as ginger and pepper tea, cayenne, and other hot beverages. The sickness typically lasted about one week.[29] As sickness afflicted the travelers, the last portion of the journey became the most challenging of the trip. The daunting Wasatch Mountains proved a formidable climb. Nevertheless, the company divided into healthy and sick groups, and an advance team entered the valley on 22 July 1847. Brigham Young arrived two days later.[30]

The first night for the advanced division was spent in a location just south of the current intersection of Fifth East and Seventeenth South, Salt Lake City.[31] The next night's camping spot was located in a city block between Main and State and Third and Fourth South streets.[32] The immediate need for these early pioneers was to plant crops for harvesting. On 23 July 1847 plows and shovels began tilling the soil for planting. The first furrow was turned at noon and planting began immediately.[33] The reason for the frantic move to plant became evident as more people arrived in the valley. In September 1847, some 1,540 persons entered the valley which put a significant strain on resources. This put the number of persons who spent the winter of 1847-48 living in the Salt Lake Valley at approximately 1,681.[34] Many who lived in the valley during the first year survived on crows, thistle tops, bark, roots, and Sego Lily bulbs. A voluntary rationing system was initiated, which limited each person to about one-half pound of flour a day. One individual described the situation that first winter as follows: "I would take a grubbing-hoe and a sack and start by sunrise in the morning and go, I thought six miles before coming to where the thistle roots grew, and in time to get home I would have a bushel and sometimes more thistle roots. And we would eat them raw." Residents in the valley looked forward to a spring harvest, but an early frost damaged the winter wheat and garden vegetables. In May and June, a mass of crickets began destroying the remaining crops. Men and women battled against the crickets, but with little success. Shortly before all the crops had been destroyed swarms of seagulls appeared and miraculously began devouring the crickets.[35]

**Trips Back to Winter Quarters**

On 2 August 1847, a group of four men left the valley to meet with the next company of emigrants from Winter Quarters. The next set of eleven men left on 11 August and were called as hunters for the others who were heading east. Driving ox teams, seventy men left on 16 August. Brigham Young led the last group to leave the valley. This party left 25 August and was composed of 107 individuals.[36] The unit selected as hunters were captained by Norton Jacobs and the troupe consisted both of pioneers and former members of the Mormon Battalion. Brigham Young sent instructions with the group that Norton, as the leader, should have his instructions followed implicitly. The band was also instructed to not travel in haste and to supply the ox teams that were following behind them.[37] The earlier trip west was almost flawless in the vanguard group. However, the later groups traveling back to

Winter Quarters experienced internal bickering, as many of the men involved in the trek east desired to travel faster than the other groups. Prominent among those who wanted to increase the speed of travel were members of the Mormon Battalion. Just eleven days after leaving the Salt Lake Valley, Norton Jacobs noted in his journal that members of the Battalion were all full of cursing and swearing. Norton added the men also threatened to leave the company and move ahead to Winter Quarters upon arrival at the Sweetwater River.[38] The ox teams that left on 16 August also dealt with those who desired to reach Winter Quarters faster than the main body was moving. The ox group actually caught up with the hunters, but the reunion was anything but sweet. The ox team members felt the hunters did not provide for their needs, and the hunters, who were short on supplies themselves, justified their actions as reasonable. The result was bitter feelings and a lack of unity. An encounter with Native Americans caused the hunters and ox train members to travel together until they reached Winter Quarters. For the return trip, Brigham's group left the valley 25 August, and arrived at Winter Quarters by the end of October 1847. His group made this trip to the Missouri River with relative ease and little bickering amongst themselves. The one individual who seemed able to mold people into a cohesive unit for the western gathering was Brigham Young, and it was his leadership for thirty years that allowed the mass migration and settlement of tens of thousands of believers.[39]

**Growth of Utah Territory**

The Salt Lake Valley and surrounding areas were quickly populated by the immigrating Saints. In 1847 alone, thirteen additional companies settled in the Utah Territory. The year 1848 witnessed seven pioneer companies enter the Great Basin area. By 1850, an additional 32 pioneer trains had entered the greater Salt Lake City area. Thus, between 1847 and 1850, 52 companies of pioneers had left the east for what would become the Utah Territory.[40] The Utah Territory was organized in 1850, and peace between the Mormons and the government was tenuous from the beginning. As early as 1846, Brigham Young had written President

James K. Polk stressing that members of The Church of Jesus Christ of Latter-day Saints were loyal Americans, and desired to establish a U.S. territorial government once they arrived in the Great Basin which then was held by the government of Mexico.[41] Several times in the intervening years, Young petitioned the federal government to establish a territory with church members filling political appointments. When these tactics failed, Young threatened to create an independent state.[42] Five years of sending petitions finally resulted in a new territorial government. Brigham Young was appointed governor, and several church leaders held key positions in the new administration. However, in 1851, Washington sent several non-Mormons to the new territory. One filled the position of territorial secretary, a second served as an Indian subagent, the third acted as a federal judge, and the fourth would serve as a Utah judge.[43] Leaders in Washington did not trust church leaders, and the settlers in the Great Basin felt betrayed by those serving in the federal government.

During the first years in the Salt Lake Valley, residents lived in wagons and tents. Those who lived in cabins found their existence very primitive. Mary Isabelle Horne described the log houses as small and further explained the circumstances in the home. "The ground was full of snakes which used to crawl around our houses, but these were soon killed or frightened away." She further noted, "The timber was so full of bugs that it was years before they were entirely subdued. The mice also were very numerous, running over us by day and by night, and destroying considerable clothing."[44] Proper clothing was also in short supply during the early years. Talking about his footwear, Parley P. Pratt noted, "Myself and some of them were compelled to go with bare feet for several months." Another resident of the valley stated, "I have all the clothes I have on my back."[45] As noted earlier, seven pioneer companies settled in the Salt Lake Valley in 1848. Three men, Brigham Young, Heber C. Kimball, and Willard Richards' trains brought 2,417 souls to the Basin.[46] This brought the total number of residents living in the valley to approximately 4,600 people at the end of 1848.[47] By the end of 1852, the majority of Saints who had been driven from Nauvoo migrated to the valley. Then gatherings began from Great Britain and Scandinavia, which added an average of three thousand new arrivals each year. By 1857, about thirty-five thousand Latter-day Saints had gathered to the Great Basin and the Utah Territory. In 1869, three years following the 1866 European migration about 75 thousand Saints were located in the valley and surrounding areas.[48]

During the second year of settlement, hunger continued to plague the Saints living in the Great Basin area. The arrival of more than two thousand people taxed food supplies to the limit. While the winter of 1847–48 had been mild, the winter of 1848–49 turned severe. One report indicated that one to three feet of snow covered the ground for several weeks and the temperature fell to 33 degrees below freezing.[49] Cattle starved and people reverted to eating rawhides, sego lilies, and thistles. By February 1849, a committee appointed to investigate the food supply determined there was enough flour on hand to provide about three-quarters of a pound of breadstuffs a day until the next harvest. A voluntary rationing was implemented, and those who had excess food were asked to turn their surplus to the bishop for distribution to the poor. The cold winter, nagging hunger, and the preceding fall's poor harvest caused some settlers to question whether or not the Great Basin was the right gathering place of the Saints. A few began openly declaring that California was superior "in every way" and that the Saints should relocate. A number of valley residents actually moved to California. Evidence indicates that a great majority of those living in Winter Quarters also were skeptical of the future of the Great Basin Colony. However, Brigham Young would not be influenced by the views of those who desired to relocate to California. In his typical direct style, he stated, "We have the finest climate, the best water, and the purest air that can be found on the earth; there is no healthier climate anywhere."[50] Brigham Young was unwavering in his determination that the Salt Lake Valley was to be the gathering place for the Saints.

The continual influx of emigrants created a need to find suitable locations outside of the Salt Lake Valley. Parley P. Pratt guided a large exploring party to southern Utah, which led to the expansion from the Salt Lake base. Soon settlements were organized in the northern and southern portions of the Salt Lake Valley. Following the founding of these towns in 1847 and 1848, other areas were located such as Provo, Utah Valley, Nephi, Salt River Valley, Manti, Sanpete Valley, Richfield, Cedar City, Las Vegas, and San Bernardino. Eventually settlements were pushed into southern Colorado, New Mexico, eastern Utah, Idaho, and Arizona.[51] During the first decade following the arrival of the vanguard group to the Salt Lake Valley, nearly one hundred communities had been organized and settled. Most of the settlements were under the direction of Brigham Young. However, there were also many self-directed migrations to different locations in the Great Basin.[52] These self-directed settlements were often spin-offs from established towns. A family sought to improve their situation by finding better locations on the fringes of an existing village. The primary justification for seeking a better setting was for housing and feeding the family.[53] Thus, a site would need good soil, sufficient water for crops and livestock, grass for grazing, and ample building materials to construct a dwelling.[54] Whether the colonies were by decree from Brigham Young or individuals relocating independently, there was always a form of religious purification enveloping the settlement process. As one respected historian noted, "Making the waste places blossom as the rose, and the earth to yield abundantly of its diverse fruits, therefore, was more than an economic necessity; it was a form of religious worship."[55]

**Perpetual Emigration Fund**

Heber C. Kimball facilitated the establishment of a program called the Perpetual Emigration Fund (PEF). Heber reminded people during the October 1849 conference that earlier in the Nauvoo Temple they had covenanted to always help the poor to gather. The fund was formally organized in September 1850, and throughout its existence relied on voluntary donations. Those who used the fund were expected to repay the account after settling in their new homeland. Thus, the plan would be self-sustaining and could continually support those who left their native soil for Utah Territory. In the years between 1850 and 1859, the fund assisted 4,769 immigrants at a cost of $300,000.[56] Unfortunately, the Saints were slow in repaying their advances, and by 1877,

$1,000,000 was owed to the fund. Many of those debts were written off during the Jubilee Year of 1880.[57] During General Conference, leaders frequently thanked, cajoled, pleaded, scolded, and threatened members in an effort to make the Perpetual Emigrating Fund self-sustaining. Over the course of its existence, the fund directly assisted some 26 thousand immigrants, or about 36 percent of the total church migration of those who emigrated from Europe to the United States between 1852 and 1887.[58]

On 12 January 1856, the territorial legislature "amended, confirmed, and legalized" the PEF. The First Presidency of the church, which constituted the church's highest governing body, appointed no less than thirteen men to oversee the organization. This group was given power to sue persons, if necessary, in an effort to collect any loans that had been made to those needing assistance. The law affirmed an annual settlement should be made regarding the previous year's loans and collections. The stated purpose of the company was to "promote, facilitate, and accomplish the migration of the poor." The final section of the bill declared, "All persons receiving assistance for the Perpetual Emigrating Fund Company shall be held responsible thereafter until paid."[59] One of the biggest challenges that faced the PEF during its thirty-seven years of service was the collection of loans from those who had utilized the funds to emigrate from Europe. Three years after the organization of the PEF, at the 6 October 1853 General Conference of the Church, Brigham Young chastised those who had used the funds, yet made no effort to repay the loans. During his remarks he stated,

> We have helped men, women, and children from England, to over the amount of $30,000. Except one individual, and that is a man by the name of Thomas Green, who lives in Utah, and one young woman, who came from England, there has never been a single person who has paid one dime towards cancelling a debt amounting to over $30,000, besides other notes, accounts, and obligations we hold.[60]

## Utah War

In 1857, President James Buchanan sent twenty-five hundred army troops to Utah, in what became known as the Utah War, or Mormon War.[61] As knowledge of the impending troop movement reached Utah, reaction from church members was swift. On 13 September 1857, Brigham Young addressed members regarding the possibilities of facing the troops sent from Washington. During his remarks he declared, "Admit of corrupt administrators sending troops here, and what would be the result? All hell would follow after." Young further thundered, "We have no desire to kill men, but we wish to keep the devils from killing us."[62] The conflict ended without armed conflict as the government and Brigham Young negotiated a settlement. One of the results of the agreement between the two parties was the establishment of Camp Floyd, a military outpost which was located between Salt Lake City and a second important town in the territory, Provo.[63]

Colonial Thomas L. Kane, who was not a member of the church, influenced the outcome of the dispute between the Church and the federal government by almost single-handedly brokering a resolution between the two parties. As the dispute between the church and the government escalated, Kane interceded on behalf of his friends. Contacting those in political office who held influence, talking to friends in the newspaper business, and writing President Buchanan constituted only the beginning of his efforts to stop what could have developed into an armed conflict. Kane further mediated by traveling to the Utah Territory, under an assumed name, to meet with the key individuals involved in the dispute. He arrived in Salt Lake City 25 February 1858, at which time he met with Brigham Young. Kane later met with Thomas Cumming, the Utah Territorial Governor and military leaders. In April, the parties involved agreed to a settlement and bloodshed was averted. Of Thomas Kane, Brigham Young wrote, "The Lord sent you here, friend Thomas, and he will not let you die . . . Your name will live with the Saints in all eternity."[64] Without the efforts of Thomas Kane to avert an armed conflict between the government and the church, the immigrations of 1864 to 1866 might have been completely different.

## Mountain Meadows' Massacre

While federal troops were heading to Utah Territory, a despicable act took place in September 1857 when a group of church members living in the southern part of Utah annihilated 120 men, women and children from Arkansas who were migrating to California. This heinous event became known as the Mountain Meadows' Massacre, and it took place while the travelers from Arkansas were seeking refuge from the trials of traveling west. Although nine men were indicted for the tragedy, only one prominent member of the church was put to death for his involvement in the annihilation. John D. Lee was executed at the site where the tragedy occurred in March 1877 which was almost two decades after the slaughter.[65] In Lee's first trial, the prosecution sought to implicate George A. Smith who traveled throughout southern Utah several weeks before the massacre.[66] By tying Smith to the crime, they were hoping to implicate Brigham Young. The first trial ended with a hung jury. A second trial two years later resulted in a guilty verdict and Lee was sentenced to death at the spot where the atrocities took place. While traveling to the execution site, John D. Lee offered his final confession. He told the minister who was riding with him that he killed five emigrants and possibly six. Although many hoped Lee would implicate Brigham Young during the ride to the massacre site, Mr. Lee repeatedly denied that Young ordered the slaughter.[67] What precipitated the actions by those living in southern Utah against a group of pioneers passing through the area, may never be understood. However, this horrific encounter and anger against the church for the actions of those participating in the murders still evoked strong emotions when the pioneers of the mid 1860s entered the Utah Territory.

On 11 September 2007, the 150th anniversary of the Mountain Meadows' Massacre was commemorated. Elder Henry B. Eyring, representing the First Presidency of The Church of Jesus Christ of Latter-day Saints, expressed deep remorse for the victims, the perpetrators, and their descendants. His statement was offered at the site of the massacre. He began his remarks by noting he was speaking "on behalf of the First Presidency of The Church of Jesus Christ of Latter-day Saints." Elder Eyring continued, "We express profound regret for the massacre carried out in this valley 150 years ago today and for the untold suffering experienced by the victims then and by their relatives to the present time." To Native Americans who for several years were blamed for the murders Eyring stated, "A separate expression of regret is owed to the Paiute people who have unjustly borne, for too long, the principal blame for what occurred during the massacre." Next, Elder Eyring addressed the challenges faced by those who committed the killings. "We know, too, that many of those who carried out the massacre were haunted all their lives by what they did and saw on that unforgettable day. They and their relatives have also suffered under a heavy burden of guilt." The final portion of Eyring's remarks sought understanding for all sides. "Having reflected and commented on both the past and future of this hallowed meadow, we conclude by expressing our love and desire for reconciliation to all who have in any way been affected by what occurred at Mountain Meadows 150 years ago today."[68]

## Down and Back Church Trains

Perhaps due in part to the handcart disasters of 1856, on 6 October 1860, Brigham Young announced the formulation of a revolutionary new plan to bring people and freight across the plains to Utah Territory. In a bold move to reduce costs, improve freighting opportunities and provide a means to bring more people from Europe, Young stated that the church would begin to send teams from Utah to outfitting stations, on the banks of the Missouri River, pick up the waiting immigrants, and return to Utah the same year. Local church leaders would be asked to donate the needed oxen, mules, supplies, wagons, and men to complete the 2,200-mile round trip. President Young stated, "If we can go with our teams to the Missouri River and back in one season, and bring the poor, their provisions, etc., it will save about half of the cash we now expend to bring the Saints to this point from Europe."[69] Young stated that additional benefits included the ability to ship freight back east from Utah, increase immigrants that could be moved west, and pick up needed supplies on the Missouri River.[70] In a trial run earlier in the spring of 1860, 29 wagons under the command of Joseph W. Young, had traveled back to the Missouri River, completed necessary work in the area and returned 3 October 1860.[71]

This short announcement during the church's General Conference in Salt Lake City began a period from 1861 to 1868 in which thousands of immigrants were transported from outfitting stations in Nebraska to Utah Territory at significant savings. Occasional handcart companies had been one previous method of transporting pioneers across the plains inexpensively. However, that process had met with varying degrees of success and was never popular with most of the Saints who migrated to Utah. Thus, in one bold move, the method of transporting pioneers was changed to church trains. Independent wagon trains were still used by some who traveled west, but after 1860 the vast majority of immigrants used the church trains as the means to reach Zion. These convoys became known as the down and back trains. After 1861, immigrants who traveled on church trains no longer needed to purchase their own oxen, mules, wagons, and supplies.

Following Brigham Young's announcement about the formation of the down and back trains, The First Presidency sent out a circular to local church leaders throughout Utah Territory detailing how the new transportation system would work. During the first full year of operation, the First Presidency requested that "two hundred wagons with four yoke of cattle each," be sent back to Florence, Nebraska Territory. Additionally, loose oxen were sought to accompany the wagons on the trip for the opportunity of selling them to any immigrants that may wish to buy them—thereby keeping the additional cash out of the "hands of strangers." Each train would be led by a captain and would include the needed teamsters and support personnel. The teams would be organized into companies of approximately fifty wagons each. The local leaders, or bishops, were requested to donate all the needed items, including the necessary manpower to run the trains, by seeking donations from their local congregations. Furthermore, the bishops were responsible for selecting the individuals who would make the round trip.[72]

The circular continued with very specific instructions concerning how each wagon was to be outfitted. "To each wagon, one tar can or keg, and at least one gallon of grease; two good whip lashes, with buckskin to splice and for crackers."[73] Furthermore, each teamster should be provided with 250 pounds of flour, 40 pounds of bacon, 40 pounds of dried beef, butter (as much as he can take safely), sugar, coffee, tea, beans, salt, yeast cake, pickles, and vinegar. In addition, one good buffalo robe, two good blankets, two good pairs of boots or shoes, three pair of pants, six shirts, five pair of socks, three overshirts, and coats enough for comfort were to be included in the teamster's provisions. One good gun, preferably a double-barreled shotgun, with a sufficient supply of powder, balls, and shot were to accompany each wagon. The instructions further stated that six men should form a mess group and agree upon how to furnish the necessary cooking utensils and medical supplies. It was further recommended that each teamster receive ten dollars in cash for the purpose of buying groceries and other necessities during the long trip. This money was to be placed in the hands of the wagon master for disbursement. If the bishops could not raise the money, then sending an extra 100 pounds of flour would be an acceptable alternative.[74]

All men involved in the down and back trains were considered missionaries and received credit on the tithing books for the value of their service. During the period this system was used, approximately 18,466 immigrants were brought to Utah. Almost 1,956 wagons, 2,483 men, and 17,443 oxen, mules, and horses were needed to transport the European pioneers to Utah Territory.[75] Florence, Nebraska Territory was used as the outfitting station during the first three years church trains were utilized to assist immigrants in their travel west. In addition, Florence served as an outfitting station for the church from 1857 to 1860. The impact of Mormon migration on the little town was significant. The pioneers' need for oxen, horses, wagons, and supplies kept many busy in Florence. Repairing broken wagons, corralling animals, and providing food brought needed income to those who lived in the area. A comparison of the U.S. federal census in 1860 and 1870 illustrates the impact of the move to Wyoming on the town of Florence. The 1870 census listed 395 people living in the town of Florence, a total which was 800 less than the number of residents listed in the 1860 census.[76] Wyoming, Nebraska Territory served as the outfitting station for the down and back trains from 1864 to 1866.

In addition to transporting European converts across the plains, church trains also hauled products and cattle from the Utah Territory to the Missouri River where the items were converted into cash or traded for needed provisions. Likewise, on the return trip back to Utah Territory, the wagons were loaded so fully with freight that most of the travelers walked from the Missouri River to Utah Territory. As noted earlier, using the PEF and church trains was not a free gift. Each person who traveled on the down and back trains signed a promissory note agreeing to repay the church the cost of traveling to Utah. Many of those immigrating did not understand English or the document they were required to sign. During the half-dozen years the church trains operated, almost one-third of the total church migration from 1847 to 1868 utilized this method to reach Utah Territory.[77] The use of down and back trains had a significant impact on the western pioneer migration for the church. For example, the round trip to the Missouri River and back to Utah, for church trains, took about four months—the same time needed by the vanguard wagon train of 1847 to travel from Winter Quarters to the Salt Lake valley.[78]

### Colorado River Emigration

Due to the high cost of traveling across the plains, another method of transporting immigrants and freight was examined in earnest. The plan involved crossing the Atlantic Ocean, traversing the Isthmus of Panama, traveling up to the mouth of the Colorado River and steam boating up the Colorado with both freight and church members. From the landing location near the mouth of the Rio Virgin River (near present day Hoover Dam), both freight and immigrants would be taken overland to the Salt Lake Valley. In a letter dated 19 October 1864,

Brigham Young explained to Daniel H. Wells his views of the possible change in transporting Saints and freight to Utah. In part the letter read, "It is our intention to select brethren immediately and send them down to the head of navigation on the Colorado River, near the mouth of the Rio Virgin, to establish a settlement and build a warehouse there."[79] During the General Conference in October 1864, Anson Call was directed by the First Presidency to establish a colony near the Colorado River for the purpose of founding a landing site for steamboats as far north on the Colorado River as possible. In addition, certain merchants of Salt Lake City, seeking a method to lower freight costs to the Utah Territory, created a fund to build a warehouse at the site selected by Call. Accordingly, Call located the site, built the warehouse, and established a settlement. By February 1865, an 18x20-foot warehouse was constructed at Call's Landing, and prospects appeared bright. Sadly, the site was abandoned after only a few years. This was due in part to the difficulty of traversing the rapids of the Colorado River which was limited to times of the year when steamboats could actually travel upriver. The completion of the transcontinental railroad also could be considered a cause for the abandonment. The vision of transporting immigrants and freight up the Colorado River evaporated into the hot summer sun of the desert southwest.[80]

# 3
# WYOMING, NEBRASKA TERRITORY SELECTED AS AN OUTFITTING STATION 1864

The village selected in 1864 as the outfitting station for emigrating pioneers known as Wyoming, Nebraska Territory was situated on a plateau above a long sweeping bend of the Missouri River. This small community near the southeast corner of Nebraska stood just below where the Weeping Water Creek flowed into the mighty river. Otoe County, Nebraska claims the right to call Wyoming one of its first towns. Patrick Gass, of the 1804 Lewis and Clark expedition, left the following account of their first glimpse of the area in July. "Friday 20, We embarked early; passed high yellow banks on the south side and a creek called the Water-which-cries, or the Weeping Stream, opposite a willow island, and encamped on a prairie on the south side."[1] The topography in southeastern Nebraska is varied. However, one word defines the dominant geographic form, which is the curve. Undulating hills, bluffs, rivers, and streams all follow curves and the result is a land of stunning beauty. Rainfall amounts to just over 33 inches a year, while the area receives approximately 26 inches of snow annually. The average high temperature in July is 88 degrees, while the average low temperature in January hits 13 degrees. There are 216 sunny days per year in Otoe County.[2] Ample rainfall, relatively comfortable temperatures, plenty of sunny days, beautiful rolling hills, and abundant wildlife created the perfect location to establish a town.

The founding of Wyoming, NT offers a unique glimpse into a portion of early Nebraska history. Jacob Dawson, who launched the town of Wyoming, NT, was born in Ohio in the year 1818.[3] In 1848, he left Ohio, settled in Pittsburgh, Pennsylvania, and married Editha Jane (Ross). During that same year, the newlywed couple moved to McKeesport, Pennsylvania.[4] Evidence suggests that while living in Pennsylvania he gained newspaper experience by working for the *Pittsburgh Gazette*.[5] Like so many others during this time in American history, Dawson moved west where land was abundant and where he felt there were greater opportunities to improve his circumstances. By 1850, Dawson, his wife Editha, and their one-year-old son John were living in Fremont County, Iowa.[6]

**Wyoming, Nebraska Territory Established**

Jacob Dawson filed a plat for the town of Wyoming, NT which lay seven miles north of Nebraska City, on 26 August 1856. Dawson, along with five other men, filed the plat in the recorder's office at Nebraska City.[7] The town site was nestled against the banks of the Missouri River, in Southeastern Nebraska—just south of where Weeping Water Creek emptied into the river. The settlement had property set aside for a town park and a public square. The park was shown between Fifth and Sixth Street, while the public square was drawn between Second and Third streets. Most of the lots in the city were just over 53 feet wide and ran 131 feet in depth. The municipality also contained view lots that ran along the banks of the river. These lots were narrower than the others in the city, running approximately 30 feet wide and 120 feet deep. Dawson's platted town contained a total of 683 lots. The focal point of the town site was the levee which ran for several hundred feet along the river. This natural landing site for riverboats was over 160 feet in width and provided ample space for unloading freight and passengers. This levee would have been the arrival point for the church-sponsored pioneers who landed at Wyoming.[8]

. . .

## A Doomed Town

When Jacob Dawson first presented the plat for Wyoming, NT, five other men affixed their signatures to the original document. Stephen F. Nuckolls, Allen A. Bradford, William E. Pardee, John H. Maxon, and William McLennan signed their names as proprietors for the town of Wyoming.[9] Unfortunately for Dawson, both Stephan F. Nuckolls and Allen A. Bradford were involved in facilitating the establishment of Nebraska City in 1853.[10] Evidence indicates the very individuals selected to work with Dawson to build up Wyoming actually sought to stifle the growth of this new village. Credence to this conclusion is found in a letter written by Nuckolls on 10 June 1874 from Salt Lake City, Utah, in which Nuckolls discussed some early history of Nebraska. The letter reads in part, "In 1856 the proprietors of Nebraska City, fearing that the town of Wyoming would eclipse Nebraska City, concluded to buy that town, and did so, but they did not pay much for it."[11]

Of the six original proprietors of Wyoming, only Jacob Dawson lived in the town itself. The other five all lived in Nebraska City—the very town that sought to keep Wyoming from prospering. The 1856 Nebraska territorial census listed Stephen F. Nuckolls' occupation as a banker. Allen A. Bradford, William E. Pardee, and William McLennan indicated their occupations were lawyers, while John H. Maxon was a surveyor.[12] Clearly, the men who were partners with Dawson had both the skills and motivation for keeping Wyoming small. Perhaps Dawson recognized early on the futility of his venture. In 1856 he wrote,

---

> Caution to the public—all persons are hereby notified that all sales of lots, shares or otherwise in the city of Wyoming proper, without my signature are illegal and will not be recognized, as the premises belong to me and no person is authorized to dispose of any part thereof.[13]

---

Dawson's claim to own all the property in Wyoming was not

accurate, and he was essentially powerless to stop the other proprietors from throttling Wyoming's growth. Ownership was split with both Dawson and Nuckolls owning one-quarter of the property each, while the other four partners possessed one-eighth of the land that encompassed the town site.[14] Thus, Jacob Dawson owned one-fourth of the Wyoming Town Company, while the other five men possessed three-fourths of the company's equity. He would be incapable of creating the type of vibrant town along the river he had envisioned. One final act occurred in the early 1860s that stripped Dawson of his ability to control the future of his village. On 14 May 1861, Sheriff William Birchfield of Otoe County recorded a Sheriff's sale against Jacob Dawson. Dawson lost 103 of his lots as a result of this action. The auction was brought about because Dawson had a judgment placed against him in 1858, and he was unable to pay the $750 awarded in the judgment. Dawson's business partner, Stephen F. Nuckolls, purchased those lots for $450.[15]

Census records provide valuable insight into the population, work, and birthplace of those living in the vicinity of Wyoming, NT during its short existence. The 1860 Federal Census revealed the town had shrunk in population to 99 residents. This census also pointed out that ten of the ninety-nine occupants were born in Europe. The town now had two ministers, three blacksmiths, a school-teacher, one carpenter, two grocers, a saloon keeper, one mail carrier, one editor (Jacob Dawson), seven farmers, six laborers, and one county commissioner. The 1860 Federal Census also noted 26 unoccupied dwellings out of a total of 48 visited during the census.[16] In other words, fifty-four percent of the dwellings at Wyoming were uninhabited at the time of the 1860 census. By comparison, Nebraska City's population in 1860 was estimated to total 1,922 inhabitants.[17] Thus, in 1860, after four years of existence as a town, Wyoming stood at only five percent of the population of their rival—Nebraska City. Wyoming never could make up the population gap with Nebraska City.

**Life in Wyoming, NT**

Two newspapers, *The Wyoming Post* and *The Wyoming Telescope* provide some fascinating glimpses into the lives of those who called Wyoming home. Jacob Dawson was involved with both papers, and some of his views on what he wanted Wyoming to become can be found in the weekly paper. For example, when the town was only a few months old, Dawson advertised for 50 day-laborers and 20 carpenters to come to Wyoming. In the same article, Dawson issued a call for shoemakers, tinners, saddlers, and tradesmen. He promised a good choice of lots for those who answered the call to settle in Wyoming.[18] Ever the optimist, Dawson wrote that as of 10 April 1858, the town of Wyoming contained 80 houses and between 450 and 500 inhabitants.[19] The 1860 federal census demonstrates, neither the call for skilled craftsmen and carpenters was met, nor did the population achieve the level Dawson was suggesting.

The *Wyoming Post* advertised that Biddleman's Pioneer Saloon, operated by George Biddleman and located on Park Street, offered oysters for lunch every day.[20] The *Post* also noted the upcoming construction of a Methodist Church in the summer of 1858. The structure would be 40 feet in width and 50 feet deep. Unfortunately, the new school year would have only one operating school instead of the two that had been utilized the previous winter. According to the newspaper, the steamboat landing at Wyoming was "equal to any on the Missouri." A new warehouse was soon to be completed, and the lone hotel in Wyoming would soon see another one, which would reach three stories in height. The paper noted that a local steam sawmill was in operation. The announcement in the paper concerning the new "steam ferry boat," which was due to arrive in Wyoming on the 29th or 30th of April 1858, likely created lively discussions on the streets of the town.[21]

The newspapers also provided views of everyday life in Wyoming. For example, Winn, Wasson, & Company announced the opening of a new store in the town. The new business offered hats, boots, dry goods, cutlery, cooking stoves, doors, and windows.[22] One week later, the paper publicized the arrival of an A. Rogers, who advertized he was a physician and surgeon. His practice would be out of his home located on Walnut Street in Wyoming.[23] Thomas E. McDonald, who served as Justice of the

Peace, announced he was permanently located in Wyoming City.[24] Another person who offered his services through the newspaper was J. B. Boone, a local bricklayer and plasterer, who indicated he also lived in the city.[25] The paper publicized the upcoming election for a mayor, three aldermen, one recorder, one treasurer, an assessor, and a town marshal which was set for 3 May 1858. The election would take place at the schoolhouse located on Wood Street.[26]

The 8 May 1858 issue of *The Wyoming Post* noted that A. A. Brookfield was elected the mayor of Wyoming by a margin of eleven votes.[27] A later issue wrote about a wagon repair shop located on the corner of Walnut and Fourth Street, which was operated by N. H. Whitehead.[28] In other news of the day, George Biddleman was adding on to his saloon on Third Street, John McFarland was digging a cellar on Water Street (over which he planned to build a home), Isaac Miller was completing his building, and Jacob Dawson was in the process of completing his hotel. A warning was placed in the paper for town residents to beware of rattlesnakes in the area.[29] Regarding the conflict in Utah Territory, the last issue printed in the month of May 1858 declared the "Mormons have submitted to the rule of the authorities." The article went on to state that the general desire of the people seemed to be "for a war of extermination against these polygamists, murderers, and imposters at any expense."[30]

## Cemetery Created

Sometime during the early years of Wyoming's existence a cemetery was established. The location of the cemetery is now a cultivated field growing alternating crops of corn and soybeans. In 1998, the John Watts Barrett Family Genealogical Organization, with the cooperation of the Jim and Harold Johnson families (property owners), placed a marker on a site 0.6 of a mile southwest of the actual cemetery.[31] The burial site was set on a hill approximately one and one-half miles north of where the town of Wyoming once stood. To bury those who died, individuals coming from Wyoming would have traveled northward along a ridge line after moving up from the river.[32] At one time, two cedar trees marked the precise location of the cemetery, and many of the old grave markers were stacked against the two trees. Mrs. William Taylor, who indicated she had three brothers and two sisters buried in the old cemetery, explained to an unnamed newspaper reporter that she had helped plant one of the two trees 50 years earlier.[33] Unfortunately, no one took responsibility for the upkeep of the cemetery, and it fell into disrepair after only a few short years. Multiple headstones once marked the final resting place for those interred at the Wyoming burial site.[34] Sadly, because of vandalism, decay, the use of broken tombstones to block ditches, and people stealing headstones it is nearly impossible to determine with any degree of certainty who was buried in the cemetery outside of the village of old Wyoming—including those who traveled in the mid-1860s church migrations.

**Memories from Early Residents**

In latter 1929, Mrs. Emma McCarthy, who lived in Wyoming with her parents, Peter and Sarah Grosjohn shared her memories of early Wyoming with a reporter from *The Nebraska City News*. Emma affirmed that when she arrived in 1857, there were only three stores and the newspaper was printed in a small one room building with only a dirt floor. She remembered a stage line ran from Nebraska City to Omaha, making regular stops in Wyoming and there was a ferry boat operated by Ed Neeley. She recalled that F. W. Robb was one of the first settlers, and he started a sawmill. There was also a stone quarry nearby. Mrs. McCarthy indicated the first teacher in the town was Miss Jane Hathaway, and she was followed by Earl Moore. She recalled Mormons passing through Wyoming during the summer of 1864.[35] Her sister, Mrs. Anna Grosjohn Fey, also recalled early days of Wyoming. Anna also remembered boatload after boatload of Mormons docked at the town. Anna and her sister Emma would visit the camps where the Mormons stayed. Anna recalled Swedes, Danes, Germans, and French parading through the little town in great numbers. She said the Mormon's "greatest joy always was the corn fields which seemed to be laden with means of an elaborate livelihood."[36]

### Joseph W. Young Appointed to Lead Immigrating Saints

In a letter dated 16 February 1864, under the signatures of Brigham Young, Heber C. Kimball, and Daniel H. Wells, Joseph W. Young was appointed as "an assistant to our agent Joseph A. Young . . ." Joseph W. received authority to aid Joseph A. "in the business pertaining to this year's immigration in the United States, particularly on the Frontiers at such point on the Missouri river as he may select . . ." The letter further declared Joseph W. was responsible for members of the church and others that might want to cross with them. Young received exclusive control over loading the trains sent from Utah Territory for both freight and passengers. In addition, all persons traveling west, whether on independent trains or in PEF Fund Companies, were counseled to heed the direction of Joseph W. Young. The shortness of cash in Utah Territory was addressed in the letter by stating, "It is probable that the grocery, tobacco, and medicinal outfit of those needing assistance to cross the plains may have to be some less in quantity than heretofore . . ."[37] This appointment letter reveals two important situations. First: no decision had been made concerning the move from Florence, NT to Wyoming, NT as the outfitting station for 1864. Second: Utah Territory was strapped for cash and sought steps to improve the situation.

### Wyoming Selected as Outfitting Station

The selection of Wyoming as an outfitting station for the 1864 church train migration was set in motion when Joseph W. Young and Joseph A. Young (a son of Brigham Young) met at Kearney, NT on 3 March 1864. From Kearney the pair traveled to Omaha and checked on the situation in that town. Concluding their business in Omaha, they traveled to Nebraska City and the village of Wyoming. After thoroughly investigating Wyoming they determined they had found the location for the outfitting station. Wanting to take advantage of the income that could be generated by the thousands of immigrants that would pass through the town of Wyoming, and because of the competition between towns south of the Platte River and Omaha, businessmen in the southeastern Nebraska Territory promised to fix up the buildings in Wyoming for use by the church. In addition, a commitment was given that no liquor license would be issued in the village for the sale of spirits.[38] Brigham Young desired an outfitting station that would be "a quiet secluded, good, convenient and sufficiently-near-civilization outfitting point for our freight and immigration."[39] The village of Wyoming met the criteria and reaped the benefits of having pioneers pass through the town during the years 1864 to 1866. The village of Wyoming realized little or no growth following the departure of the church immigrants. Andrew Jenson visited the town in 1871 and wrote that he found the place "very much the same as when he first saw it in 1866—only a small cluster of farm houses with no importance whatsoever as a place of business."[40]

Evidence indicates that Florence, NT, which had been used as the outfitting post for the down and back trains since 1861, would also be utilized in 1864. In February 1864, Brigham Young wrote a letter to Bishop Edward Hunter, the individual with direct responsibilities to organize the massive down and back church trains with each bishop throughout the Utah Territory. In the epistle, Young told Hunter the requested 300 down and back teams for freight and the poor would again use Florence, NT as the outfitting station. Young wrote, "You may inform the Bishops that my nephew Joseph W. Young is appointed to go to Florence as our agent in the affairs of our immigration there . . ."[41] Interestingly, as Joseph A. Young and Joseph W. Young traveled separately by stage coach to their meeting in Kearney, Joseph A. wrote to Brigham from Denver, Colorado Territory. In his letter dated 28 February 1864 he wrote, in part, to verify that Joseph W. would "layover at Kearney until we come up." Furthermore, Joseph A. noted that from Omaha "we will go down river and locate the outfitting point, and from there to Saint Louis, and Chicago, to decide about the wagons—where we will separate he to the frontiers and me to N.Y."[42]

Following the meeting at Fort Kearny, Joseph A. and Joseph W.

arrived in Omaha at 1:00 a.m. 6 March 1864. In a letter written that same day, Joseph A. noted how they passed roughly 350 wagons loaded with freight and passengers for Denver, Bannock, and points beyond. Joseph expressed to his father that the merchants in Omaha were very liberal in their offerings for warehouses, and other items related to the immigration season. He noted they were headed to Nebraska City via carriage the next day and hoped that the owners of the town of Wyoming would be very liberal in regard to land, warehouses, and other accommodations.[43] From St. Louis, Missouri, Joseph A. wrote that he and his nephew did not take a buggy on the 7th of March. Instead, they traveled on the steamer *Denver* to Nebraska City, and from there they were taken to the village of Wyoming. After negotiating with a Mr. Fulton and a Mr. Hawley, Joseph A. and Joseph W. Young concluded to establish Wyoming, NT as the outfitting location for 1864. The specific justifications used by Joseph A. Young were first; Wyoming contained the "best steamboat landing I know of on the river." Second; a high dry hilly country surrounded the village. Third; settlers were scarce. Fourth; a closer road to Fort Kearny by 20 miles, which also avoids the Elk Horn and Loop Forks of the Platte River. Fifth; "a kinder spirit among the people—owing to there not being so many apostates all of which were taken into consideration in determining the points."[44] Thus, Wyoming was selected instead of Florence.

### Joseph W. Young's Responsibilities

Young's primary responsibilities were to purchase cattle, wagons, and other items needed for crossing the plains. Young arrived in the early spring to transact the needed business. His description of Wyoming offers insight into the condition of the village in 1864. Young wrote that Wyoming was not much of a town, but that it was beautifully situated on the banks of the Missouri River, and is very well adapted for camping and outfitting purposes.[45] Elaborating further, Young wrote that the town contained about a dozen houses, and that he had obtained two large warehouses of three stories each, which provided him with a needed storehouse, office, and living quarters.[46] On 7 July 1864, Young wrote a letter to his uncle, Brigham Young, in which he explained the immigrants sleeping arrangements. Describing a scene that would be repeated by those traveling later, he wrote, "The Saints have commenced camp life already. Some are sleeping in wagons, others under tents, and others, again, with nothing but the sky to cover them."[47] Besides transporting immigrants, Young also described another valuable purpose of the church trains to those living in Utah Territory. "There is considerable fitting out this season by merchants, and a great deal of merchandise and machinery will be taken on to Great Salt Lake City."[48]

Young faced a monumental task as the immigration agent at Wyoming, NT. His responsibilities included organizing, implementing, and supervising all aspects relating to the immigration of 1864. To successfully complete the year's immigration, he purchased supplies, food, wagons, oxen, and all items needed. He also accomplished all this during the last full year of the American Civil War, when supplies such as wagons, oxen, and key food items were consumed by the war effort.[49] Two additional components provided a justification to move from Florence, NT to Wyoming, NT. First, Wyoming was closer to St. Joseph, Missouri than Omaha, shortening river travel. In addition, the Nebraska City Cut-off Trail shortened the travel distance to Fort Kearny and the Utah Territory, as compared to the original Mormon Trail out of Florence. Therefore, freight and passengers could be shipped to Wyoming, NT cheaper than to Omaha on the Missouri River, and church trains would save travel days going both east and west.[50]

Joseph W. wrote to Brigham Young numerous letters during his stay in Wyoming, NT. A better understanding of the pressures he faced, and events taking place in 1864 is gleaned from those communications. In a 24 May 1864 letter, Joseph described to Brigham Young the magnitude of the gold mine immigration taking place as follows: "The steam ferry at Omaha averages two hundred and fifty teams per day for the last thirty days. Then the Ferrys of Plattsmouth, Nebraska City, St. Joseph and Atchison will at least cross as many more."[51] In the same letter, Joseph informed his uncle that livestock prices will likely remain high due to the large government contracts for freight at the many military posts in the west.[52] Interestingly, in a letter dated 27 May, Joseph may have been second-guessing some of his earlier thoughts about Wyoming when he wrote, "Perhaps I was too positive in giving my opinion about Wyoming as an outfitting place, but whether correct or not, I got the inference from Bros. Hooper & Eldridge that perhaps the town would grow and property become valuable, hence I wrote as I did and am glad to know that my views are in unison with your own on the subject."[53]

According to extant information, Joseph W. Young wrote more than 90 hand-written letters during his time as the immigration agent at Wyoming, NT.[54] Joseph's search for wagons seemed never-ending. In a letter written to Peter Schettler, a manufacturer of wagons out of Chicago, Illinois, Joseph lamented, "Our first mule train from Salt Lake is now here and depending on you for some 25 wagons before we can load and start them back . . . I have already had to purchase ten wagons to start out an early train and pay for them the highest price with agents and commission added."[55] Concerning the durability of some wagons from Utah, Joseph wrote, "The teams sent this year are very light and are not capable of taking heavy loads such as have been taken in former years. Many of the wagons are old and broken and have to be repaired. Very few of them have covers sufficient to protect the loading, and I am compelled to furnish them from this office."[56] Yet, with all the challenges faced by Joseph and his associates the overland migration continued.

The immigrating Saints of 1864 to 1866 who arrived in the town of Wyoming, NT found a village in the twilight of its existence. Jacob Dawson's dream of building a vibrant city on the banks of the Missouri River faded like a Nebraska sunset. Business leaders in Nebraska City had accomplished their stated goal of keeping Wyoming from becoming a rival. Other ghost towns dot the landscape of Otoe County. Towns such as El Dorado, Minersville, Oto, Woodville, Saltville, Swift, Erie, Groveland, and St. Peters joined Wyoming as locations that have vanished into history.[57] Yet, unlike the other ghost towns in Otoe County, Wyoming holds an important standing in Nebraska's history for the part it played as an outfitting station for several thousand church pioneers seeking to reach their Zion in the Utah Territory. Andrew Jenson, who immigrated with the 1866 Latter-day Saint pioneer migration, visited the site of Wyoming in 1934. Accompanied by Dr. A. E. Sheldon, secretary of the Nebraska State Historical Society, and other dignitaries, Jenson explained why Wyoming was so important to the immigrants arriving in 1866, "They set out from there because they desired comparative seclusion for their rest before starting their long journey, rather than starting out from the hustle and bustle of the new town of Nebraska City."[58]

## 4

# THE NEBRASKA CITY CUT-OFF TRAIL

Insight into how the Nebraska City Cut-off Trail came about gives a better understanding of travel across Nebraska in the 1860s, including variants of the trail itself and identifying the various qualities that made the trail attractive to both freighters and immigrants. The genesis for the establishment of the Nebraska City Cut-off Trail resulted, in part, from the Utah War of 1857. The country was mired in a serious economic recession, and many communities were suffering from business failures and bank closures. Like other towns bordering the Missouri River, Nebraska City suffered from the downturn. However, the freighting company of Russell, Majors and Waddell was awarded the government contract to freight millions of pounds of supplies to Utah Territory to support the troops that were involved in the war. During a meeting in February 1858, Nebraska City promised to meet the criteria set by the freighting company to repair the town's levee for accepting the expected large volumes of freight. In addition, a resolution was adopted to suppress liquor shops in the city. Perhaps most importantly, Mr. Majors, not satisfied with the Oxbow Trail, extracted a promise to survey and improve a shorter route to Fort Kearny. Thus, Nebraska City escaped economic disaster, and a new shorter route was eventually developed.[1]

The promise to locate a shorter route to Fort Kearny did not materialize during the time of the Utah War.

Alexander Majors was the driving force behind Russell, Majors and Waddell Freighting Company. Mr. Majors noted in his memoirs that in 1855, after freighting on the frontier for many years, he partnered with William Hepburn Russell and William Bradford Waddell. This was while Majors continued to live in Jackson County, Missouri. For three years, the firm operated under the name Majors and Russell. However, in 1858, when the government granted the contract to haul supplies to Utah Territory, the firm name was changed to Russell, Majors and Waddell.[2] One condition of the freighting contract allowed the company to locate another starting point in addition to Fort Leavenworth, Kansas. In Majors' opinion, Fort Leavenworth was unsuitable due to a lack of herding grounds for the thousands of livestock that would be needed to transport the massive amount of supplies needed for the army. The supplies sent to Utah in 1858 amounted to over sixteen million pounds, which required more than 3,500 large wagons and the appropriate men and teams to transport. Majors, along with a Lieutenant Dubarry of the Quartermaster's Department, traveled up the Missouri River as far as Plattsmouth to locate a suitable location for a freighting depot. Following the trip up the river, his conclusion was Nebraska City presented the best option for a freighting terminal.[3]

**Fits and Starts to Create the Nebraska City Cut-off Trail**

Because the assurance from the 1858 town meeting to find a shorter route to Fort Kearny did not materialize, the freighting firm of Russell, Majors and Waddell was forced to use the Oxbow Trail which went north from Nebraska City rather than directly west. A large portion of this trail bordered the slow moving Platte River. This caused an inordinate amount of mud—particularly during bad weather—making progress for freighters and emigrants extremely slow. In addition, the Oxbow Trail was a longer trip to Fort Kearny than a direct route. By 1860, the Utah War ended and the huge government contracts evaporated. Nevertheless, many freighting opportunities still existed.

The need to find a shorter route to Fort Kearny became even more crucial to keep the freighting business profitable. One or two days of travel could save thousands of dollars in expenses for the freighting companies. During the Utah War, Alexander Majors had moved to Nebraska City, and he stated that he never did business more pleasantly than with the gentlemen whom I met during my residence of nine years there.[4] Majors not only enjoyed his associates in Nebraska City, but the firm of Russell, Majors and Waddell spent thousands of dollars building warehouses, stables, corrals, stores, and all the associated items needed to support a large freighting concern. Selling the existing real estate and buildings would have caused significant losses for Alexander Majors. Evidence indicates each wagon train sent out from Nebraska City to points west could at times show a profit of two thousand to three thousand dollars. Thus, the desire to abandon a profitable route seemed foolish. Nevertheless, a shorter route needed to be pursued to support the needed profits.[5]

In an attempt to find a shorter route to Fort Kearny, a meeting was held 14 February 1860 in Nebraska City. Two key participants in this gathering were Alexander Majors and Samuel W. Black, governor of the Nebraska Territory. Governor Black urged those attending to locate and clear a well-defined road to Fort Kearny. During this conference, five men were appointed to request prescriptions for money, lumber, merchandise, and labor to build needed bridges and improve the road. Just as the get-together in 1858 produced no results, this meeting also fell woefully short of producing tangible movement in building a shorter road. With no progress forthcoming, Mr. Majors hired Augustus Harvey, city engineer of Nebraska City to lay out the road. Interestingly, in 1858, Ward B. Burnett, surveyor general of the United States Land Office, measured almost the same route, and on 11 January 1859, Burnett wrote he expected this road to be used the next season.[6] Harvey followed almost the exact route as Burnett, and this new road offered a firmer passage than the existing Ox Bow route.[7] One part of Harvey's job was to examine existing bridges, fords, and stream bottoms to verify their viability for heavy freighting trains.[8] Of interest, many who lived in Lancaster County traveled to Nebraska City for groceries and other supplies, so when Harvey began laying out a new road to Fort Kearny, he found a well-beaten path from Nebraska City to a settlement known as Olathe on Salt Creek (near present day Lincoln, Nebraska).[9]

No trail or road existed past Olathe, so Mr. Harvey's work started from there and continued to Fort Kearny. Beginning in present day Lancaster County, the route passed through the western portion of Lancaster County through present day counties of Seward, York, and Hamilton, concluding in the eastern edge of Hall County, where the trail merged with the Oxbow Trail. Augustus Harvey and his assistants rode on horseback ahead of the others, marking the course for the trail to follow. Another person followed with four mules "hitched to a breaking plow" who turned over a furrow.[10] Upon Harvey's return the local newspaper wrote effusively concerning the new road. The paper noted that within two weeks, work on bridges and culverts would be completed and there would be no better road in Nebraska. The total distance from Nebraska City to Fort Kearny came to 181.5 miles. In addition, the paper noted, perhaps with some hyperbole, "there is no section where wood, water, and grass cannot be found within one mile." Furthermore, "Every person going west will find it to his interest to take the direct road, and save thereby from seventy to eighty miles of dreary, lonesome travel."[11] One of the names attached to the trail was an "air line" route. This moniker stuck for several years, because the new road was "as direct as a road can be made in this region, being but a few miles longer than an air line."[12] Another early name attached to the trail was The Central Route. In addition to the church pioneers of the mid 1860s, evidence indicates that after 1861 most emigrants availed themselves to the new route, with Nebraska City, rather than Wyoming, NT, being the outfitting point.[13]

**Freighting on the Nebraska City Cut-off Trail**

The new road profoundly impacted freighting. From 25 April to 13 October 1860, Alexander Majors transported 2,782,258 pounds of freight over the new central route. In the process 5,687 oxen, 515 wagons, 72 mules, and 602 men were needed to complete the freighting operation.[14] Thus, each wagon could carry approximately 5,400 pounds of freight. During the freighting year of 1864, 23 million pounds of freight utilized the trail.[15] By 1865, the height of the freighting boom, a staggering 44,023,598 pounds of goods shipped over the trail. This record amount of freight required 10,311 wagons, 76,596 oxen and 11,730 men.[16] During its relatively short existence, the Nebraska City Cut-off Trail was instrumental in the success of Nebraska City. It helped populate the Nebraska Territory south of the Platte River and provided a means for immigrants to travel to their destinations in California, Oregon, or Utah. Figures from 1865 indicate that 75 percent of all overland travel through Nebraska Territory utilized this direct line between Nebraska City and Fort Kearny.[17] One should understand that this direct route was not a straight highway, but a serpentine trail that meandered along hillsides, changed directions resulting from weather conditions, and at times the wagons would run three to four abreast as they tumbled west. Unfortunately, by 1867 the expansion of the railroad would cause the demise of frontier freighting over the Nebraska City Cut-off Trail.

**Road Ranches**

Road ranches played an important role for those who traveled the Nebraska City Cut-off Trail. These ranches were of varying sizes, but the intent of those who owned these over-night stations was to create income by providing a place to lodge, eat, purchase supplies, stable animals, and rest from their day's journey. These resting points were spaced close together, because freighters could cover about 12 to 14 miles in a day.[18] Ranches in Otoe County included the Wilson Ranch, just north of the present town of Dunbar, Nursery Hill, located twenty-two miles west of Nebraska City, and the Meacham ranch, which was located on the Otoe and Lancaster county line.[19] Lancaster County ranches comprised the Salt Creek ranch, eight miles south of Lincoln and Cheese Creek Ranch which lay in the western portion of Lancaster County.[20] John E. Fouse, and Daniel Millspaw, William J. Thompson, and Roland Reed all established ranches in Seward County.[21] York

County ranches were known as Porcupine Ranch, the Jack Smith Ranch, the McDonald Ranch, and the Antelope Ranch.[22]

Hamilton County historians note that three significant road ranches existed to serve travelers on the trail. In 1861, Daniel Milspaugh established a ranch in the eastern part of the county. Six miles west of Milspaugh stood the Prairie Camp ranch. John Harris and Alfred Blue, two Confederate war veterans, founded the Deep Well ranch in 1865.[23] Evidence indicates Hall and Adams Counties were unable to establish ranches during the time the trail existed due to Indian hostilities. Dogtown and the Ben Holladay ranches were located in present day Kearney County. Dogtown stood at the junction of the Nebraska City Cut-off Trail and the Oregon Trail, while the Holladay ranch was located two miles west of Fort Kearny.[24] Most of the road ranches folded following the loss of freighting and immigrant travel on the trail due to the completion of the railroad. Ranches, the directness of the route, good water sources, and the flat terrain offered weary travelers a relatively efficient route from Nebraska City, NT to Fort Kearny.

**The Steam Wagon Experiment**

On Monday, 14 July 1862 a massive steam powered machine was unloaded at the Nebraska City levee that would impact the future of the direct route to Fort Kearny—even to the point of changing the name of the road. This colossal contraption weighed almost ten tons, moved under the power of four ten-horsepower engines, and contained rear wheels that reached a height of over ten feet. The rims measured eighteen inches wide, and the front wheels had a diameter of six feet.[25] Arriving at the same time was the proprietor of the machine, Joseph Renshaw Brown. Three men drove the wagon and Daniel Dangerfield, who served as Brown's nurse for an infectious skin condition, accompanied Brown.[26] Brown entered Nebraska City as somewhat of a mystery man. However, he was a person of notoriety in Minnesota where he served in politics for the Democratic Party; he was Minnesota's first wheat farmer, and he assisted in codifying the territories laws. Brown even attained the rank of major general in the state militia. Brown's critics considered him unscrupulous, while his colleagues found him hard-working, enterprising, thoughtful, and extremely intelligent.[27]

The unit that was unloaded at the Nebraska City wharf was actually the second steam wagon Brown had financed. Brown paid John A. Reed of New York City $4,000 to build a similar one in 1860. This particular wagon was freighted from New York City to Red Wing, Minnesota in May 1860. Preliminary tests showed the wagon moved too slowly to be effective in hauling freight, so Reed and another gentleman adjusted the gears so the machine could reach speeds of about two and one-half miles per hour—about the pace of mule-drawn wagons.[28] Brown was determined to test the machine's ability to travel over an existing trail between Henderson, Minnesota and Fort Ridgeley, about forty miles west. Twenty-eight agonizing days later, after placing plank roads across sloughs, the machine reached a creek within four miles of the fort. Unfortunately, the steam wagon sunk into the mud during the season's first heavy snow. The mammoth wagon remained in that bog when Mr. Brown arrived in Nebraska City with his second wagon. The second machine built by Mr. Reed was lighter, faster, and it purportedly could reach speeds of four-and-one-half miles per hour. The steam wagon allegedly reached speeds of almost eight miles per hour while traveling down a steep hill on present-day Central Avenue in Nebraska City.[29] Mr. Brown's total investment in the second steam wagon was $7,583.62, which included charges to ship the machine from New York City to Nebraska City.[30] The citizens of the town seemed almost delirious at the thought of the steam powered wagon lumbering over the route to Fort Kearny at twice the speed of oxen. Nebraska City's claim as the freighting capital of the west could reach even greater heights.

As noted earlier, Brown had attained the rank of major general in the Minnesota militia. Many living in Nebraska City called him General Brown, a title he seemed to like. During the Civil War, the label of general seemed important, so one can appreciate Brown's attachment to the name. Interestingly, Nebraska City's two newspapers seemed to temper the expectations of the venture. Both papers warned their readers that this was a voyage to establish water stations and improve the stream crossings. Once this needed infrastructure was in place, the trip from Nebraska City to Denver, Colorado could be made in about four days. Excitement ran from Nebraska City all the way to Denver. The enterprise began on 22 July 1862. With great fanfare, the steam wagon left Nebraska City pulling three wagons. Two carried about four tons of flour, while one was used as a tender for the boiler. The steam wagon limped out of town and was unable to pull the freight wagons up or down the short inclines just outside of the city. The driver was forced to run the steam wagon alone and then pull the tender and freight wagons up with a rope. About three miles west of the city a crank on one of the engines broke, and the giant machine ground to a halt. The crank could not be repaired in Nebraska City, which meant Brown must ship the broken part to Reed in New York City. Knowing he needed the support of the citizens of Nebraska City, Brown stayed in town for several days.[31]

Just five days after the steam wagon disaster, a community meeting was held in Nebraska City, where a number of people at the meeting expressed satisfaction with the results of the experiment. In addition, they declared their belief that the steam wagon would bring the freighting time between Nebraska City and Denver to within three days —even though Denver stood roughly 535 miles away. The attendees unanimously approved a motion to ask the Otoe County commissioners to approve building a public road to the borders of Lancaster County. In return, General Brown would create regular steam wagon service to Denver, which entailed building more steam wagons. Brown promised the Nebraska City citizens he would deliver a new steam wagon by October 1862, and would complete the sixth and final steam wagon by April 1863. Unfortunately, his commitments were conditioned upon receiving the needed investment dollars—money which never materialized. Interestingly, Brown knew from the beginning the shortcomings of his machine. It was too heavy, and the power driving the steam wagon was not sufficient. He also understood his contraption, which burned a chord of wood every four hours and needed to pull a tender, would necessitate extensive wood stockpiles for the journey. In addition, numerous water tanks would be required along the trail to support the steam-powered behemoth. The needed funding failed, the broken crank never came back to Nebraska City, and Brown never returned.[32]

### Improvements to the Trail

Fortunately for the new direct route, now known as the Steam Wagon Road, improvements came as a direct result of Mr. Brown's experiment. Otoe County voters approved the sale of $2,500 worth of bonds to finance improvements to the road. In addition, the county commissioners asked Frederick C. Morrison to survey the road and lay out a better course. Morrison completed his survey by the fall of 1862. County commissioners asked Silas E. Smith, the county treasurer, to sell Steam Wagon Road bonds. The bonds, created by Smith, bore an annual interest rate of ten percent and were payable on the first day of January and July, starting 1 July 1863. Also, William E. Hill was appointed as road superintendent, and by mid-summer six bridges had been built along the trail in Otoe County.[33] Trail improvement also took place in several counties west of Otoe. A law approved by the territorial legislature on 15 February 1864 named William E. Hill, David L. Osborn of Otoe County, and Anderson Davies of Seward County as commissioners to locate a territorial road, beginning at the western boundary of the Steam Wagon Road, on the western line of Otoe County, running west on the most practicable route to strike the territorial road running from Nebraska City to Fort Kearny, where the same crosses Walnut Creek, in Seward County.[34] Thus, even though the steam wagon trial was unsuccessful, the efforts of Joseph Renshaw Brown and the people of Nebraska City proved crucial to improving the trail now known as the Nebraska City Cut-off Trail.

### Freighting Stories

The *People's Press*, a Nebraska City newspaper, described the crucial impact of the freighting business on the local economy during the year 1862. The July 3rd issue noted that during the preceeding four weeks, emigrant traffic had fallen over 90 percent from the spring rush.

Consequently, business from pioneer traffic dropped substantially. However, the freighting trade expanded significantly during the same period of time. For example, the week of 7 June witnessed no less than 110 government wagons roll through the town. The following week experienced 146 wagons, with 131 wagons heading west during the week of 21 June. The last week of June experienced 152 wagons travelling through the town. The article stated that just these wagons alone amounted to over 3,170,000 pounds of freight heading west on the "Great Central Airline from Nebraska City via Fort Kearny to Denver." The article concluded by noting the fact that the merchants in Colorado had realized the advantage of the direct route from Nebraska City over all other trails heading west from the Missouri River.[35]

The trail was created primarily for freighting. The stories of those who traveled the Nebraska City Cut-off Trail and worked on the massive freight wagons, provides the opportunity to envision what life was like on the trail. One early freighter, Deforest P. Rolfe, addressed a meeting of the Nebraska Historical Society on 10 January 1900 in which he shared some of his experiences from the early days of freighting. He learned quickly after his arrival in Nebraska City that freighting constituted the best and only business for building up the town and adding value. It seemed that every person involved with business in the city was ready to do all in his power to advance the interests of Nebraska City as a freighting point.[36] Concerning the wagons used in freighting, Rolfe stated they were specifically made for plains transportation, were built from the best lumber, were wide tracked, strong and tight, and were covered with heavy canvas over the bows. In addition, he noted:

---

Seven thousand pounds was the load drawn by five yoke of good cattle; six yoke if cattle were light. A good team consisted of one yoke of heavy, well-broken cattle for wheelers, a good second best came next; two pair in the swing could be made up from partly broken cattle, with a good pair of leaders.

---

Rolfe remembered that Texas Steers made the best leaders, because they held their heads high, were quick on their feet, and could run like a horse when alarmed.[37]

Rolfe describes one of his successful trips from Nebraska City to Denver in the early spring of 1862. His wagons were the first to leave the city that season, and the trip to Denver was completed in twenty-eight days. Upon the conclusion of his trip, he received a payment of just over $10,000 in Cherry Creek gold dust which he placed in two-pound oyster cans. He rolled the cans in his blanket, secured the valuable gold dust at the back of his saddle, and headed out to catch up with his freight wagons that were now heading east. On the second day out from Denver, he met a war party of Ogallala Sioux traveling to raid against their old-time enemy, the Utes. The chief and Rolfe used sign language to communicate. The leader of the war party explained in sign language that they intended to surprise the Utes by "sneaking up on them like snakes, and getting many scalps." After about half-an-hour of sign language, Rolfe treated the war party to tobacco, which was received with great appreciation. Then, as suddenly as they came, they galloped away as Rolfe states, "[I sat on my] mule and gazed after them until they passed from my sight."[38] Food consumed on the trail was simple. The daily ration for men employed was 2 pounds of flour, one-and-one-half pounds of bacon, one-and-one-quarter ounces of coffee, and two-and-one-half ounces of sugar. Monthly wages paid during the freighting season of 1865 equaled $150 for wagon masters, $85 for his assistant, and $70 to $75 for drivers. The freighting period also benefited the farmers who lived in Iowa and Nebraska near the Missouri River. Many small traders with a single team of mules and a wagon could load their wagon with corn, oats, poultry, butter, eggs, and even dogs and cats for the western trade. These small traders often realized good profits for their efforts."[39]

Thomas Alfred Creigh kept a diary of his 1866 freighting adventure from Nebraska City to Montana. The Montana gold rush brought thousands of people to the area, which created a tremendous demand for equipment and supplies. The population of the Montana Territory by 1865 reached 120 thousand people, and gold was virtually the only item produced there. Creigh traveled west as a clerk on a wagon train carrying machinery to the mines. His entries offer a unique view into the life of a member of a freighting wagon train. The train that Creigh worked on carried boilers and quartz stamping machinery to the mines. His particular wagon caravan consisted of 52 wagons and 250 yoke of oxen. The freighters traveled over the Nebraska City Cut-off Trail to Fort Kearny, crossed over the Platte River near Julesburg, Colorado Territory, and journeyed to Fort Laramie where they took the newly-opened Bozeman Trail to Montana. The journey took 107 days and covered a distance of 1,115 miles.[40] Some of his more out-of-the-ordinary experiences, during the months of June and July, on the Nebraska City Cut-off Trail are recorded as follows:

---

[June] 23 – Breakfasted at 3 A.M. Pulled out second wing of train at 7 A.M. Considerable trouble crossing slough—a number of tongues broken . . . There is 81 tons of Machinery including 2 Boilers—5 wagons of Provisions & 5 private wagons of Christenot (family accompanying the freighters to Montana).[41]

June 25 – Monday—Clear. Hot: Broke camp at 4 A.M. . . . Camp on Wolf Creek. Passed a train of 250 wagons coming from Salt Lake City to take out Mormons from Wyoming. Crossed the Nemaha River at 6 P.M. having broke camp at 4 P.M. Halted at 7 P.M. . . . Cook overtook us, having remained in Nebraska City.

June 26 – Tuesday—Clear—Pleasant. After a night of perfect torture from myriad of mosquitoes, both to man and beasts, keeping us up all night, we broke camp at 4 A.M. Had a fine bath in a creek one mile from camp—Reading Harpers & Beadles Monthlies. We are new and will be for a long time entirely lost as to what is going on in the world around us. Would like to see an occasional daily paper.

July 5th 1866 Thursday—clear—Broke corall at 4:30 AM drove till 9 A.M. Passing through Valley City (Dogtown, near Fort Kearny), bought and issued clothing to men. Camped on bank of Platte. Broke corall at 2:45 P.M. halted at 5:30 two miles from Fort Kearny

[sic] . . . Fort K. contains only about a dozen soldiers commanded by Brig Genl Wessel of U.S.A.[42]

---

In 1866, one of the more recognizable figures who hired out as a freighter was William Henry Jackson. Years following his freighting experience, he wrote an autobiography. In addition, he painted many pictures from his memory and from sketches he drew while on the trail. Jackson and his friends arrived at Nebraska City 2:30 a.m., Tuesday, 26 June 1866. After departing from the steamboat *Denver* with his two friends Rock and Billy, the trio napped on steps and in doorways until day light. The freighting wagon train he and his friends worked for was owned by a gentleman named Matt Ryan. He knew virtually nothing about the owner of the wagon train, but as soon as they were officially signed up to work they were whisked off to the company store to purchase outfits for the plains. Every new teamster began their journey from Nebraska City with a pair of blankets, white rubber coat, shoes, stockings, pants, shirts, an old-fashioned carpetbag, a Colt .44 revolver, and a supply of cartridges. The total cost for outfitting equaled about $40, which was subtracted from the monthly pay.[43]

The first early morning began with calls for the new teamsters to roll out of their beds and prepare for the incoming horde of bulls. The oxen, which Jackson and most of his associates had never yoked up, came thundering into the circular enclosure of wagons. In his own words, "Each driver had his own twelve bulls to identify, beginning with the 'wheelers,' then the 'pointers,' the 'swing cattle' (three yokes), and the 'leaders,' six pairs in all, each of which had to be yoked and bowed and chained in proper position." The first morning of yoking required a full eight hours to complete—only then could the exhausted freighters began their journey west. Fortunately, after a few weeks the time for yoking had fallen to about forty minutes. During the first few days only one drive a day was completed. During the early part of the trip, a hot dry wind blew continually, choked the freighters with dust, and burned their faces and lips with a powdered alkali. Jackson described his first two weeks on the trail as "the severest physical hardship I have ever known, and every day I cursed the folly that had prompted me to throw up my well-shaped career in Vermont.[44]

As noted, millions of pounds of freight passed over The Nebraska City Cut-off Trail during its short existence. The trail also proved crucial in the efforts for members of The Church of Jesus Christ of Latter-Day Saints to reach their desired Zion between the years 1864-1866. During that time, the down and back church trains provided the means to walk to Salt Lake City. No down and back trains were sent in 1865, so emigrants depended on their own reserves, or the goodness of others to put them on the road to Utah Territory. Here is their story.

# 5

# THE FIRST WAGON TRAINS OF 1864

1864 witnessed significant changes from the previous year's emigration. The outfitting station (rest area) was moved from Florence, NT to Wyoming, NT. Seven down and back church trains, four independent wagon trains, and six freight wagon trains carried members of the Church of Jesus Christ of Latter-day Saints to their desired destination in Utah Territory. Church trains accounted for about 2,200 of those who traveled. Independent and freight wagon trains transported roughly 315 additional trekkers. An additional 383 pioneers, whose names currently are not connected to a particular wagon train, add to the number of travelers. Thus, approximately 2,898 individuals left their homes in Europe, South Africa, the United States, or other parts of the world for their desired settlement in Zion.[1]

Composition of the wagon trains for 1864 is as follows:

### CHURCH TRAINS SENT FROM SALT LAKE CITY TO WYOMING, NEBRASKA TERRITORY, 1864

| Wagon Master | Departure from Missouri River | Arrival in Utah Territory | Estimated number of passengers |
|---|---|---|---|
| John R. Murdock | 29 June 1864 | 26 August 1864 | 115 |
| William B. Preston | 4 July 1864 | 15 September 1864 | 439 |
| Joseph S. Rawlins | 15 July 1864 | 19-20 September 1864 | 435 |
| William S. Warren | 22 July 1864 | 4 October 1864 | 436 |
| Isaac A. Canfield | 27 July 1864 | 5 October 1864 | 251 |
| William Hyde | 9 August 1864 | 26 October 1864 | 365 |
| Warren S. Snow | 13-17 August 1864 | 2 November 1864 | 160 |

### INDEPENDENT WAGONS TRAINS CARRYING IMMIGRANTS

| Wagon Master | Departure Date and location | Arrival in Utah Territory | Estimated number of passengers |
|---|---|---|---|
| John D. Chase | 26 June 1864/Wyoming, NT | 20 September 1864 | 101 |
| John Smith | abt. 25 July 1864/Wyoming, NT | 25 Sept – 1 Oct 1864 | 117 |
| Joseph W. Young | 21 August 1864/Wyoming, NT | 29 September 1864 | 14 |
| William D. Pritchett | 4 June 1864/Virginia | 31 Aug – 1 Sept 1864 | 38 |
| Unknown | 1864 | 1864 | 383 |
| **FREIGHT TRAINS** | | | |
| Soren Christoffersen | 1864/Wyoming, NT | 13 October 1864 | 14 |
| William Dallin | 1864/Wyoming, NT | 1864 | 3 |
| John Judge Kerr | 1864/Wyoming, NT | 1864 | 1 |
| Kimball and Lawrence | 1864/Wyoming, NT | 5 September 1864 | 17 |
| Seely Freight Train | 1864 Wyoming, NT | 30 October 1864 | 1 |
| Sharp and Spencer | 1864/Atchison, KS | 6 October 1864 | 9[46] |

Of the 17 wagons trains that transported members of the Church of Jesus Christ of Latter-day Saints to Utah Territory, 13 used the Nebraska City Cut-off Trail. One freight wagon train began its trek west at Atchison, Kansas, while an independent wagon train actually began traveling west from the state of Virginia. The first wagon train to leave Wyoming, NT constituted an independent wagon train under the direction of John D. Chase. His train was followed by the seven down and back trains, another independent train captained by John Smith and four wagon trains transporting freight to Utah Territory. In addition, one independent wagon train passed through Omaha, NT (from its starting point of Virginia), and one freight train initiated their trek west from Atchison, Kansas.[2] Those who left Europe during the 1864 migration sailed on three vessels. *Monarch of the Sea* carried 974 immigrants from Liverpool, England to New York City. The *General McClellan* left Liverpool with 802 converts, while the ship *Hudson* departed London, England with 863 anxious passengers. These two sailing vessels also landed at New York City. The total number of members of the church who traveled on the above-named sailing ships totaled 2,639 passengers, or approximately 90 percent of those who traveled west from Wyoming, NT. In addition, two other sailing ships left Port Elizabeth, South Africa for Boston, Massachusetts in 1864. The *Echo* and *Susan Pardew* carried a combined 27 passengers to the American continent.[3]

**Ocean and Rail Travel**

Those who traveled across the ocean on sailing ships in 1864, experienced violent storms, poor food, overcrowding, putrid water, accidents, seasickness, cholera, explosions, births, deaths, and a host of other painful experiences.[4] Andrew Christian Nielson describes his travels from Denmark. He and his companions took a steamer from Alborg to Copenhagen, Denmark. After leaving the European continent by steamer, the group arrived at Hull, England. From Hull the pioneers traveled to Grimsby, England where they stayed for about a week. A train took the immigrants from Grimsby to Liverpool, where the group could board the *Monarch of the Sea* for the voyage to Castle Garden in New York City. Nielson noted that measles broke out on the ship during the Atlantic crossing, which claimed the lives of 50 children and one old Scotsman. In addition, he described the crew as "the most cruel and wicked set of sailors that I have ever seen in my life."[5] After arriving at Castle Garden and following inspection, the passengers sailed to Albany, New York. From Albany, trains and ferries were used to take them to Quincy, Illinois where they traveled in cattle cars to St. Joseph, Missouri. Nielson observed the desolation caused by the American Civil War by stating, "Here was [sic] the ruins of whole towns as had been laid waste by the terrible struggle."

Mary Roberts Roskelley, who sailed on the *General McClellan,* vividly describes a storm that wracked the vessel after 15 to 20 days on the ship. Mary's parents traveled in steerage, while her brother, John, stayed one floor below with other small boys. She describes the storm as almost a hurricane, and how the violent rocking of the ship caused great tension among the passengers. During the storm, her mother worried about John sleeping below, so she made a special place next to her out of trunks and boxes placed in a row down the middle of the room between braces. She hoped this special built-up area would be a safe location for her son. As the storm intensified other people in steerage were now crying, praying, or singing. Suddenly, a powerful wave caused the ship to rock and lurch, which sent John's bed on the floor and rolled him under the bunks. The mother cried out, "O my boy, my boy." Conversely, the boy's father responded with "Oh never mind mother, he'll come back when we roll the other way." Her mother thought John had rolled out of the ship into the ocean. The ship did roll back and John came out from under the bunks, with bedding and buckets, whereupon his mother grabbed him. Shortly, John was tied to boxes and posts, which allowed the mother to stop worrying about her son. This violent storm lasted three days and two nights. Upon arrival at New York City and following inspections at Castle Garden, Mary, her mother, father, and siblings traveled up the Hudson River to Albany.[6] The trip from Albany to St. Joseph, Missouri happened mostly by rail train. After arriving at Wyoming, NT, Mary and her family traveled on the Warren S. Snow down and back church train.[7]

## John D. Chase Independent Train

On 22 June 1864, Joseph W. Young issued instructions for those who would travel in the first independent wagon train for that year. John D. Chase, who was returning as a missionary in England, received the authority to supervise those who would travel west with this private wagon train. Young declared those traveling with Chase should "rally around and sustain Bro. Chase and harken to all his council." In addition, those on this train should find him "a good riding animal, saddle, etc., which I want you to give Bro. Chase as his individual property." Furthermore, Chase should be provided with a "comfortable place to board while on the journey."[8] Chase and the mule train, with approximately 97 immigrants, began the long trek west on 26 June 1864 and arrived at Salt Lake City on 20 September 1864.[9] Travel went smoothly until a few days from Ash Hollow, when a disagreement between two men traveling on the train blew up into a full-scale guns-drawn fight. A shoe merchant from St. Louis, Missouri, who desired to immigrate to Utah, made an agreement with a fellow named Isaac Nash. The arrangement stipulated that if Mr. Nash would take charge of the merchant's eight wagons of boots, shoes, and hats during the trek to Utah, then Mr. Nash and his wife could travel for free. The deal was finalized, and all merchandise was placed under the direction of Mr. Nash.[10]

The shoe merchant supplied the money, inventory, and wagons. Nash hired the teamsters and made the necessary arrangements for the western migration. Shortly, Nash was selected as sergeant of the guard for the entire wagon train, which in the shoe merchant's eyes took him away from what he was hired to do. As the wagon train neared Ash Hollow, NT, the vendor's dissatisfaction with Nash's work boiled over into a full-blown fight. The merchant confronted Nash, and said, "[he would] not go on any farther and I could quit as he had no more use for me." At this point, Nash and the teamsters he had hired threw their whips on the ground and agreed to quit. Cooler heads prevailed, when one member of the company suggested another person could act as sergeant of the guard for Nash. This worked for a few days until the group arrived at Ash Hollow. Upon arriving, the disgruntled marketer sought out a group of soldiers who were camped nearby. After visiting with the soldiers, the merchant returned to Ash Hollow and told Nash that he and his teamsters were fired. An argument escalated until the owner of the shoes allegedly drew a revolver on Mr. Nash and stated he would shoot him down. The merchant cocked the gun and placed his finger on the trigger. A bystander knocked the gun out of the merchant's hands. This infuriated the merchant, so he instructed his son to retrieve another gun from his wagon, which gun was promptly knocked to the ground by another member of the Chase Company. At this point, the merchant, along with his stock of shoes and wagons, left the scene for nearby soldiers' camp. Nash, the teamsters, and the balance of the wagon train continued their journey west.[11] They arrived in Salt Lake City, along with the rest of the Chase wagon train.[12]

## John R. Murdock Down and Back Church Train

The first down and back church train to leave Wyoming, NT was under the captainship of John R. Murdock. The wagon train departed 29 June 1864 and arrived at Salt Lake City 26 August 1864. The number in the company totaled approximately 78 individuals and 18 teamsters. During the journey west, three adults and two children died. In addition, a teamster named Sidney Beckstead died by an accidental discharge of his rifle.[13] Captain Murdock's mother and father were among the first converts to the church in Kirkland, Ohio. His father graciously offered Joseph and Emma Smith his twins to raise following the death of his own wife. Subsequent to the expulsion from Nauvoo, Illinois and the trek west, John R. Murdock enlisted in the Mormon Battalion and walked the entire distance from Winter Quarters to San Diego, California. In 1856, John actively participated in the rescue of the ill-fated Martin-Willie handcart companies. On five different occasions Mr. Murdock captained down and back church trains. He hauled mail from Salt Lake City to Independence, Missouri. In addition, he carried wagon trains of merchandise across the plains for Livingston & Bell. In total Captain Murdock completed eleven round trips across the plains. John Murdock likely brought more members to Utah than any other leader. Murdock also served in many church and civic positions during his lifetime.[14]

Captain Murdock's down and back train remained in Wyoming, NT for about ten days, all the while loading freight and emigrants, before beginning the return journey to Utah Territory. Most of the freight contained in the wagons went to Brigham Young and Hooper and

Eldredge. He relates that during the first night on the trail the horses stampeded all across the country, and it took four days to relocate the animals. Following this episode, men were constantly kept mounted on animals to prevent another stampede. Murdock noted that once the horses and mules were scattered over a large area of ground and were quietly feeding, any small sound would cause the animals to jump together and run away in a flash. As the Murdock train continued west, they were overtaken by two families. Captain Murdock once noted, "[I was] most successful with my teams and lost but very few."[15]

Phebe Ann Wooley Davis, was not a member of the church, but had several family members living in Utah Territory. Phebe yearned to see her brothers (who had joined the church during the Nauvoo period), so she and her family departed from northeastern Ohio 18 May 1864. They were filled with high hopes and great expectations of seeing the Woolley kin again. Little did the family know of the heartbreak that awaited them on the trail. Phebe's husband, Moses Davis, possessed sufficient funds to secure the best lodging and gear for the trek to Utah Territory.[16] Nevertheless, Phebe's accounts of the experiences that took place during their travel west under the direction of John R. Murdock are heartbreaking. Shortly after the family's arrival in Wyoming, NT, Phebe Ann's daughter Sarah Jane died. The family came ashore at the Wyoming town levee Monday, 23 May 1864. They had traveled on the riverboat *Denver*, from St. Joseph, and Sarah Jane was already very sick. Just four days later, Sarah Jane died. The grief-stricken mother wrote, "May 27, Friday. Weather clear, Sarah Jane died at 7:30 a.m. The last word she said that I understood was, 'Mother!' about midnight. Here she died, away from home, amongst strangers: not a face which we had ever seen, not another woman in the room." A coffin was purchased in Nebraska City, and the body was placed inside. The next day Phebe Ann, Moses, and the children buried Sarah Jane "on the prairie where there never was anyone laid near. No one can imagine our feelings at this time." Phebe Ann further writes, "It seems as if we don't know what to do. It seems mysterious to think that the one among us who was the most anxious to come on this trip must be taken, just at the start of our journey."[17]

As the family waited in Wyoming to begin the trek west, Phebe Ann provides one of the more explicit descriptions of a birth in camp. She wrote, "Some stakes were put in the ground, and something like a wagon cover thrown across—not high enough to get in without stooping. There was a kind of trench dug in the ground, some leaves put in, and something thrown over it; this was the bed, lower than ground level." Phebe further explains that everything the mother owned was contained in one box, including clothes. She saw the mother and new baby later in Salt Lake City. Phebe was very anxious to begin the walk to Utah Territory. On 11 June, Phebe wrote that she dreamed of seeing her daughter. In addition, as she looked around the area surrounding Wyoming, she wrote, "[I did not] see any place where I would like to live." She noted seeing a field of corn and one of wheat, which stood about four miles outside of the outfitting station of Wyoming. She visited Sarah's grave on the morning the down and back train began its journey.[18]

By 3 July, the company arrived at Salt Creek, NT. At this point, after just a few days on the trail, her son Eli contracted diarrhea, which Phebe believed was caused by drinking the slough, or standing water. Eli's condition continued to worsen, and by 11 July, Phebe stopped writing in her journal. However, a few months after arriving in Salt Lake City she updated her journal.[19] Her words that describe caring for Eli on the trail and his subsequent death are haunting. They reveal a mother's love for her son. As Phebe Ann and Moses trudged along the trail, Moses also became sick and needed to ride in one of the captain's wagons. Their daughter Susan was now forced to drive the family's personal wagon— as she was the only family member well enough to do so. Phebe explained that traveling on the plains is very challenging for everyone, and that people seemed to have so many personal burdens that helping sick people was very difficult, so her family helped themselves as best they could. Eli's condition continued to deteriorate, and he grew weaker. The heat became almost unbearable. Phebe noted that during noon breaks, other company members would "lay Eli and me under the wagon in the hot sand for a change." Eli's body was now "reduced to a skeleton" and the "mosquitoes and flies were very troublesome." Eli died 25 July, and Phebe shared her feelings with these heartrending words:

---

I was so weak that I could not move the light so that it would not shine in his [Eli's] eyes. They thought that I would not live from one day to the next. About midnight, I saw that he was going. I called Moses, but Eli was gone by the time he got there. He died very easy.

Stop dear reader and think a moment! There, hundreds of miles from civilization, we must leave him. He lay with me in bed till three in the morning, when he was taken out by the captain. No one can tell my feeling when his little feet was drug over me. He was taken to a tent where there was a little boy that had died the afternoon before and was fixed for burial. They took two cracker boxes and put them together, put a blanket in them, and laid him on —then lapped another 'round. They carried me to the grave so I might see him laid in. Here we left him, a little after sunrise on the 25th of July, and pursued our journey from day to day.[20]

---

One final tragedy to strike Phebe Ann during her travel to Salt Lake City was learning of her twin brother's tragic death when she arrived at the Green River, in Wyoming.[21] His death occurred in Little Cottonwood Canyon when a runaway log crashed into a stone pile, causing fragments to strike John Wooley on the side of the neck and face. He survived fifty hours, but never gained consciousness.[22]

Not all who traveled on the church trains journeyed for religious reasons. One such family was relocating to California, and they actually began their trip in Newton, Iowa. Samuel Gilcrest, along with his wife Mary Ann, and their four children began their passage west from Newton on 2 July 1864. They crossed the Missouri River at Plattsmouth, NT three days later, and continued to Fort Kearny. Shortly after crossing the Missouri River, the family realized how ill-prepared they were for the trip west. The family possessed two wagons. One was a light spring wagon, which was never intended for heavy cross-country travel. Their supply of provisions was totally insufficient with only enough for about two weeks. The family's intent was to purchase food at trading posts, or ranches along the trail, but the cost proved inordinately high, and the family soon ran out of money. In addition, the family was not aware of the seriousness of the situation between the pioneers and the Native Americans. In relating the family's predicament many years later, Frank Gilcrest indicated the news was upsetting and the fact the family was traveling alone only made matters worse.[23]

While stopping at Fort Kearny the Gilcrest family purchased a Smith & Wesson revolver with plenty of cartridges and a lot of buckshot for the gun which placed themselves in a better—but not excellent—position for protection from the Indians. Their choice was to either hurry to catch up with an actual wagon train, or wait for another wagon train to arrive. Once they learned about a large party of immigrants ahead of them bound for Salt Lake City, the family determined to drive ahead. After driving hard for a couple of days, the Gilcrest family caught up with another family heading west by themselves. The two families joined up, finally reaching the Murdock church train near Julesburg, Colorado. The Murdock train had crossed the South Fork of the Platte River and was resting for a day before proceeding west when the Gilcrest family reached them. Upon arrival at the Murdock camp, the Gilcrest family asked permission to join forces, which Captain Murdock agreed to. Accidents occurred regularly during the trek west. One heartbreaking example involved Sidney Beckstead, a blacksmith who served as one of the horse guards. He was on the first watch of the night and told to come into camp at daylight to repair a wagon. After waking up and mounting his horse, Sidney reached for his gun which was leaning against a greasewood bush when the gun accidentally discharged causing the one-ounce ball to enter just below his ear and come out at the top of his head.[24] He died instantly.

To help pay their share of the cost of traveling with the wagon train, Frank and his father were asked to work as camp guards. Frank Gilcrest was serving as a night guard when he experienced both fear and laughter in one incident. He began his night guard service at 8:00 p.m. by putting on his shotgun, checking to make sure everyone was inside the wagon enclosure, and putting out all the fires within the wagon train. About 11:00 p.m., Frank noticed the typical night noises such as coyotes and other animals ceased. Dropping down on all fours, Frank began crawling, so those who might be stalking him or the train could not see him. He heard a commotion down in the bushes. His immediate impulse was to call out for some assistance from some of the men, but he felt others would laugh at him. So, he decided to investigate the noise himself. He recorded, "[I] jumped down on the bank into the bushes, making quite a noise, following which I saw five or six heads pop up through the bushes, only ten or fifteen feet from me." Immediately, he drew his shotgun on the group of men. As the gun reached his shoulder, and he prepared to get as many of them as he could, before they got him, he heard a voice scream, "Don't shoot!" The embarrassed group explained they were teamsters who had crawled out from under the wagons to find a warmer location to sleep within the bushes. When cooler heads prevailed, the teamsters' biggest fear was that Frank would report their disobedience to Captain Murdock, which would result in severe punishment. Frank never reported the teamster's indiscretion.[25] The Gilcrest family rested in Salt Lake City for ten days before proceeding on to California.[26]

**William B. Preston Down and Back Church Train**

The second down and back train to leave Wyoming, NT departed 4 July 1864 and arrived in Salt Lake City, Utah Territory 15 September 1864. This particular wagon train came under the direction of William B. Preston. Captain Preston's responsibilities included about 400 immigrants, an enormous amount of freight, numerous teamsters, and 50 wagons.[27] Of the roughly 400 immigrants who journeyed west in Preston's wagon train, slightly more than half of the immigrants originated in Denmark followed by Sweden, Norway, and Germany.[28] Much of the freight assigned to Captain Preston's wagon train went to Brigham Young. According to the freight manifest, 35 wagons held freight for transporting west. Items sent to Brigham Young included stoves, machinery, hardware, steel bars, iron, tinware, tobacco, lye, soap, raisins, sugar, cod fish, oysters, candles, and a host of other items. In addition, Preston's train carried a new type-script for the *Deseret News*.[29]

An interesting traveler in Preston's wagon train included Jens Moller Haugaard Borglum, who emigrated from Denmark with his wife and seven-year-old daughter.[30] Jens traveled to Utah Territory and settled in the northern portion, near the Idaho territory border. Jens eventually became dissatisfied with his prospects in the territory and moved his family to Nebraska. Shortly after arriving in Utah, Jens married a second wife who bore two sons. John Gutzon De Le Mothe Borglum was born to Jens and his polygamous wife, Christiane Margrethe Mikkelsen, in 1867. His brother Solon was born one year later. Both brothers became famous for sculpting. Gutzon attained fame for his efforts in carving Mount Rushmore, while Solon focused on subjects related to the outdoors—particularly the plains of the Midwest. Noted author, Dr. Jean A. Lukesh wrote the following about these two brothers.

> Solon and Gutzon are both gone, but their Borglum name lives on, in carvings, in art, and in legends—across the prairies and plains, across America, and around the world. They were men who carved in sand, stone, clay, iron, wood, and more, and they left a deep impression on the land and on people who knew them.
>
> How proud their Danish woodcarver father, James (Jens) Borglum, would have been of his two once-secret sons Solon and Gutzon, who would never have been born if their parents had not been Mormons.[31]

Upon his arrival at Wyoming, NT Nils Flygare, who began his journey from Sweden, described the village as a wilderness. Previous to leaving his homeland, he and his fiancée determined to marry each other after their arrival in Utah Territory. It was at Wyoming where Nils noted he was introduced to western civilization. Before coming to the United States, Nils had never set eyes on cowboys, bull-whackers, prairie schooners, lassos, or other uniquely frontier activities. Nils also indicated the Utah boys who traveled on the down and back trains to "bring up the emigrants, did not impress us with much." Nils felt the time on the plains where the teamsters experienced dust, rain, and sunshine had hardened their appearance and caused them to appear rough. However, as Nils became more acquainted with these fascinating young men from Utah, he learned that beneath their rough exterior beat a kind heart. Upon arriving at the village of Wyoming, Nils and those traveling with him received flour, pork, dried apples, rice, sugar, and soap from the church agent. Those traveling west needed to learn the art of cooking without stoves or fireplaces while traveling. Nils noted, "[I was] satisfied from my own experience that most of us never did learn it while traveling across the plains."[32]

Nils described the challenge of walking across the plains. "It was a very weary and long journey. The wagons were loaded with merchandise, besides our luggage, so very heavy that the emigrants had to walk all the way on foot." He explained that the travelers from the old country were unaccustomed to the physical demands of walking day after day, week after week in heavy morning dew, scorching sun, torrential downpours, and freezing nights. The trekkers were supplied with very light shoes that soon gave out. This caused many to travel for days and weeks on their bare feet. He noted that the women traveling in the group would "pick up dry buffalo chips and carry them for miles in their aprons so to have something to make fire with at noon or night." The camp enjoyed real bread if the dough would rise. Since the dough often did not rise the travelers often ate something called flapjacks.[33]

Caroline Martine Anderson and Charles Keilgaard Hansen were married 14 December 1860 in a Lutheran Church at Saeby, Denmark.[34] Prior to their marriage and following their relocation to Randers, Denmark, both Caroline and Charles joined the Church of Jesus Christ of Latter-day Saints on 1 December 1860. Following their baptism, their desire to emigrate to Utah Territory, or Zion, substantially increased partly due to the war between Denmark and Prussia. In 1864, with a promise of needed money from a local church member, the young couple felt their desire to immigrate to Zion would become a reality. Unfortunately, the pledged money fell through, and there was only enough for one to travel to America. After much discussion, the couple determined that Caroline would travel first, and Charles would attempt to come the next immigration season. Caroline left her husband, friends, and homeland to travel thousands of miles into an unknown territory with a completely different culture, geography, and setting. She left Randers 8 April 1864 bound for Copenhagen, Denmark, and from there she continued her journey to the United States. Charles noted he received three letters from Caroline during her journey. The first came from Copenhagen, the second originated in Grimsby, England, and the final communication was written at Wyoming, NT as she waited to travel west with the William B. Preston wagon train.[35]

Her letters reveal a woman of great faith and one who deeply loved her husband. In her first letter from Copenhagen, Caroline wrote, "Oh! My dear husband let us be patient and pray to our Heavenly Father that we will be faithful through all things. Dear husband let the Lord bless you and all that wish to do the Lord's work." Earlier in this letter Caroline pined, "Dear husband, I wish that you could go with me." She concluded with, "Now dear husband, live well and God bless you that you will be faithful that is what I hope for. Write to me and live well."[36] Her second letter from Grimsby, England was written 18 April 1864. Caroline described an awful storm the group encountered from Copenhagen, Denmark to Hull, England. "There was [an] awful storm, the waves washed over the deck all the time. You can believe me dear man that I was very sick, but I was not the only one." In this endearing letter, Caroline tells Charles, "I will prepare a lovely home in Zion, if the Lord will give me the strength to earn a little, and he will—that I know. I have that feeling. He has always given me the things I have ask [sic] for and he will always hear my prayers that I ask of him with a sincere and righteous heart." In closing she stated, "I hope that both your days and mine will be long upon the earth . . . Live well, and I will think of you as we sail across the water."[37]

Letter number three was written 17 June 1864. She shared with Charles her struggles with sickness as she crossed the Atlantic Ocean. "We sailed aboard the large ship thirty-one days. I was only sick eight days. It wasn't sea sickness, but it was climate fever. I was very sick and missed you. I needed you here to take care of me." In an effort to put on a brave face for her husband she continued:

---

The worst is past and I must not grumble against the Lord, he has given me so much and I must be thankful for the many blessings I have, but I can't hold my feelings back and I am homesick for you … I hope that I will be among the worthy to reach the mountains.[38]

---

She described her living conditions in Wyoming, NT, "We have it good her [sic], we live in a leaf hut, it is named Bag Bystedt. I can't remember the street where we live at." With tender feelings and heartfelt earnestness, she continues, "I will try to earn some money over here. If you can't come over here it would be the greatest test for me, anything else I could take." Caroline continues:

---

Dear husband the happiest days we have lived together, if only these would come again so we can be together in Zion. I pray to Heavenly Father that the way will be opened … Dear Husband, I miss you so much, if only I could hear from you and find out how things are with you.[39]

---

Tragically, Caroline died on the trail only six days before reaching Zion. Her death occurred 9 September 1864, and the Preston wagon train arrived in Salt Lake City 15 September.[40] Upon hearing of the death of his wife, Charles was devastated. However, he noted that he repeatedly experienced in dreams that they would not see each other again. However, Charles still clung to the flickering hope that he and his dear Caroline could be reunited again.[41] Charles remarried in 7 April 1867 and immigrated to Utah Territory that same year.[42]

# 6

# ADDITIONAL WAGON TRAINS HEAD WEST DURING 1864

**Joseph S. Rawlins Down and Back Church Train**

The Joseph S. Rawlins down and back church train departed Wyoming, NT 15 July 1864 and arrived at Salt Lake City between 19-20 September 1864. Approximately 400 immigrants and 50 wagons constituted the company. During the journey, nineteen people died and two births occurred. The group experienced no serious accidents but lost roughly 30 head of cattle from disease.[1] Christopher Alston described some daily challenges faced on the trail.

> Think of cooking your supper, after a long day's walk, over a fire of 'chips' with the wind blowing over the great plains, and sometimes rain putting out the fire, and going to bed without any supper, getting up in the morning at daylight to find everything soaking wet and nothing to burn to cook your breakfast with, hooking up the oxen and traveling until noon, trying to find some dry 'chips' to make a fire to cook dinner! Such was our life on the plains before we reached the mountain country where we procured sticks to use with the 'chips.'[2]

Christopher described the joy of walking out of the mouth of Parley's Canyon where the train was met by a group of men. One of the men handed Christopher a handful of peaches, which he shared with others. About the experience Christopher wrote, "Now imagine, if you can, an eleven-year-old boy who had walked 1,100 miles and had a 1,100-mile appetite, and had never tasted a peach before in his life, having half a dozen nice peaches to eat!"[3]

Richard Daniels Brown Jr. left England by working as a sailor on *Monarch of the Sea*, and then hired out as a teamster to a private individual to cross the plains, which worked for about one month. The person who hired Richard had a disagreement with the captain and determined to turn back. Richard decided not to turn back but to stay with Captain Rawlins and his train. Unfortunately, he had no money, so he relied on the goodness of those traveling in the company to move farther west. To pay for his food, Richard agreed to herd from 3:00 a.m. until they broke camp, during the noon hour, and from the time they camped in the evening until 10:00 p.m. This left Richard with only five hours of sleep each night. As the wagon train moved farther west, cattle began dying due to alkali. Several of the travelers were required to leave goods on the ground, because there were fewer oxen to pull the wagons. At a certain point the company split up, and a few traveled their own course. Richard was left alone, which caused him to retrace his steps for about 50 miles to a ranch the group passed earlier. He arrived at the ranch and worked for about three weeks. During his stay at the ranch, another emigrant company passed by in which his mother and father were traveling! Richard noted, "Oh! what joy I had, as well as they, in meeting again with my parents—words cannot tell for I had never been away from home before starting on the journey."[4] Richard and his parents arrived in Salt Lake City 19 September 1864.[5]

Gideon Murdock received his mission call to drive a team to the Missouri River to help bring emigrants and freight back to Utah Territory. During the trip from Utah Territory to Wyoming, NT, Gideon served the pilot on the trip east. Mr. Murdock was selected to serve as an assistant to Joseph Rawlins on the return trip from Wyoming, NT. During the trek west, about three miles below the upper Platte bridge, some night herders lost several cattle. Gideon wrote that he and Captain Rawlins saddled their horses and tried to find the lost oxen that evening, but to no avail. Fortunately, the cattle were soon located, and Gideon brought them back to the wagon train when he noticed the wagon train was stopped, and the drivers were not allowed to cross the bridge. Upon further examination he learned soldiers had ordered the wagons to stop so they could search for stolen cattle. The military had orders to examine all Mormon trains and take all cattle branded with the letter C on the left shoulder and ribs. This examination was created because a man named Croffer had lost some of his cattle at Deer Creek, which lay about 30 miles back on the trail. Gideon tried to reason with the soldiers by stating the brand for the Rawlins' oxen was an HB, not a C.[6] During one portion of an exchange between Gideon and the military officers the discussion became heated, with accusations flying back and forth. Eventually, cooler heads prevailed, and the wagon train was able to continue on to the Salt Lake Valley. Once the argument concluded, a Lieutenant told Gideon that the Civil War was winding down and the next item of business for the Federal Government was to "clean the Mormons out." He then offered Gideon a job that would be "as good a position as you can ask for." Gideon thanked him for the offer, but declined to accept.[7]

As with all down and back church trains, hauling freight constituted a crucial part of the journey. The wagon train led by Captain Rawlins proved no exception. For example, stoves and their castings filled three full wagons of the train. Another wagon carried 12 small heaters, two small bottoms, four stove grates, a box of soap, a stove, and one box of tinware. Coal oil and a book bindery filled one wagon, while three boxes of coal oil filled another. Boxes of glass, lye, olive oil, fish, sewing machines, song books, shoes, additional machinery, and items listed as "sundries" constituted the balance of the freight being hauled on the Rawlins wagon train. The customers for the freight included companies such as Hooper and Eldridge, the Salt Lake Theatre, and the cotton factory. The freight was also consigned to individuals. Among the more notable names were Brigham Young, George Q. Cannon, and Hiram B. Clawson. Freight manifests indicated 19 wagons were utilized to haul the needed freight.[8]

**William S. Warren Down and Back Church Train**

William S. Warren's down and back church train departed Wyoming, NT 22 July 1864 and arrived in Salt Lake City 4 October 1864. Warren's train carried about 391 individuals, freight for Utah Territory, and utilized roughly 65 wagons during the journey. The majority of those traveling in this wagon train came from England, Wales, and Scotland.[9] Much of the freight hauled on this down and back train was consigned to Hooper & Eldredge. Included were such items as nails, glass, clocks, bolting cloth, leather, and other needed supplies.[10] Like many other wagon trains of 1864, this one traveled along the Nebraska City Cut-off Trail. Sadly, just a few days after reaching Fort Kearny, the travelers witnessed the aftermath of a terrible massacre that occurred near a station called Plum Creek, NT. A teamster named Orley D. Bliss kept a diary and recorded the events as the wagon train passed Plum Creek. The date was 9 August 1864, and in his own words Orley described the scene,

> Traveled 6 ½ miles; came to the place where the Indians attacked a train of 11 wagons; they killed eleven men a [sic] burned the wagons; the wagons was [sic] still burning; the soldiers had just buried the men all in one grave; the Indians took off a woman belonging to the train; traveled 1 ½ miles farther and nooned at plum creek afternoon; traveled 9 miles and camped on the Platte.[11]

The event described by Orley came to be known as the Plum Creek Massacre and initiated a war that according to one writer "burned on the Great Plains for more than a quarter-century."[12]

One of two survivors of the attack, Nancy Jane Fletcher Morton, later described the events of 8 August 1864 and her subsequent release about five months later. Unfortunately, her husband, brother, and cousin were among those who lost their lives during the attack. Nancy was making her third trip across Nebraska Territory from Sidney, Iowa to Denver in a small group of freight wagons. Early in the morning of 8 August 1864, the eleven wagons pulled out of Plum Creek Station, and Nancy drove while her husband slept. The freight wagons had only traveled about 1 ½ miles along the trail when the attack took place. Her words describe the almost unimaginable scene.

---

> With wild screams and yells, they circled around and around which frightened our teams so they became uncontrollable. Thinking there might be some faint hope of escape, I sprang from the wagon. When my husband called, "Oh my dear! Where are you going?" Those were the last words I heard him say. But our team was running, and I jumped. I fell to the ground and before I could recover myself one of the back teams came dashing by and the wheels passed over my body . . . With all the strength I could procure I started for the river. When I met my brother and my cousin and they said we have no hope of escape. As the Indians had encircled us, and the air was full of arrows. At that moment an arrow struck my cousin . . . and he fell dead at my feet. In another instant three arrows penetrated my brother's body, he too fell at my feet and his last word were, "Tell Susan I am killed. Goodbye my dear sister."[13]

---

In January 1865, Nancy gained her freedom near Fort Laramie, Wyoming Territory. The price of her freedom was horses, supplies, guns, and ammunition. Nancy made her way back to Sidney, Iowa 9 March 1865. She remarried and had three children. Nancy died near Jefferson, Iowa in 1912.[14]

Hannah Pritchard traveled with the Warren train in her efforts to reach Utah Territory. Hannah began her journey in Wales and traveled with two sons and one daughter. Her daughter, Rachel was 18 years of age, one son Thomas was 16, and David was 13 at the time of leaving their homeland. Hannah's story is like so many others who left their homes for their sought after Zion. Her husband Thomas was killed during a horrific coal mining accident along with 68 other men on 10 May 1852, at a coal pit located near Cwmbach, Wales. The explosion took place as poisonous gasses were trapped in the firedamp, and with no method of escape, the fumes ignited, killing the helpless miners. Of the 69 men who lost their lives in this tragic accident, Thomas and 18 others were members of the local branch of the Church of Jesus Christ of Latter-day Saints. Explosions such as this were common in the mining regions of Wales with countless miners being killed, burned, or badly maimed.[15] Because of poverty, young boys were forced to work in the mines. Tragically, of the 69 men who lost their lives, 20 were between the ages of 10 and 16. Recovery of the bodies took 18 months to complete for the 26 men and boys who drowned when water flooded the night shaft.[16] Interestingly, even though their father had died in 1852, Hannah's two sons were still listed as colliers (coal miners) when they signed up as passengers on the *General McClellan*.[17] Happily, this widowed mother and her three children completed the trip west.

Thomas Waters Cropper served on the down and back church train with Captain Warren beginning in Utah Territory. After arriving at the Missouri River, the train and all the teamsters were compelled to wait seven weeks for the arrival of immigrants. During this time, many of those with the Warren train hired out to local farmers to cut and bind grain. One particular day a group of men were standing by the Missouri River when a Mr. Hans Jasperson challenged those around him to swim across the river and back. Thomas accepted the challenge and swam across the swift-flowing river. According to Mr. Cropper, the river "ran swift and was filled with driftwood. The stream ran about half a mile wide. It took us down stream four miles. While walking back to camp the group ran races against each other. Cropper noted he beat everyone except one person, He also wrote he ran the 100 yards in 10.5 seconds.[18]

Regarding the trip west, Mr. Cropper remembers 18 individuals placed their belongings in his wagon. He also mentioned passing the Plum Creek station. Shortly after passing the Plum Creek massacre, the train came to a ranch where the house was burned and a man lay dead.

The individual was buried and the wagon train was now on high alert for any Indian troubles. During that night's camp, a heavy guard stood around the cattle and camp. As Thomas stood guard, he counted 14 Indians crossing the river not far from camp. He also noticed that as he passed the wagons in camp, he could hear people's teeth chattering with fear. The travelers were able to complete the balance of their trip without significant issues with the Native Americans.[19]

One impartial observer traveling with the Warren wagon train, was J. W. P. Stannard who was a member of the Church of England and offered his observations of traveling across the plains with members of the Church of Jesus Christ of Latter-day Saints. Stannard wrote that Joseph W. Young furnished the emigrants with excellent provisions. In addition to a good food supply, the wants of the soul were not neglected as the wagon train chaplain called people together mornings and evenings for public worship. The writer also took exception to an article in the *Chicago Tribune* that stated "Mormons believe in Joseph Smith, but do not believe in Jesus Christ!" The traveler was particularly impressed with Captain Warren, describing his ability to temper "authority with benignity" as a key attribute of his character and which "secured for himself general respect."[20] Concluding his review of traveling across the plains, Dr. Stannard wrote, "With such physical and spiritual provision; under such able guardianship; and with the beneficent protection of our Heavenly Father, we at length arrived at this far-famed city; and here my expectations were completely surpassed." Sensing a need to write more, Stannard noted, "Surely such a people; so industrious, as surrounding objects indicate; so religious as their crowded bowery evinces, eminently deserve to have their *'Territory'* formed into a 'STATE.'"[21]

### John Smith Independent Wagon Train

John Smith, captain of this independent wagon train was the son of Hyrum Smith and Jersha Barden. John began his life 22 September 1832 in Kirtland, Ohio. Although only 31 years old at the time of his captaincy, John Smith brought a wealth of experience to his responsibilities. Following the slaughter of his father and Joseph Smith, young John found his way to Utah Territory, settling there in 1848. John Smith was ordained to the office of Patriarch by Brigham Young in 1855. Mr. Smith captained a wagon train that left Florence, NT in 1860. During this particular western migration, Smith led about 150 individuals to the Salt Lake Valley, and 20 wagons were part of the company when the journey west started.[22] In April 1862, he was called to fill a mission to Scandinavia, where he faithfully served until 13 April 1864. John sailed to America with hundreds of emigrants on the sailing ship *Monarch of the Sea*. Following his arrival at Wyoming, NT, he was asked to lead an independent group of Saints to Utah Territory.[23] Smith's train left Wyoming around 25 July 1864 and arrived in Salt Lake City between 25 September and 1 October. This independent wagon train likely carried freight, along with teamsters and emigrants.[24] Concerning the need to move freight, Joseph W. Young wrote the following to Brigham Young shortly before the Smith wagon train departed.

---

I think no one will complain this year because his team is not loaded. The only grumbling I hear is that I am loading the wagons so heavily that they can never get through with the teams they have. But the teamsters do not realize that from ten to twelve hundred pounds of the aggregate loading of wagons are provisions that will be eaten up. I aim to have an average of 1,000 pounds of freight and ten passengers to a team, all except about five provision wagons. Thus, with passengers, luggage and a proportion of flour (or other loading in its place, as most of the flour is taken in wagons with nothing else) makes pretty solid loads. We shall have a great deal of freight left when the Church trains are all loaded. Bro. Eldredge thinks not less than one hundred tons.[25]

---

Joseph Young's letter certainly indicates the need for every wagon leaving Wyoming, NT to carry necessary freight for merchants and others in Utah Territory.

John Peter Rasmus Johnson kept a diary while traveling with the Smith wagon train. One of the more intriguing aspects of his diary is his semi-regular recording of how many miles each day the company traveled. His record indicates the wagon train began their journey west 25 July 1864. John's recording of mileage began 28 July. "We left Clearcreek about 7 a.m. and reached a place called Carter's ranch about 11 a.m. Here we remained till about 3 p.m. because a man died from diarrhea—he was from Scotland—and we then proceeded about six miles farther, to a place called South-Platte ranch, where we camped for the night."[26] Thus, on a day when a burial took place the wagon train traveled 13 miles. On the 29th of July, stock wandered off during the night, and the animals were rounded up before starting the day's journey. The wagon train traveled 14 miles—even with the need to locate stock that had strayed during the night. On Sunday 31 July, the company traveled 20 miles and camped where they found plenty of grass and good water. Perhaps in reference to no Sunday church meeting, John added that on this particular Sunday "No meetings was held."[27] A 22-mile travel day happened 3 August as the group passed Dog Town, Fort Kearny, and a small town, called Kearney City, which is where the trekkers camped for the night. Mr. Johnson faithfully recorded in his diary until 30 September, when the daily entries cease. They had reached their destination. Interestingly, his final entry reads, "We entered the City about 1 p.m. and formed our camp on the general Emigrant camp place. There were some Gentiles camping there when we came."[28]

Andrew Christian Nielson, who traveled from Europe on the *General McClellan*, hired out as a teamster in Atchison, Kansas with the Sharp and Spencer Freight Train. While Andrew and others hired to assist in taking freight to Utah Territory, other emigrants continued to Wyoming, NT to continue their journey to the Salt Lake Valley. Mr. Nielson recalls how each freight wagon needed three to six yoke of oxen and hauled between 3,500 to 8,000 pounds of freight in each wagon. Most of the men who hired on as teamsters were from the European continent and could not understand a word of English. Thus, the captain's shouting and commanding, only caused more confusion.[29] Evidence indicates the Sharp and Spencer freight wagon train traveled with or near John

Smith's independent train during a portion of the trek west.[30] Tragically, Joseph Sharp, captain of the freighting outfit, died suddenly at Willard Springs, Wyoming. Following Sharp's death, his brother James traveled 50 miles to a telegraph station and sent a dispatch to Salt Lake City requesting a metal coffin and 80 yoke of oxen. Meanwhile, a temporary coffin was made and John Smith along with a few others began hauling Joseph Sharp's body in the temporary coffin. Because of the hot weather, the body began decomposing, so Captain Joseph Sharp was buried near Devil's Gate, Wyoming. Once the metal coffin arrived, the body was exhumed and brought to Salt Lake City.[31]

**Isaac A. Canfield Church Train**

The next down and back wagon train to leave Wyoming, NT fell under the leadership of Isaac A. Canfield. Captain Canfield left with about 251 persons, 30 teamsters, and approximately 50 wagons. His departure happened 27 July 1864, and the arrival in Salt Lake City took place 5 October 1864.[32] His arrival was announced in the *Deseret News* in the following manner: "Capt. J. [Isaac] A. Canfield's train of some 60 wagons, laden with 208 Scandinavian immigrants, a large amount of freight for Messrs. Hooper and Eldredge, and a power press, caloric engine, etc., for the *Deseret News* office. During the journey, 12 deaths and two births occurred. They also lost 23 head of cattle.[33] Of the 30 wagons hauling freight, all but five were loaded with inventory for Hooper and Eldredge. Teamster Fred Coombs hauled 18 boxes of soap, which weighed 1,152 pounds. Chris Larson loaded 22 boxes of soap weighing 1,408 pounds. In addition, his wagon transported tea, glass, and a sofa which added 1,114 pounds of freight. Wagon number 23 (teamster unidentified) carried three boxes of machinery weighing a combined 3,685 pounds. [34] The boxes carried by wagon number 23 contained the power press and caloric engine for the *Deseret News*.[35]

One of the more interesting accounts of the 1864 migration comes from H. N. Hansen, who emigrated from Denmark. Hansen traveled with the Canfield wagon train. Several years later, he wrote about his experiences with complete candor. His difficulties began even as they left Denmark. He described his crossing from Denmark to England as follows: "The wind became stronger again, and we had a very rough sea; the waves constantly rolling over the deck, and found before we reached England that I had overestimated the pleasures of a sea voyage."[36] Concerning meals on the ocean voyage to America Hansen wrote, "Our condition was most deplorable. The meat we got could be smelled from one end of the vessel to the other when barrels were opened, it was almost a wonder that it did not explode the same beforehand, so strong as it was."[37] As Hansen and the others onboard *The Monarch of the Sea* continued their voyage across the ocean, the treatment of the crew to the passengers became reprehensible. "I have mentioned the ungentlemanly conduct of the crew as examples of their meanness would mention, that if an attempt would be made by anyone to wash their clothes and to have they [sic] dried on the deck, the sailors would without the least provocation throw the same overboard as soon as they came across it."[38]

Hansen's experiences did not improve after arriving at Wyoming, NT. After expressing gratitude for a tent given to him by John Smith, Hansen wrote about the difficulties faced during the constant storms. "I remember several nights that I together with my father when the storms came up would get up and cling to the poles with all our strength in hope of holding it secure, but it would only be for a while and then it would go down notwithstanding our efforts." After six weeks in Wyoming, NT, Hansen noted that the teams from Utah to "bring the poor to Zion" were "loaded with merchandize [sic] almost to their full capacity" before any of the belongings of the travelers could be loaded. Hansen was extremely disappointed that thousands of pounds of freight would be loaded on wagons, but each person "was only allowed fifty pounds and that included bedding and all."[39] Hansen voiced his most serious complaint as he witnessed the head of each family signing a promissory note ". . . agreeing to pay $60.00 for each person carried across the plains and these notes drawing interest at the rate of ten percent, paid interest to be added to the principal yearly and drawing interest at the same rate until paid, it looks like an expensive privilege." Hansen noted that all who desired to cross the plains signed the document even though, "The masses coming from foreign lands of course could not speak nor read English, but they asked no questions but did as they were told, and no one explained what their signature meant."[40]

Mr. Hansen did notice that as the wagon train reached a higher altitude, the overall health of the company improved. However, his father became sickly and lagged behind the rest of the wagon train. His father had "become so tired and having been left behind, that he very near had given up in despair not thinking himself able to reach us." Fortunately, his father's health improved. As the wagon train moved further west, Hansen's mother fell under a wagon, and she was run over. Sadly, he did not find out about the accident until the group camped for the evening. Hansen asked what happened, but his father was so overcome with grief he could not respond. "His two youngest children had died on the road, his only daughter lay sick and entirely helpless, lingering as it were between death and life, himself wornout [sic] and sick and mother he thought was killed or would die, or if not was ruined for life."[41] The accident happened about 200 miles from Salt Lake City. By the time the Hansen family arrived in the city, mother, daughter, and father were much improved.[42]

### William Hyde Down and Back Church Train

The down and back church train of William Hyde left Wyoming, NT 9 August 1864 and arrived in the Salt Lake Valley between 26–30 October 1864. The journey began with 62 wagons, and the *Salt Lake Daily Telegraph* noted 60 wagons finished the journey. The journey began with 375 people. However, due to the war between Native Americans and settlers, Hyde's train was instructed to go no farther than Salt Creek until Warren S. Snow's company caught up with them. Snow's wagon train was the last organized group to leave Wyoming, NT in 1864. Hyde's company followed a new route, up Lodgepole Creek, to Utah Territory after crossing the South Platte River at Julesburg. This course took the trekkers roughly 70 miles south of Fort Laramie through present-day Laramie Mountains. The road also took them through the current site of Laramie, Wyoming. From here the path merged with the Overland Stage Road, then joined the Oregon Trail near Ham's Fork. The Hyde church train experienced a high mortality rate during the crossing with an estimated 47 deaths.[43]

Freight carried by Hyde's company constituted a significant aspect of needed supplies for Hooper and Eldredge, a Salt Lake City retail firm. One bundle of plow beams (to be drawn by horses and used to turn up soil for planting crops), a box of dry goods, and a 660-pound box of glass comprised freight hauled by the wagon labeled as #2 in the freight manifest. Wagon #3, which shows as the "13th ward wagon" carried nine boxes of soap, one roll of three-coil rope, four boxes of hats, one box of olive oil, one box of pepper sauce, and one box without a label. Additional wagons hauled boxes of axes, scales, candles, tobacco, candy, blankets, sheeting, and a host of additional items for Hooper & Eldredge's inventory.[44] An advertisement appearing in the *Deseret News* in August 1864 noted the company's address was on Main Street, Salt Lake City. Their offerings, according to the ad, included hats, shoes, clothing, coffee, glass, soap, tobacco, hardware, and candles.[45] Other retail establishments that advertised in the *Deseret News* included Walker Brothers, W. S. Godbe, W. Jennings, and Kimball & Lawrence. Each of these businesses relied on either down and back trains, or freight wagon trains to ship their goods from the east to Salt Lake City.[46]

John T. Gerber kept a diary during most of his travels across the plains, and he noted the Hyde train left Wyoming, NT 6:00 p.m. Tuesday, 9 August 1864. The company only traveled about one mile before camping on the prairie where the grass wood and water were good and plentiful. The next day the group moved about 4 miles, where several independent wagon trains caught up, and became a part of the Hyde down and back train.[47] There were times when Gerber stopped keeping his diary. For example, he stopped from 18 August to 28 August and from 13 September to 24 October 1864. While keeping his diary, Gerber noted a total of 15 deaths and burials. Undoubtedly, deaths occurred during the time John did not write his thoughts. On 28 August 1864, Mr. Gerber did share events surrounding his marriage to Anna Marie Ruopp. Although somewhat sparse in detail, his entry paints a picture of a wedding on the plains. The wedding took place on a Sunday. John noted he had been very busy during the previous days "attending to camp duties, waiting on the sick, etc." Joseph W. Young entered the camp, whereupon John asked for permission to marry his bride-to-be, which permission was cheerfully granted. He describes his marriage in the following words:

> Mary and myself dressed up preparatory to being married. We attended [the] meeting in the center of the corral about 8 p.m. After singing, Capt. Hyde made a few remarks concerning camp duties. Bro. Smith announced to the Saints my desire to be united in marriage to Miss. Anna Mary Ruopp and asked if there were any objections. There being none, he performed the ceremony making Sister Ruopp and myself man and wife. After this, Bro. Joseph Young preached and counseled the saints. After the meeting, a number of the Elders and Saints congratulated us. We retired to our tent where Bro. and Sis. Schramm and Sis. L. Dodler took supper with us. I retired with my wife about 11 o'clock. The weather was fine.[48]

His entry presents a fascinating glimpse into how weddings while crossing the plains were sandwiched between his daily duties, camp requirements, and the need to continue the journey.

**Warren S. Snow Church Train**

Warren S. Snow was returning from a mission to the British Isles when he was called upon to direct a down and back church train from Wyoming, NT to Salt Lake City. Mr. Snow was called to leave Manti, Utah Territory and serve a proselyting mission to England in 1861.[49] This particular company accommodated approximately 160 emigrants. However, because this was the last wagon train to leave Wyoming, NT for the season a tremendous amount of freight was also transported. Included in the freight being transported were four pianos.[50] One can only imagine how out-of-tune the instrument would be after bouncing inside a wagon, crossing numerous rivers, and enduring the overall hardship of the 1,100-mile journey. An organ weighing 234 pounds traveled in this particular wagon train with the destination shown as Brigham City, Utah Territory. One can surmise that this wagon train carried material left over in the warehouse at Wyoming, NT by how many names appeared on the consignee list. For example, wagon #16 carried nine stoves detailing eight different names as owners. Joseph W. Young transported freight in some of his own wagons.[51] In addition, the freight manifest noted Joseph W. Young left several items in the warehouse before he headed west. Inventory left behind included but was not limited to, 12 kegs of nails, several boxes of coal oil, 22 pieces of iron pipe, 12 sacks of sugar, carpet, rice, coffee, and one box of machinery.[52] Snow's church train left Wyoming, NT somewhere between the 13th and 17th of August1864, and arrived in Salt Lake City 2 November 1864.[53] As noted earlier, the Hyde and Snow train traveled together during a large portion of the trek west.

Richard Crowther left England on the sailing vessel *McClellan*. After landing at Castle Gardens, New York City, he began his cross-country train journey to Wyoming, NT. Upon arriving at Rochester, New York, Crowther noted he "had twelve cents left at the time." His company continued traveling day and night until reaching Wyoming, NT 4 July 1864. After arriving at this destination, Crowther met an individual named William F. Cooke who left Fountain Green, Utah Territory as a teamster on the church train that Warren S. Snow would captain on the return trip.[54] When Richard left England, he paid for his passage across the ocean to Wyoming, NT, yet like so many others, he needed assistance to finish the balance of the journey west. Fortunately for Richard, he met a merchant from Provo, Utah Territory who was picking up merchandise for customers. Richard and the merchant, Isaac Sitton, agreed that Richard would drive a team of oxen to Provo for fifteen dollars a month and board. Mr. Crowther stayed in Nebraska City, NT while Sitton purchased the needed cattle and goods.[55]

Desla Slade recalled the hunger she and her family faced, and the assistance from an anonymous family living near the trail west during the crossing of 1864 in the following words:

> I remember one cold, wet day in particular. We had kept huddled up for warmth in the wagon all day, while the rain beat its monotonous tattoo on our canvas roof. When we stopped for the night, fires were out of the question. We were hungry and went to bed crying for something to eat. Next morning Mother climbed out of the wagon. Through the drizzling rain and mist she saw a little old shack, with smoke pushing its way out of the chimney. She made her way to it and as the door opened to her knock, there greeted her a rush of warm air, fragrant with the odor of frying meat. Will you sell me some bread? she asked of the woman who had answered the door. We haven't any to spare," she replied, but seeing how weak and sick Mother looked, she said, "We are just going to have a bite, come and eat with us. I cannot eat; my children are hungry. You shall eat, she insisted, and you shall have bread for your little ones even if we have to go without. When Mother came back, we all were out on the wagon tongue. She broke the bread in chunks and handed us each a piece.[56]

Traveling with her mother and six siblings, Desla shared some memories from their trail crossing. One day she heard her sister Rhoda scream. Her sister had stepped on a prickly pear, and the blood was falling in drops from her wounded foot, but her sister refused to let Desla pull the thorn out. As the pair began walking back to the wagon train Desla cried out that Indians were coming. As Rhoda turned in terror to look Desla pulled the cactus out of her foot, before she had time to say ouch. Two brothers died on the trail. When her infant brother, John, died, he was buried in a shawl which the mother had torn in half to wrap his little body in. Later, her other brother Eddie was buried in the other half of the shawl. Eddie died as the company neared the Green River in present day Wyoming. Desla noted, "Sick, disheartened, and weary, we had to carry on." Following Eddie's passing Desla's mother became "very, very ill." Many believed her death was imminent. Desla recalled grabbing her sister's hand and running off into the sagebrush to pray. With the simple faith of children, they pleaded, "Please, Heavenly Father, don't let mother die. Please make her better, in the name of Jesus, Amen." The two sisters finished their heartfelt prayer confident their mother would be healed. Desla and Rhoda's mother was feeling better the following day and continued to heal during the balance of the journey. Desla noted the passing of John Kay, a missionary returning from his labors, who was stricken and died on the trail. "A side was taken from a wagon to make him a coffin."[57]

Jesse N. Smith recorded his experiences as they happened in the village of Wyoming and on the trail. On 12 July 1864, Jesse wrote that he hauled some flour from Nebraska City for J. W. Young. For the next several days, Jesse prepared to move west. According to his account, his wagon train consisted of six wagons, one carriage, 13 men, and 15 horses and mules. Joseph W. Young asked Jesse to dispense medicines contained in a medicine chest, but Jesse refused the offer. Smith describes traveling with "a vast caravan of wagons some 200 in number" as they continued west from Fort Kearny. Ten days after traveling with other wagon trains for protection, Smith's group left the ox trains. At the Laramie Fork of the Platte, J. W. Young and H.B. Clawson concluded to move at a faster pace with the mail, so they parted company. Jesse N. Smith actually entered the valley 29 September 1864 and reached the state road as Brigham Young and his party were returning from a trip south. He fell in behind this group and drove into the city.[58]

**Freight Wagon Trains of 1864**

In addition to the thousands of pounds of freight hauled on the down and back church trains, six freight wagon trains also used Wyoming, NT or Nebraska City as either a loading or reloading point for their merchandise. Soren Christofferson began his journey in Manti, Utah Territory by taking orders from local citizens before heading east. On the trip east, Soren took sellable products owned by the local residents and exchanged those items for either cash or the product desired by his customer. Christoffersen's wagon train consisted of six wagons and 20 yoke of cattle. Soren hired several emigrants to act as teamsters on the crossing from the Missouri River to Manti, Utah Territory. One of the teamsters, Jens Christian Lauersen Breinholt, noted he and four other young men worked as teamsters for Christoffersen's wagon train. Jens friend's names were Peder Jensen, Niels L. Lund, Soren Thomsen, and Charles Rover. Rover's sweetheart, Catherine Festesen, was hired to cook for the traveling freight wagon train. Sadly, Niels Christoffersen, a stepson of Soren, died in the Green River two years later when he returned to retrieve two wagons left at Fort Bridger during the 1864 crossing.[59]

Another freight wagon train of 1864 was led by William Dallin, who took orders from residents of Springville, Utah Territory for merchandise from the east. Dallin hauled wheat, cattle, horses and other produce to Montana Territory and exchanged the items for cash. With the acquired cash he would purchase plows, stoves, groceries, and other items from the east for his customers. The merchandise would be shipped to the Missouri River. The new products would be loaded onto freight wagons and hauled to the waiting customers.[60] The John Judge Kerr freight wagon train of 1864 hauled a significant amount of freight for Brigham Young. Stoves, castings, machinery, rice, sugar, coffee, several roles of coil rope, and a host of other items were charged to Brigham Young. Also included in Kerr's freight wagon train were three organs. One of the organs, listed as a "church organ," weighed 1,420 pounds, while the second one came in at 317 pounds, and the third one noted a weight of 314 pounds.[61]

Thomas Briggs, a member who had immigrated to St. Louis, Missouri in 1851, signed on as a teamster with the Kimball Lawrence freight wagon train of 1864. Thomas began his journey from St. Louis to Salt Lake City in 1862. However, conditions caused him to turn back. He traveled with his family to Springfield, Illinois where he stayed with his sister until 9 April 1864 when he renewed his travel west. Thomas and his family eventually arrived at Wyoming, NT, and the family rented a house in Wyoming where they stayed until the time came to head west.

During his time in Wyoming, Thomas helped assemble the wagons that arrived on the paddle wheelers. He eventually was placed as a night guard over the freight. Regarding his travel with the Kimball Lawrence freight wagon train, Mr. Briggs wrote, "Brother Henry Lawrence persuaded me to go along with his company of about 25 wagons, and he hired my sister's husband to drive a team across the plains." The wagon train with its freight and several emigrants arrived at Salt Lake City 4 October 1864.[62]

The vast quantities of incoming freight can be gleaned from a *Deseret News* article during the week of 7 September 1864.

---

ARRIVAL OF MERCHANDISE—W. S. Godbe's first train, consisting of drugs, groceries and general merchandise arrived on the evening of the first, in charge of Cap. C. [Claudius] V. Spencer.

Hooper and Eldredge's first train of the season come into town on Saturday noon.

A train of 22 wagons, for Barrow and Co., came on to the Public Square on Saturday night.

Kimball and Lawrence's train of 35 wagons got in on Monday.[63]

---

The hazards of hauling freight are noted in the same issue of *The Deseret News*. A Captain A. P. Patterson, who was transporting needed freight for individuals in the Salt Lake City and surrounding areas, placed the following in this issue. "A Freight Train, Capt. A. P. Patterson, is tied up at Deer Creek through cattle dying, and the Captain requests those owning freight in that train to send him oxen and provisions."[64] With the arrival of all freight by church and independent wagon trains, the immigration year of 1864 came to a close.

# 7

# MIGRATION TO ZION 1865

The year 1865 differed substantially from both 1864 and 1866 in one very significant manner. No down and back church trains were sent to the outfitting station at Wyoming, NT. Notification was sent out early in 1865 concerning the fact that no church trains would be sent to pick up the emigrating Saints. Several crucial reasons existed for the decision to cease church train activity for this particular year. The need to build up depleted herds in Utah, the impact of the country's Civil War on locating suitable landing points for emigrating Saints, and the territory's Black Hawk War all contributed to the cessation of the down and back trains.[1] Nevertheless, more than 700 emigrants from England, Europe, and South Africa still managed to make the journey.[2] Many members of the church in Europe knew there would be no church sponsored trains from the outfitting station at Wyoming, NT, yet 1,272 members left their homes by sailing ship hoping to find their way to Salt Lake City.[3] Elder Thomas Taylor served as the Church Emigration Agent for 1865. He and several assistants greeted the arriving Saints in New York City and assisted with the departure of freight and independent wagon trains from Wyoming, NT.[4]

. . .

## Crossing the Atlantic Ocean

Five sailing vessels left Europe and South Africa for the United States in 1865. The ship *Mexicana* left Port Elizabeth, South Africa 12 April 1865 and landed at New York City 18 June 1865. The ship carried 47 members, and the voyage took 67 days to complete. The *Belle Wood* departed Liverpool, England with 636 members and pulled into the New York City harbor 32 days later on 14 June 1865. This ship carried the largest immigration company of the year with 636 emigrants. The *B. S. Kimball* sailed from Hamburg for New York City on 8 May 1865 and arrived 14 June 1865 with 558 passengers. Two other ships, The *David Hoadley* and the *Bridgewater* transported 23 and between one and seven passengers, respectively. The *David Hoadley* concluded its journey in 40 days and the *Bridgewater* finished in 37 days. The largest sailing vessel to carry the emigrants in 1865 was the *Belle Wood* at 1,399 tons. The smallest ship of this year was the brig *Mexicana*. This ship registered at 276 tons, yet it traveled the longest distance of the sailing ships of 1865.[5]

## The Sailing Vessel *Mexicana*

According to the captain of the *Mexicana*, the voyage from South Africa was the most pleasant, peaceful voyage he had ever experienced. One traveler, Elizabeth McDermott Sims, lost her baby girl as she waited for the ship to arrive. Her daughter Elizabeth died 2 January 1865 and was buried on a beach. According to her own account, during the first days of the voyage the mother "laid in my bed and sobbed and prayed earnestly to God for comfort in this direction." She further noted,

---

> Sometime during the night, I dreamed that I held the baby in my arms and that she was coming with me. So real was this dream that I awoke and on awakening I felt the baby so plainly in my arms that I looked to see if it was really there. I felt comforted and from that time on whenever I thought of my little girl, I felt like she was coming with us.[6]

Elizabeth indicated that after crossing the equator the "sailors played jokes and had their own fun." Furthermore, very little sea sickness occurred during the ocean crossing.[7]

Miner G. Atwood, who presided over the Saints during the ocean voyage and again as the captain of an independent wagon train that left Wyoming, NT for Salt Lake City, kept an excellent diary about his ocean crossing and his time on the trail. His record pinpoints some more dramatic events during the crossing. His entry for Tuesday, June 6 noted he and Elders Noon, Smith, and Priestley administered to a Brother George F. W. Kershaw, who sadly died at 4:00 p.m. that day. A short memorial service was held at 7:00 p.m. that evening. George was survived by a wife and six children. Concerning Sister Kershaw, Miner wrote, "Sister Kershaw is very destitute and grieves very much for the loss of her husband." One day later, June 7, Atwood wrote, "The bugs [bedbugs] are very bad in the sister's compartment so that they get but little rest at night." Apparently as the voyage was ending, nerves became frayed and people began to argue with each other. On Tuesday, June 13, Atwood recorded, "I advised the Saints to be careful about each other's feelings and do right and go off of the vessel with as good a feelings [sic] toward each other as they had when they came on board. The devil has been busy for a few days but so far all is well."[8]

**The *Belle Wood***

The passengers who sailed on the *Belle Wood* were organized into nine wards before beginning their journey across the Atlantic Ocean. In an effort to create a positive atmosphere to the long tedious voyage, three gentlemen were asked to make arrangements for social parties for the recreation of the Saints. To further create an upbeat atmosphere, a small brass band was assembled. Instruments included in the fledgling group were violins, a flute, and a clarinet. Amazingly, a small newspaper was published entitled the *Belle Wood Gazette*. This small paper was published daily under the direction of Elder George Sims. Poetry, political contributions, possible upcoming marriages, lost property, essays, and editorials were topics considered worthy for the newspaper. Sadly, three deaths occurred during the ocean crossing. John Edwin Hefferan, William James Hazell, and Ann Eyre lost their lives during the 31-day journey. After arriving at New York City, W. H. Shearman noted the trip was "an exceedingly pleasant voyage thus far, having experienced very little rough weather, but considerable rain."[9] Because the church sent no down and back trains in 1865, the consensus for this year's emigration was that about one-half of those who traveled across the ocean would not complete the 1,100-mile trek to Salt Lake City. Of the 1,271 who left their homeland and sailed to America, approximately 700 began the trek from Wyoming, NT.

### The *B S Kimball*

The *B. S. Kimball* also seemed to have a fair sail from Hamburg to New York City, with few violent storms, and sufficient wind power. Sadly, 29 deaths occurred during the voyage allegedly due to measles and scarlet fever. In a letter written 15 June 1865, John Swenson indicated, "The Jutland Saints brought these diseases with them, which caused many deaths." Swenson went on to note, "I think many of the cases have ended with inflammation of the brain and bowels." Mr. Swenson did appreciate the kindness of Captain Henry C. Dearborn and all the crew who traveled with the immigrating Saints. He also felt the provisions provided for the passengers were of a "good quality" with excellent availability. Swenson also singled out the first mate, and lesser officers on the ship as being very helpful during the voyage.[10]

Like other sailing vessels used by the Church of Jesus Christ of Latter-day Saints during the migration years, issues continually came up —even during good sails. One matter was a lack of fresh water. Indeed, the water deteriorated to the point where vinegar was mixed with it to try to make it palatable. A unique solution to the problem was proposed and accepted. The captain told several leaders of the ship to go to the steersman and get some whiskey to divide among the sick people. According to Peter A. Nielson, when he told members of his group the captain's offer, "They all got sick so they could get whiskey." Nielson goes on to say, "I gave it freely because I could go and get it replenished any time." Another concern for the voyagers was the lack of any pipes for fresh air below deck. Concerning this issue Nielson wrote, "What I called the most trouble on the ocean was the fact that we had no air pipes, all the air had to come through the stairways. The stink coming from below was very hard to withstand and there was vermin so we could not rest." [11] Remembering the difficulty of leaving family comes from words written by Maria Lofdahl Andelin, many years after departing from her loved ones in Sweden. "I saw no more of the land of my birth. Now it was my turn to shed tears. I thought, how cruel, how could I ever leave them, their only daughter, only sister, no one to care for them . . . Oh how my heart yearned for them. Why hadn't I stayed?"[12] She traveled alone from Sweden to Salt Lake City.

### The *David Hoadley* and the *Bridgewater*

According to extant records the *David Hoadley* transported 23 individuals from Liverpool to New York City. William Underwood served as the church leader for this small group of Saints. Underwood, who listed his occupation as a laborer, was accompanied by his wife Cecilia and four small children—seven years and younger. Charles Yard, his wife Jane, and their three young kids also traveled on this sailing vessel. Charles worked as a shoemaker before leaving England. Thomas Bullock, also a shoemaker by trade, boarded the ship with his wife, Jane, and four children ages 12 and under. A widow, Ann Alston sailed with the group, along with her three youngsters. Two young men, John Mitchell and Thomas Horne, round those who sailed on this ship.[13] The *Bridgewater* transported few passengers, so little information is available for this vessel.

### Events at Wyoming, NT

As noted earlier, due to a lack of funds some individuals who arrived at New York City were unable to continue west. One such family sailed on the *Belle Wood*, but was unable to proceed further after arriving at Castle Gardens. The father and widower, John Hagell, determined there was only enough money to send one child west. He selected his oldest daughter, Catherine Hagell Naisbitt, to leave the family and travel to Salt Lake City. She describes her feelings concerning the separation from her family.

> I never will forget the homesick feeling I experienced when they bade me goodbye. We were detained in Castle Gardens ten days after this, and I can assure you if it had been possible I would have gone back . . . When we arrived at the frontier I found a letter from my uncle asking me to return to those poor motherless children. I was overjoyed at the prospect, but it seems I was destined to disappointment, for when I told the captain that I was going back with the missionaries who were going East from Utah, he said, "No, my girl there is no going back in this Church." So once more I was headed toward Utah with no prospect of returning to my family in New Jersey.

Fortunately, her father and siblings traveled to Utah the next year, and the family was reunited.[14]

In a letter written from Wyoming, NT to Brigham Young, one can capture a picture of life for the Saints heading west. At 6:00 p.m. 26 June 1865, the steam packet *Denver* dropped off about 550 of the Danish company. Sadly, the bodies of three people were also unloaded on the levee at Wyoming. These people died during the ride from St. Joseph, Missouri to Wyoming. Tragically, a child died within two hours of the ship's arrival. The arriving group was composed of Danes, Norwegians, and Swedes. George Sims, who wrote the letter on behalf of John G. Holman noted, "The Danish Saints have brought with them several good tents, and they are pretty well armed, and have considerable luggage with them." The English company arrived on 15 June and numbered nearly four hundred. Upon arrival this group was immediately conveyed to dwelling-houses, where they were made as comfortable as practical. Among those who were now at Wyoming were many who are actually destitute, depending upon being assisted through. With no down and back trains coming, special arrangements were made to help as many as feasible continue their journey west.[15]

Having many who were destitute and unable to pay their way west, Thomas Taylor and John Holman sought to help as many Saints as possible. One solution involved the men who signed on as teamsters for the various freight wagon trains heading west from either Nebraska City or Wyoming. Sixty to seventy men were hired as teamsters for the various trains at a rate of $50 per month. In return for their pay, these men would drive the assigned wagons to Salt Lake City. John Holman convinced the men to turn over their pay (with the exception of needed clothing articles for the plain crossing) to the church. A portion of this money would be used to help those who were destitute continue the journey west. Ten men were assigned to Mr. Overton's freight wagon train. Overton carried product for W. S. Godbe and Company. Nine men worked as teamsters for the D. J. McCann train. Sixteen men worked on Mr. Street's wagon train. Five individuals went to work for John Judge Kerr's freight wagon train. Each group of men working on the freight hauling wagon trains were presided over by another church member. Married men and their families also worked their way through, receiving as wages the transportation of their families.[16] In sharing some of their earnings with others, many were able to continue to Salt Lake City.

The village of Wyoming was surrounded with many freshwater springs including a small stream known as Weeping Water that emptied into the Missouri River just north of town. Often emigrants would use the springs or the small stream to clean clothing and to bathe. Some travelers had not bathed since beginning their journey. Lars Pederson, who arrived with his family at the outfitting station of Wyoming, decided to bathe in the small Weeping Water stream. At the time, Lars was unmarried and about thirty years old. Lars helped twenty Danish Saints emigrate and was looking forward to reaching Salt Lake City. Those who were with Lars did not see anything out-of-the-ordinary that day—until they noticed his clothes folded on the bank of the stream.

Immediately a search ensued. The searchers located his body in the bed of the stream. Lars Pederson was buried 29 June 1865. His possible burial place is the cemetery located about one-and-one-half miles out of the town of Wyoming. A record of the event noted, "Today he was buried, and a large concourse of Danish Saints followed him to the grave who feel to mourn his loss, as he was greatly respected by them."[17]

**Miner G. Atwood Independent Wagon Train**

An independent wagon train captained by Miner G. Atwood left Wyoming, NT 31 July 1865 and arrived in Salt Lake City on three different dates. The first group, led by Elder Charles B. Taylor, a returning missionary, entered Salt Lake City 31 October 1865. The balance of Atwood's company arrived at Salt Lake City on the 8th and 9th of November. Atwood's train was comprised of roughly 245 individuals, and their journey across the plains offers great insight into the challenges of life on the trail for these intrepid pioneers.[18] Although this wagon train left Wyoming, NT 31 July 1865, the first few days were spent moving a few miles west, then going back and picking up stragglers that had been left behind. During this time, Henson Walker told Miner Atwood that there was considerable sickness raging in Wyoming. It wasn't until Sunday 6 August that the wagon train passed over a couple of creeks and one rather dangerous bridge; all got over safe. As the train continued its western movement various points along the Nebraska City Cut-off Trail were noted. Nemaha Creek, Salt Creek, Beaver Crossing, and Beaver Creek are a few of the natural water drainages mentioned. While camped one evening, during an early part of the journey, Atwood wrote that a stampede of cattle took place, which he believed was caused by mosquitoes. Lightning and torrential rains also caused delays and general irritation during the early part of the journey.[19]

Walker noted three days before reaching Beaver Crossing that Brother B. Hampton's train of ten wagons caught up with his train. Davis's (Albert Westley Davis) mule train, consisting of ten wagons, came alongside the Walker train and both wagon trains intended to travel with the Walker train. The now larger wagon train continued its westward march, reaching Fort Kearny 22 August. Atwood entered the fort to obtain a pass. Officers at the fort granted permission to continue heading to Salt Lake City. As the pioneers left the area surrounding the fort, several soldiers traveled out on horseback to see the train pass by. They made many remarks about the young sisters, and some tried to get the sisters to converse with them.[20] Two days after leaving Fort Kearny, a young lady traveler who was walking near one of the wagons fell down, and four wagons ran over her. She died almost instantly. Earlier in the day, another sister was buried following a long bout of sickness. Monday, 28 August, three soldiers entered Atwood's camp soon after the corralling was completed. The three men stated they had fought in the Southern Army for the previous three years; they wanted to join the wagon train and travel to Utah Territory. One of the young men even told Captain Atwood that he was a member of the church. The captain listened to their pleas to join him, but flatly refused their request. The intruders told Atwood he was very hard-hearted, and it was a pity that he was appointed captain. The gentlemen quickly left. Other soldiers later came searching for the three deserters.[21]

Atwood's wagon train continued plodding west. Unfortunately, two ladies died within one day of each other in early September. A common grave was dug, inside the corralled oxen, and both women were buried in this shared grave. By 13 September, the wagon train passed Chimney Rock and meandered their way by Scott's Bluff on the 15th. Upon arriving at Fort Mitchell, a young lady approached Captain Atwood with a request to continue with the captain's wagon train to Salt Lake City. She noted she and her child had been traveling with a freight wagon train, but had been left at the fort. She told Atwood she was not a member, but had relatives in Utah Territory. Captain Atwood wrote that if "she could get anyone of the independents to take her she could go, but the church wagons were full and she could not go with them." She asked everyone she could find if they would allow her to travel with them, but no one could take her.[22]

. . .

### Events Around Fort Laramie

Miles P. Romney wrote a humorous description concerning an encounter with some soldiers on the trail. During the afternoon of 16 September, Anders W. Winberg and about 30 other men from the Atwood train were left near Horse Creek to butcher an ox and bring the meat to the next camping spot. Without warning, a wagon from a local mine which was guarded by about a dozen soldiers, came barreling by, heading east. As they roared past the men who were butchering the ox, the soldiers yelled and cursed in a shallow attempt to show their bravery. Surprisingly, a few hours later the same mine wagon came thundering back, going the other direction—heading west. Romney noted that the wagon ran at full speed and the horses were being pushed to their limit by the riders and drivers. One of the soldiers, from the mining wagon, entered the camp area with his face pale as death, and he told the travelers of the Atwood wagon train that about 200 Indians were crossing the river with the intent to attack their wagon train. The messenger quickly hurried away, totally convinced he had helped prepare the wagon train for an attack. One hour later, Anders Winberg, who had stayed back with the 30 men to butcher the ox, came striding into camp. Winberg meekly admitted that he and his group of 30 men had unintentionally frightened the soldiers by waving their hats and shouting at them.[23]

Albert Westley Davis, who earlier had traveled east from Salt Lake City to Omaha with 13 wagons full of missionaries preparing to leave on their missions, traveled west with the Atwood train. Davis carried freight bound for Salt Lake City. Albert noted "Nothing happened more than is usual to large trains traveling across the plains, until we arrived at Laramie on the return trip." Shortly after dark, some persons pretending as though they were Native Americans, stampeded our animals, causing us to stay an extra day hunting them, and then we were unable to recover all of them. Davis further noted, "Some of the Laramie people said the government was going to kill the 'Mormons' off within two years and thought they might as well begin there and then, yet no one received any bodily injury from their hands at this time."[24] Shortly after arriving at Fort Laramie, the travelers were called together for a meeting where the officers of the fort warned the group that the Indians were on the warpath, and we had better not go further on the trail. The soldiers offered free passage to any part of the United States we wished to go. The declaration was made in three different languages. Once all in the caravan heard the announcement and the attached conditions, a vote was held. All members of the wagon train voted to reject the offer and continue forward.[25]

## The Attack

A tragic event took place 22 September 1865, during a noon watering, which resulted in seven men receiving wounds and a woman being captured by the Indians. Several eye-witness accounts offer their view of the events of that fateful day. However, the most poignant description comes from Frants Christian Grundvig, husband of the captured woman. Frants and Jenssine Hostmark were married in 1856, and their son was born two years later. All three left Denmark in 1865 for Salt Lake City. Concerning the events Frants wrote, "Sept. 22nd we had to travel a long way to get to water. My wife got very tired, and we fell behind the train. Our son stayed in the wagon." The wagon train reached a creek, lined with brush along the banks, which offered a great hiding place for the Indians. The attack did not last very long, but the outcome was devastating. Later Grundvig wrote about that heartbreaking day.

---

> At the time my wife and I were about a quarter mile from camp. And some of the Indians came towards us and with a blood-curdling yell started to shoot at me, while some of them took my wife, put her on a horse and took her away. I was hit by five or six arrows, the last one lodged in my hip. I pulled it out and dropped it, thinking it was all out. However, the whole arrowhead was left in the hip bone, and it caused a running sore. Two years later Dr. Anderson came to Salt Lake City and took it out. It was 3 ½ inches

long and ¾ inches wide at the top. Thinking I was dead the Indians left me. I was far from camp, but managed to hobble in, but it was three weeks before I could get around again with a cane. But all the bodily suffering I passed through for nearly two years was small compared to the anguish and sorrow for the loss of my wife. I have often stood by my work bench with tears running down my cheeks. I can never forget it. My boy was all I had to live for.[26]

---

Captain Atwood listed the wounded as John Swenson, Peter Oluf Holmgren, Sven Neilson, Peter Christensen, Jen C. Peterson, Andres Erickson, and Frants Grundvig.[27] Regarding the status of the wounded, Peter A. Nielson wrote,

---

[Johan Swenson] came into camp with two arrows, in his left arm and Peter 'Doctor' with one arrow in his cheek and one clear through his neck. A Swedish brother came in with an arrow in the small of his back and was not able to walk again on the journey.

---

A Brother Holmgren was shot by a bullet and taken for dead. And a fellow by the name of Anderson was hit by a bullet that took off a piece of his cheek and a piece of his nose.[28] Albert Westley Davis provides a graphic description of how an arrow was removed from one of the wounded. After two men tried to remove the arrow from Peter Holmgren's face, they asked Albert if he could remove the iron spike. He said he'd try to do so.

---

We laid an ox yoke on the ground and had the man sit on it. Albert then asked two men to take him by the head and hold him tight and he would do the pulling. Albert then got hold of the spike with the pincers (a pair of long-handled blacksmith's pincers) and pulled with all the strength he had until the spike came out. The wounded man then stood up, took Albert by the hands, and said thank you in broken English.[29]

---

When the wagon train under the direction of Captain Miner Atwood left Wyoming, NT, the company was equipped with food and provisions for an eight-week journey.[30] However, due to cattle losses, weather issues, and the uncertain nature of Native Americans along the trail, the journey to Salt Lake City took an additional seven weeks. Food for both the pioneers and the livestock began running low as the wagon train reached the higher elevations in Wyoming. The reason Miles Romney and 31 men butchered an ox on 16 September was because the company's food supply was running out. How little some people ate and still walked each day is shocking. Anthonette Olsen Lybbert remembered eating no supper the entire journey, and she stated, "For breakfast I had a biscuit and a cup of black coffee. At noon I had even less than this."[31] Lars Fredrickson remembered being placed on half rations after traveling past Fort Laramie. He also remembered, "Every night some weary traveler would lie down to sleep and wake up no more." In addition, Lars added, "Our shoes was [sic] worn out and we walked with our bare feet in the snow and mud through the mountains on half rations."[32]

Miner Atwood's excellent journal ended abruptly 29 September 1865. His company was camped at Deer Creek Station, which lay near the North Platte River. Atwood's company was still east of Casper, Wyoming. The last entry he wrote centered on the lack of food. "I telegraphed this evening to Brother Thomas Taylor that we had but ten days provisions on hand for the Church people and requested him to meet us at Green River without fail."[33] Atwood's next telegraph appeared hopeless. This message was sent directly to Brigham Young. "My company here only three days rations. M. G. Atwood."[34] Fortunately, mule team rescue wagons arrived before complete starvation set in. Thomas Taylor and Orson Arnold brought much needed relief to the starving pioneers. According to *The Deseret News*,

Thomas Taylor telegraphed Brigham Young that 45 people were sent on to Salt Lake City with the faster moving mule teams. In addition, Charles Taylor arrived in the city with some immigrants.[35] The food crisis was narrowly averted, and the balance of Captain Atwood's company entered Salt Lake City early in the month of November 1865.

**Henson Walker's Independent Wagon Train**

Thomas Taylor and John G. Holman organized the second independent company to leave Wyoming, NT. Henson Walker was appointed captain. Robert Pixton was chosen as chaplain with John Hammer captain of the guard and Joseph Hammer as assistant captain.[36] The wagon train departed 12 August 1865 and arrived at Salt Lake City 9 November 1865. The journey took almost 13 weeks which proved difficult towards the end of their travels. This company contained about 200 individuals and 50 wagons when it began.[37] Both Walker and Pixton were returning to Utah Territory following a release as full-time missionaries in England. Included in the 200 persons, the wagon train was occupied by approximately 109 immigrants. In addition, three others were selected as leaders on the wagon train. Those included were Brother Eastham as "captain of the first ten," Brother Conrad as captain of the second ten; with Adolphus H. Noon (from South Africa) as captain of the third ten.[38] Ten freight wagons accompanied Walker's wagon train.[39] Many of those arriving at Wyoming were delayed several weeks, for a variety of reasons. During the delay, individuals began pairing and breaking cattle, assembling wagons, and purchasing needed supplies.[40]

Thomas Alston was seven years old when he traveled with his widowed mother and two siblings. He wrote about some of his experiences later in life. He recalled how many young people had never seen an ox, or a cow, and they would climb fences to watch the older men work the livestock. Alston noted that the men would "lasso steers, tie them to a post, put the yoke on one, bring up another in the same way, put him at the other end of the yoke and after completing the yoking, turn the pair loose to kick around the corral." Many times, while the cattle ran wildly around the corral the yoke would fall beneath their necks, instead of on top, which quickly caused the animals to stop thrashing wildly.[41] He further noted that there were about 1/3 as many cows as oxen, so each team with three pairs would have one pair of cows. Later, while on the trail, Alston's widowed mother experienced some negative interactions with Thomas Taylor during their time in Wyoming.

Thomas Alston described some interesting events about the crossing. He wrote, "[I learned to] bake apple cakes in a frying pan; they being cakes of bread dough, raised with a piece of sourdough, made into a sandwich with stewed dried apples, in which I became quite proficient." He remembered seeing only one Native American during the entire journey, and that sighting took place near Chimney Rock. The Walker train followed very closely to the Atwood train. Several times they drove through the camping place where the preceding company had started their fires, only to be driven from there by Indians. Alston noted the only taste of meat came during a time when one antelope was killed, and the small pieces were shared with the entire company. No buffalo were sighted. An incident occurred as the wagon train was plodding along. Suddenly something frightened the teams in front of the Alston wagon causing the animals to stampede. The wagon just in front of the Alston wagon jerked forward quickly causing a young woman who was sitting in the rear of the wagon to fall backward and be hung by the heels of her shoes until the team was stopped. She survived the accident. Unfortunately, many of the ox and cattle died of alkali poisoning along the trail, and the Alston wagon lost three at one time, causing them to use one-half of their team. They were able to borrow one ox, which provided four animals to pull their wagon instead of the desired six. Alston wrote, "In order to lighten our load we were compelled to throw away many of our heavier articles." Alston remembers meeting teams from the valley "at some distance East of Fort Bridger." These teams carried food and other needed items for the Walker wagon train.[42]

The Hefferan family's journey across the plains was very different from others. William Hefferan began the passage west with his wife,

Clarissa, and five young children. Twins were born to Clarissa during the later portion of the trek. Both William and Clarissa were born and married in India. Their journey to Salt Lake City began in India; the next stop was London, from there to Castle Gardens, New York, and finally to Wyoming, NT. William was referred to as "Dr." and was part of a military family. William enjoyed sufficient resources to purchase many items while still in Wyoming. Years later his daughter Agnes wrote:

> He bought 2 new wagons and a traveling carriage, this had 3 seats besides the drivers. These seats could be folded down at night and used for beds. Under the seats there was a large space to pack boxes, these never had to be disturbed. He also bought a beautiful charter oak stove and every implement used for farming in those days except a plow. Then he had the farmer make an enormous cheese, also had him pack a large stone churn full of fresh butter. He bought bacon, flour, grain as well as several pigs.[43]

Dr. Hefferan hired a young couple and a young man to drive two additional wagons. In addition, another person Jane Dick Frame was hired to look after Clarissa and the children. Agnes recalled how her father would drive in his carriage ahead of the rest of the wagon train, and the family would often stop for a picnic with the items purchased before they began their trip. She noted the children had a grand time, but her "mother was always afraid of the Indians and wouldn't let them get too far away."[44] At one point on the trail, a stampede took place, and the company was held up for two weeks while the wagons were repaired. The Hefferans had extra cattle, so when the company's cattle couldn't pull a wagon up a steep hill, their teams were unyoked to help the other wagons.

As the company passed through Wyoming Territory, snow began falling and food became scarce. At some point, Captain Walker came to Dr. Hefferan and asked if he could help other members of the company with food. Dr. Hefferan gave them the bacon and flour that he bought from the farmer. Fortunately, 24 hours later a rescue team, led by Thomas Taylor, arrived with needed provisions. All felt relieved and grateful for the arriving wagon train. That evening Mr. Taylor came to talk with Dr. Hefferan. Taylor allegedly kicked an older fellow, traveling alone, who was huddled over likely trying to keep warm. Agnes wrote, "Taylor was coming to speak to father. As he passed the man, he kicked him." Taylor apparently yelled at one of Hefferan's children, which angered the Doctor. An argument ensued and Hefferan drew out his revolver and was about to shoot Taylor, but Clarissa Hefferan ran over to the two men and begged Dr. Hefferan to not shoot Taylor. She became so excited over the unfolding events, she had to be helped to the carriage that was already prepared for the night. Twin babies were prematurely born that night, but all turned out fine. Martha and Mary Hefferan were born 4 November 1865 at Green River, Wyoming Territory. According to Agnes' written recollection, "The next morning, Thomas Taylor pulled the old man out of the wagon frozen to death. He had some men dig a very shallow hole. They were going to put the body in it with no protection." Dr. Hefferan stopped them and had them dig a deeper grave. He also pulled two of his own wool blankets to wrap the body in. The mule rescue wagon train took 25 women and children with them to Salt Lake City. Dr. Hefferan traveled with them, so his wife would consent to leave.[45]

**William S. S. Willes Independent Wagon Train**

The last independent wagon train to leave Wyoming, NT in 1865 was under the leadership of Captain William S. S. Willes. He was assisted by Frederick W. Cox; chaplain and Joseph L. Barfoot; commissary. This company left Wyoming mid-August and arrived in Salt Lake City, on the 11th, 15th, and 29th of November 1865. The group contained roughly 200 passengers and 50 wagons.[46] Willis served in the Mormon Battalion and was present when gold was first discovered by members of the battalion in central California. He served a mission in England and was returning home when he was selected to captain this independent wagon train.[47] After arriving at Fort Kearny, NT following a grueling journey of 23 days,

Willes wrote a letter explaining the issues his wagon train was experiencing. The train averaged only 8 miles per day from Wyoming, NT to Fort Kearny, a situation that was created by heavy rain, inexperienced teamsters and wild cattle. In addition, three axle trees and two tongues broke during this 184-mile march. His frustration showed as he described the teamsters he was forced to use as "old decrepit men, entirely unaccustomed to handle cattle." The company was detained for two days waiting for freight belonging to Thomas Taylor to be loaded. He further explains to Brigham Young that he is carrying many sick people. Willes also alerted President Young that he only had enough provisions to the South Pass or the Green River. He did conclude by stating that "Bro. Taylor has promised to meet us with provisions and teams."[48]

Captain Willes, and those traveling on his independent wagon train, continued their journey. Anne Maria Kershaw Thompson remembered certain parts of the trek very vividly. She described the captain's unique method of helping slower people keep up with the wagon train. When the captain noticed people lagging, "[he] would come back and drive us ahead of him on horseback cracking his blacksnake whip at us, and I tell you we never stayed back again." [49] Anne noted how the train that passed just before them would leave notes written with a piece of charcoal on buffalo skulls with the date they passed through. One message read that the "Indains [sic] had stolen a young woman."[50]

Catherine Hagell Naisbitt wrote the following about her journey, "We buried many people on the way. We were also delayed on the road, as the oxen which we had been given were not broken."[51] Catherine and the company were experiencing the situation addressed in the letter sent by Captain Willes. Tragically, George Sims, a returning missionary lost his life on the Platte River. The company was camped near the end of the Platte River. Elder Sims crossed the river to approach some livestock that stood on an island. His responsibility was to hitch the cattle up and bring them back across the river to be yoked. Sadly, his horse slipped and Sims fell into the water. Because of the cold weather, Elder Sims likely wore heavy clothes, and he was unable to pull himself to the bank of the Platte River.⁵² An article appeared in the *Semi-Weekly Telegraph* and described Elder Sims with the following words:

> Elder Sims was unqualifiedly a good man: honest; guileless and simple in his dealings and intercourse with everybody ... The deceased was a native of London, 43 years of age: came to Utah in '53: in 55 he found occupation in President Young's office and remained there as a copying clerk till May, '62 ..."

He left a "wife and numerous family of minor children."⁵³

## Rescue Efforts of 1865

Rescue trains from Salt Lake City, and surrounding areas, played a prominent role in helping the beleaguered groups arrive in the Salt Lake Valley. Thomas Taylor did keep his commitment to organize relief teams to help those trapped on the plains. He arrived earlier than the other groups in Salt Lake City and began procuring teams to assist the companies still on the plains.⁵⁴ Several teams from the valley were a part of the rescue effort. George Q. Cannon appealed to anyone who was able to help those on the plains, to send out such aid as might be within reach. Cannon also accounted for actions already taken in behalf of the incoming groups.⁵⁵

As the Willes train continued west, they passed the Platte Bridge 27 October 1865. Concurrently, the *Deseret News* reported, "A dozen mule teams were about starting out yesterday afternoon, 28ᵗʰ inst., as we were going to press, with provisions, etc., for the immigrants and grain for the animals. Blankets, groceries etc., were liberally furnished, we understand for immigrants, by several of our merchants."⁵⁶ Meanwhile, the Thomas Taylor rescue wagon train stopped at South Pass—heading east with provisions on 17 October. Taylor noted that Miner Atwood's company left that morning, and the Henson Walker train should pass through the next day. Taylor continued to search for "a company that left

Laramie a few days ago."[57] The next day Taylor sent a communication to Brigham Young requesting oats for 30 ox teams, 40 sacks of flour, and 50 pounds of bacon. Equal amounts of these items were to be sent to South Pass, Hams Fork, Bear River and Weber River, respectively.[58] Wagons from the Willes train began arriving in Salt Lake City, loaded with as many folks from the Willes train as they could accommodate on Saturday 11 November. A short article in the newspaper noted, "They had suffered a good deal with cold, and before assistance arrived, had been very short of provisions."[59] Captain Arnold's train arrived with many women and children from the Willes train Wednesday night 15 November. Almost 40 men remained with the Willis train to continue the journey to Salt Lake City.[60] In a *Deseret News* article posted 16 November 1865, the Ogden and Kaysville team of rescuers arrived in Salt Lake City, the morning of 11 November. Henry Woolley captained this particular wagon train and brought 54 of the immigrants to the valley.[61] Reportedly, the final rescue team arrived 19 November. This eight horse and mule team carried additional passengers from the Captain Willes train. William D. Chipman, who managed a down and back church train in 1866, also captained this rescue team. Chipman's team picked up the struggling passengers near Independence Rock, which location is approximately 355 miles from Salt Lake City. Interestingly, their return journey required 19 days to complete, or an average of 18 miles per day.[62] The emigration year of 1865 could now be concluded. Although this year's emigration was much smaller than 1864 and 1866, remarkable efforts were made by hundreds of individuals, living in the valleys of Utah Territory, to come to the rescue of those who were stranded on the trail. The story of one rescuer, Heber Robert McBride, who lost his father while crossing the plains during the ill-fated handcart migration of 1856, will be chronicled in the afterward portion of this book.

# 8

# FORMATION OF THE 1866 DOWN AND BACK CHURCH TRAINS

Ten down and back wagon trains left Utah Territory in the spring of 1866, traveled to Wyoming, NT, and returned to Zion with both immigrants and freight.

The following table details the essential facts respecting the ten down and back wagon trains of that year:

| CHURCH TRAINS SENT FROM SALT LAKE CITY TO WYOMING, NEBRASKA TERRITORY, 1866 | | | |
|---|---|---|---|
| Wagon Master | Departure from Missouri River | Arrival in Utah Territory | Estimated number of immigrants |
| Thomas E. Ricks | 6 – 10 July 1866 | 29 August 1866 | 251 |
| Samuel D. White | 10 July 1866 | 5 September 1866 | 230 |
| William Chipman | 11-12 July 1866 | 15-16 September 1866 | 375 |
| John D. Holladay | 16-18 July 1866 | 25 September 1866 | 350 |
| Daniel Thompson | 24 July 1866 | 29 September 1866 | 500 |
| Joseph S. Rawlins | 2 August 1866 | 1-2 October 1866 | 400+ |
| Horton D. Haight | 4 August 1866 | 15 October 1866 | 4 families |
| Peter Nebeker | 7 August 1866 | 29 September 1866 | 400 |
| Andrew H. Scott | 8-9 August 1866 | 8 October 1866 | 300 |
| Abner Lowry | 13 August 1866 | 7, 22 October 1866 | 300[1] |

The summer of 1866 was the final chapter of church pioneers using locations along the Missouri River as the preparatory point for the walk to Zion. This was the last time Wyoming, NT was used by the church as the outfitting station for the immigrants and one of the last times the Nebraska City Cut-off Trail was utilized as the road to Fort Kearny.

Five of the ten wagon masters were veterans of the down and back train system. Thomas Ricks, Samuel White, and Peter Nebeker had served as wagon masters in 1863. Joseph Rawlins volunteered as the wagon master in 1864, while Horton D. Haight led down and back trains in 1862 and 1863. The other five men, William Chipman, John D. Holladay, Daniel Thompson, Andrew Scott, and Abner Lowry served as captains only in the year 1866.[1] Those who led the down and back trains, along with the others who accompanied them, served at great personal sacrifice. The Utah Territory in the mid-1860s was struggling for self-sufficiency.[2] During this epic battle for survival, these men left their homes to bring the immigrants waiting at Wyoming, NT to Utah. Therefore, those that remained behind would assist the families of the wagon train volunteers and help harvest crops. Indeed, speaking on the reasons for establishing the church train system during the 1860s, Brigham Young wrote, "We are rich in cattle, but do not abound in money either at home or abroad and desire to plan and operate to use our small amount of money and large number of cattle in the best possible manor for accomplishing the best good."[3]

The church trains of 1866, like those in the preceding years, were well organized. Both oxen and mules were used, but because oxen were less expensive, only two of the ten trains from this year were pulled by mules. Thomas E. Ricks and Samuel White both used mules for the down and back trip.[4] Because of the rigorous journey, specific instructions were given with regards to securing quality wagons, bows, covers, axles, and oxen. As noted earlier, the teams were to be organized into companies of fifty each, with the captain responsible for the safety and welfare of all involved. Four mounted men were to take charge of the animals when not in the yoke. The teamsters were held "responsible for the teams, wagons, and other property placed in their charge, for the Church will not be held responsible for said property."[5] Those who donated teams to pick up the immigrants could send freight to the east if the expenses for the wagon-master and mounted guard were paid for. Sending loose cattle to sell was also allowed, but the person sending personal livestock paid "a proportionate share of the expenses incurred in driving, guarding, and selling said cattle."[6] In addition to hauling flour and other items to the east, individuals and companies could purchase and transport wagons, groceries, machinery and other staples for their own use, which provided an inexpensive method for freighting product to the Utah Territory.[7]

## Composition of Church Trains of 1866

Captain Thomas Ricks' church train, known as the Logan Train, was composed of wards from Logan, Clarkston, Oxford, Franklin, Richmond, Hyde Park, Smithfield, Providence, Hyrum, Wellsville, and Ogden. His group also provided passage for six independent mule trains. Ricks' team included 30 teamsters, 25 wagons, 100 mules, two horses, and five night-guards. The largest number of wagons and mules came from Logan. A total of 13 wagons and 50 mules were donated by those living in that village.[8] In a report submitted by Bishop Peter Maughen to the Presiding Bishop of the Church, Edward Hunter, Maughen noted that Captain Ricks' train received a total of $3,707.95 worth of donated goods for the trip to pick up the Saints on the Missouri River. Staples such as barley, butter, vinegar, salt, meat, and other basic food products were included in the donations. In addition, the Cache Valley also sent 35 thousand pounds of wheat to feed the poor and 5,500 pounds of wheat for the teamsters. Rather than traveling to Salt Lake City for inspection, the teams from the Cache Valley were reviewed in the local area before departing east. Shortly after departing, the group crossed the Bear River Ferry on 30 April 1866.[9] According to the report written 9 May and sent by Bishop Maughen to Bishop Hunter, a man shot one of the teamsters in the arm while at the ferry which created the need for a replacement. One was quickly located and joined the group heading east.[10] The eastern journey of the 1866 down and back church trains was underway.

Samuel White's train was composed of several Salt Lake City wards,

Heberville, Tooele, Payson, Stoker, Centerville, Farmington, Kaysville, Ogden, Millard County, Beaver County, Parowan, Pinto, Spanish Fork, and three independents. White oversaw a total of 39 teamsters and five night-guards. A total of 22 wagons and 103 mules constituted the team that headed east on 1 May 1866. The Salt Lake City 20th ward provided 16 mules for the journey.[11] We learn from Bishop Thomas Jenkins' report to Presiding Bishop Edward Hunter that the Salt Lake City 4th ward sent $600 in currency to purchase a four-mule team and $180 to buy a wagon upon reaching the Missouri River. An additional $25 was sent to hire a teamster for the return trip. Bishop Jenkins also indicated $40 was provided to purchase wire for the telegraph.[12] A fascinating glimpse into specific items needed to form the church trains is found in the report of the Salt Lake City 7th ward. Like the 4th ward, the 7th ward sent cash to hire a teamster at the frontiers. In addition to the food needed for the journey, personal clothing, boots, ammunition, a powder flask, socks, blankets, ropes, and wagon covers were provided for Captain White's team. Moreover, wagon grease, whip lashes, ox shoes, and cooking utensils formed the basic items needed by the teamsters. Even though all the articles were donated, each item was given a dollar value to establish a cost for tithing purposes.[13]

The wards from Heberville, Tooele, Lehi, American Fork, and Pleasant Grove put together the team for Captain William Chipman. Chipman's train was manned by 32 teamsters and five night-guards. His train was known as the American Fork Company and the team was made up with 36 wagons, 312 oxen, six horses, and six mules. Seven independent trains also traveled with Chipman's group, and of that group four teams indicated they were only traveling one-half of the journey.[14] The Tooele ward sent enough currency to purchase one more wagon on the frontier. The amount of food needed for the journey is staggering. Edible items supplied for the journey included 5,300 pounds of flour, 612 pounds of bacon, 90 pounds of dried beef, 340 pounds of beans, 124 pounds of dried fruit, 43 pounds of butter, 114 dozen eggs, five gallons of vinegar, 300 pounds of salt, 48 ½ gallons of molasses, and yeast powder. In addition, 45 pounds of coffee, 65 pounds of sugar, four pounds of tea, 100 pounds of crackers, potatoes and onions balanced out the food supply. Fresh water, which was not always available during overland travel, was carried in four water kegs. Spades, axes, rope, 20 whips, ox shoes, shoeing hammers, cooking utensils, medicine, and clothing completed the items needed for the trip to the Missouri River.[15]

Captain John Holladay's church train came from nine Salt Lake City wards, a Weber City ward, Summit County, Payson, and Morgan County. In addition, three independent teams accompanied Captain Holladay. A total of 40 teamsters and five night-guards made the trip with the team. In addition, 35 wagons and 300 oxen started the down and back journey.[16] Daniel Thompson's train was formed using the wards from Nephi, Millard, Beaver, Parowan, Cedar, Tocqueville, St. George, Muddy, Santa Clara, and Grafton. Approximately 49 wagons, 441 oxen, 58 teamsters and five night-guards traveled with the Thompson train.[17] The report to Bishop Hunter from the Nephi ward reveals some personal items needed by the individuals traveling on the train. Thirteen overcoats, boots, shoes, socks, undershirts, over shirts, pants, blankets, saddles, bridles, and lariats were provided for the teamsters from the Nephi ward.[18] Many individuals sacrificed to supply wagons, oxen, horses, and teamsters for the down and back trains. St. George, Utah Territory lays over 300 miles south of Salt Lake City, yet this fledgling community sent wagons, oxen, teamsters, and necessary supplies for the round trip to the Missouri River and back. Some teams left St. George on 4 April 1866 in order to arrive in Salt Lake City by the appointed departure date of 1 May.[19]

Ten wards from Salt Lake City, Sugar House, Big Cotton Wood, Mill Creek, West Jordan, South Willow Creek, and South Cotton Wood constituted the areas that provided the necessary items for Captain Joseph Rawlins' church train. Rawlins' wagon train was known by the name of South Willow Creek. The train was made up of 41 wagons, 366 oxen, two horses, 48 teamsters and five night-guards. A total of six independent wagons traveled with Rawlins' group. West Jordan supplied seven wagons, which constituted the largest amount from this group of wards.[20] In his report to Bishop Hunter, Bishop A. H. Raleigh of the Salt Lake City 19th ward described some of the challenges of putting together the church teams. He had sought oxen from two different men and the result was he received nothing from either person. Another gentleman, Phillip Bugsley, expected his father and mother to be in the group emigrating in 1866, so he tried to send a wagon and four yoke of oxen. The wagon was old, and it broke down before heading east. One of the oxen was too wild to pull a wagon. The result was Bugsley could only send one-and-a-half-yoke, rather than the four-yoke he wanted to send.[21] These types of challenges were faced throughout the church by bishops as they sought donations for the down and back trains.

Horton D. Haight captained the church train that hauled telegraph wire from Nebraska City on the Missouri River to the Salt Lake Valley. The wards that contributed wagons and supplies to Haight's train were from Centerville, Kaysville, Willard, Farmington, Bountiful, and Weber County. A total of 50 wagons, 59 teamsters, 466 oxen, and five nightguards were assigned to this down and back train. Captain Haight's train was also known as the Farmington Company and the group headed east 26 April 1866.[22] In his report to Bishop Hunter, A. Cordon the bishop of the Willard ward offered a glimpse of interesting items that made the trip east. An auger, thread, cream of tartar, saleratus, pills, painkiller, and a shoeing rasp constituted some more unique items that made up this church train. During the trek east and upon arrival at Fort Bridger, one of the night guards was taken sick and returned home. Another situation early in the journey occurred when a wagon tongue broke which caused the teamster and a mounted guard to return home.[23]

Peter Nebeker's company was composed of wards from Cache Valley, Box Elder County, and Richmond County. Wards from Cache County donated 52 wagons. Brigham City in Box Elder County assisted with 10 wagons. And Richland County presented 17 wagons for the trip to pick up the Saints on the Missouri River. A total of 364 oxen began the trip to the Missouri River. No independent trains traveled with Captain Nebeker.[24] In his letter to Bishop Hunter, Bishop Alvin Nichols of Brigham City noted he sent 4,050 pounds of flour, 294 ½ pounds of meat, 81 pounds of butter, 52 dozen eggs, and ten gallons of molasses with the teams from Brigham City. Bishop Charles C. Rich from Paris, near Bear Lake, reported to Bishop Hunter the names of 14 teamsters, four wagons with chains, two guard horses, and $300 cash to purchase cattle.[25]

Andrew Scott captained the church train that received its wagons, oxen, horses, and teamsters from Provo, Springville, Spanish Fork, Payson, and Goshen. No independent teams headed east with this train. A total of 50 teams, 35 wagons, 352 oxen and five night-guards left Provo for the Missouri River to pick up immigrants. The team began the journey east 26 April 1866.[26] The reports sent by the various bishops to Bishop Hunter reveal some interesting aspects of the composition of the teams. The bishop of the Provo ward indicated that two of the teamsters would likely not make the return trip as they were not members of the church. The Springville and Spanish Fork bishops also noted some teamsters would not be making the return trip back from the Missouri River. Captain Scott said he could find teamsters to make the return trip. Of interest, this group took 8,500 pounds of wheat to Fort Bridger at a rate of $3.00 per hundred pounds. Captain Scott was to use the money from the freight as partial payment for the teamsters on the return trip. The bishop from Goshen wrote that Captain Scott's train traveled through Provo Canyon on the trip to eastern Nebraska Territory and they had a guide help them through the ravine.[27]

The sacrifice made by so many to bring immigrants to Utah Territory is amazing when one considers that there were very few wealthy people living in Utah during the 1860s. The last down and back church train we will examine was led by Captain Abner Lowry of Sanpete County. Incredibly, during the formation of this down and back train the inhabitants of Sanpete County were involved in the Black Hawk War, yet the Saints living in this area, like those in other locations, found a way to provide the needed supplies, food, and men for the wagon trains. Wards from Mount Pleasant, Manti, Ephraim, Moroni, Gunnison, Springtown, Fairview, Fountain Green, Richfield, Marysville, Circleville, and Alma provided the needed items for Captain Lowry and his team. No independent teams traveled with Captain Lowry. Included in this train were 59 teamsters, 57 wagons, 451 oxen, and five night-guards. Mount Pleasant supplied 11 of the 57 wagons and 87 oxen.[28] While on the way from Sanpete County to Salt Lake City, one of the teams from

Mount Pleasant was sent back home on 1 May, due to illness and a broken-down wagon . Although no independent wagons traveled east with the Lowry train, records indicate that 10 independent wagons made the return trip from the Missouri River, and Lowry charged each wagon $10.[29]

In a letter written to Bishop Edward Hunter, Apostle Orson Hyde, who presided over the Sanpete County area, denoted some issues faced, because of the Black Hawk War, in putting the teams together. While returning to Sanpete County from Salt Lake City, Hyde found a dozen of the teams rendezvousing at an unsafe location, and he directed them to move to a safer spot. Hyde also met with Captain Lowry at Moroni and provided some final instructions before Lowry headed to Salt Lake City. Mr. Hyde indicated the area was requested to "furnish 50 teams for the poor and seven for the telegraph making in all 65." Hyde noted that to the best of his understanding Sanpete, Sevier, and Piute Counties sent 58 or 59 teams and five mounted guards for the down and back train. In his letter, Hyde also reported the capture of two or three wagons by the Indians as the teamsters started from home. According to Hyde, some settlements failed to make their quota altogether. He closes the letter by noting the challenges of having settlers relocate to safe havens in Ephraim, Moroni, and Mount Pleasant as the Black Hawk War caused evacuations from smaller settlements to areas with more population.[30] Against seemingly overwhelming odds, the ten down and back church trains were now ready to begin the trek to Wyoming, NT to pick up the Saints who were gathering to Utah.

9
---

# THE JOURNEY EAST

The first European Latter-day Saint pioneers of 1866 began arriving at Wyoming on 18 June 1866. Riverboats continued depositing the travelers at the town on a weekly basis until the final group arrived on 11 August.[1] By 23 June 1866, six of the wagon trains sent from Utah to pick up that year's immigrants had also arrived. Before the first wagon train departed west that summer, almost 1,600 people were encamped near the small town of Wyoming. The Church Trains accounted for an additional 348 wagons with the accompanying oxen, mules, horses, support personnel, and supplies.[2] These trains brought approximately 300 men and 1,400 oxen to the area. As mentioned, the final immigration company arrived in August. Unlike the earlier groups, those arriving late were allowed no rest, and the weary pioneers left for Utah after only two days of preparation.[3] Sadly, this final party had been infested with cholera during their voyage over the ocean and while traveling on the rails across the United States. Regarding the pain experienced by many in this company, Charles P. Anderson of Sweden penned these poignant words: "I could not help but feel sad, in seeing suffering humanity excruciating in the most horrible manor until death relieved them from their suffering."[4] The effects from the cholera epidemic would continue to haunt them for much of their journey to Utah.

One significant benefit for those participating in the pioneer migrations between 1864 and 1866 was the existence of the telegraph. Several telegraph stations existed along the trail, and the captains of the ten wagon trains of 1866 kept Brigham Young apprised of their progress as their teams traveled east. For example, Horton Haight, who was responsible for bringing telegraph wire back to Utah, noted he was at Ham's Fork on 15 May, Three Crossing on 24 May and Fort Laramie by 4 June.[5] Thus, he had traversed from Salt Lake City across the majority of Wyoming in slightly more than one month. Abner Lowry's Sanpete County wagon train reached Ham's Fork on 19 May, the Sweetwater station on 1 June, Deer Creek on 3 June, and Fort Mitchell (near present day Scott's Bluff, Nebraska) on 11 June.[6] Some captains used the telegraph more frequently than others. Extant records indicate John Holladay sent thirty-two telegrams, the most of all the captains, while Daniel Thompson sent the fewest amount of telegrams with a total of eight. Regardless of the number of times the captains communicated with Brigham Young, knowing the progress of the wagon trains as they headed east was a tremendous benefit for both the church trains and those living in Utah.

The wagons participating in the 1866 migration left Utah Territory in the spring. Most left Salt Lake City on 1 May 1866. Other trains, as noted earlier, left directly from the town of origin. An excellent account of one wagon train's travel from Utah to Wyoming, NT was kept by Moses Thatcher who departed from Logan, Utah with Thomas E. Ricks. Moses Thatcher had been called on a mission to England, and he described his feelings as he left his family. "I went down to my house today and everything looks lonely and dreary. No one there to welcome you. No babes to smile on you."[7] In the latter part of April, the mule train of Thomas E. Ricks from Cache Valley and Peter Nebeker's ox train from Box Elder began the long journey to the Missouri River together. Prior to heading east, the trains were loaded with flour and provisions for the saints who were awaiting their arrival.[8]

After loading the flour and other necessary provisions, the Ricks and

Nebeker wagon trains began their eastern journey by heading north, passing the site known as the Battle Creek Massacre where Joseph Conner and his soldiers slaughtered a group of Native Americans in 1863. Thatcher described seeing the skulls and bones of those who had been massacred still lying on the ground.[9] As they traveled during the month of April, Thatcher wrote that the roads were the muddiest he had ever encountered in his life, and it took them seven days to travel 45 miles.[10] As they neared the Green River, the train delivered approximately 12 thousand pounds of oats, which they had been freighting for Eldridge & Clawson, merchants from Salt Lake City.[11] On May 27th the travelers met an 80 wagon mule train loaded with merchandise headed for Salt Lake City.[12] The volume of pioneers and the diversity of destinations on the trail is shown by Thatcher's entry of 6 June. He described meeting a great number of travelers going west, some to the Montana mines, some to Denver, some to Salt Lake City, and others were traveling to California and Oregon.[13] On 8 June, the teams passed Camp Cottonwood, and on 10 June, they passed Fort Kearny.[14] At this point, Moses Thatcher gave his view of the Nebraska Territory he was now traveling through. "I never saw a country so beautifully covered with green grass. This is all in Nebraska Territory. There are some fine farms recently located here."[15] The wagon train arrived at Wyoming, NT towards the latter part of June and they camped within a half mile of the little town, so the livestock would have plenty of room for grazing and could rest following the long journey from Utah. Thatcher notes that the train had covered the last 200 miles in five and a half days.[16] Thatcher continued on to England from Wyoming, NT.

John Warren Pickett worked as a teamster on the William Chipman train. Due to snow and muddy roads, the trip from Salt Lake City to Fort Bridger took one month to complete. The distance between the two locations was 113 miles, which translates to an average of less the four miles a day. In addition, during the trip to Fort Bridger, some oxen developed sore necks and feet, so they had to be left behind at the Platte Bridge, Deer Creek, and Laramie. Chipman's train was loaded with grain for an overland stage stop and flour for the return trip to Utah. Pickett wrote about stopping at Fort Laramie and trading for buffalo robes and moccasins with the Indians who were lodging at the fort. He noted that 500 lodges were in the area, because the Sioux, Arapaho, and Cheyenne were all gathered at the fort for a pow-wow. This particular gathering was composed of many of the Native American tribes in and around the Fort Laramie area, and a peace commission sent to create a treaty with the Indians. Accordingly, "A treaty of peace was constructed by the Peace Commissioners on the 28th of June 1866 with the principal tribes of the Indians surrounding the fort."[17] Unfortunately, the treaty did little to bring stability to the areas along the Oregon and Mormon Trail in 1866.

When crossing the Platte River above Kearny City, Pickett noted the river was a mile wide and three wagon trains crossed at one time. He described the scene as a "grand sight to see."[18] We learn from Pickett that even as the church trains headed east and would travel in close proximity to each other, they all wanted to reach the village of Wyoming first. He noted the "Chipman and Rawlins trains kept side by side all the way down, but the last night of traveling we watch [sic] each other to see which was going to camp first like a bunch of culprits."[19] Arriving first would allow that train to load first and leave prior to the other teams. Better grazing for livestock, more access to food along the trail, and better camping sites were options for those who were first on the trail. In addition, Pickett recorded how wagons tipped over, the struggles of yoking wild oxen, meeting passing trains headed west, and the necessity to strap bedding and provisions on the top of wagons while fording rivers.

One very interesting entry in Pickett's writings was his description of frontier justice. He referred to this process as Kangaroo Courts. For misdemeanors charged against a teamster we had a court of record, with a judge, sheriff, and jury. The judge wore a stove-pipe hat and put on a pair of spectacles without lenses. Typically, the court would convene at noon and the offender would be put on trial. The judge would pass sentence, and if the defendant was convicted, the ruling would be carried out. One punishment described by Pickett was "to be bumped so many times on the wagon hub."[20] Both Thatcher and Pickett provided captivating pictures of life on the down and back trains as they traveled to the Missouri River. After leaving Utah, traveling through Wyoming, moving east in present day Nebraska, and crossing the Platte River, the down and back church trains of 1866 used the Nebraska City Cut-off Trail. The church trains heading to the Missouri River used this route to reach the village of Wyoming which lay about seven miles north of Nebraska City. The road was used again for the return trip to Utah.

## 10

# LEAVING THE HOMELAND BEHIND

Ann Gregory Marriott departed from her home in Nottinghamshire, England, on 27 April 1866 to begin the long arduous journey to the headquarters of the Church of Jesus Christ of Latter-day Saints, located in Salt Lake City, Utah Territory.[1] Ann, her husband George, and their sixteen-year-old daughter left their home in England and boarded the ship *John Bright* for the lengthy ocean voyage to New York City.[2] In her diary, Ann describes the scene at the docks in Liverpool. Large piles of luggage were stacked everywhere for weighing. Before sailing, she and her family walked the streets of Liverpool and purchased tin ware, some pickled onions, bread, butter, cheese, and eggs. After obtaining the food, the family returned to the docks and "got some water boiled and we had a nice tin of tea. All well. Fair."[3] On 30 April 1866, the day the *John Bright* set sail for New York City, Ann wrote that all passengers were called on deck, so deck hands could clean and search below decks. The search by the ship's crew located a stowaway woman and her child. The two were taken off the ship and sent back to Liverpool.[4] Another passenger, Caroline Hopkins Clark, simply wrote, "We left Liverpool, England in the sailboat named *John Bright* at four o'clock on the afternoon of April 30, 1866."[5] Ann Gregory Marriott and Caroline Hopkins Clark were two of the 747 passengers who left England on the ship *John Bright* to sail toward their Zion on the deserts of Utah. Passengers on the ships were expected to provide their own beds and bedding, and they were instructed to place clothing in waterproof bags. Instructions were given to purchase utensils for cooking, and each person was advised to use every precaution to preserve their health before boarding the vessel.[6]

Almost a month later, Christian Jenson, his wife Kirsten, and two sons, Andreas and Joseph, boarded the ship *Kenilworth* on the European continent and sailed from Hamburg to New York City.[7] To begin their journey, Christian and his family left their home in Copenhagen, Denmark, along with other church immigrants, on the steamer *Aurora* 17 May 1866. The company arrived in Kiel, Schleswig-Holstein and took a train to Altona; from there the men walked to Hamburg, while the women rode a small steamer. The *Kenilworth* lifted anchor and set sail from the River Elbe 25 May 1866. The ship charted a course across the North Sea and Atlantic Ocean. On board were 684 pioneers bound for Utah. 583 were from Denmark, 73 from Sweden, 23 from Norway, and five from Germany.[8] Caroline Pederson Hansen, a fellow passenger, wrote the following about the beginning of the journey. "The ship sailed north on the east of England to go up north of Scotland. We had fierce head winds and were driven back out of our course until at one time we could see the mountains up in Norway."[9]

The *John Bright* and *Kenilworth* represent two of the nine ships loaded with converts to the faith that left England and continental Europe during the spring and summer of 1866. As noted, the *John Bright*, with 747 church member passengers, was the first to depart. The ship *Caroline* left London on 5 May with 389 immigrants bound for Utah Territory. The *American Congress* set out from London on 23 May, and 350 intrepid souls called this ship home for the next 43 days. On 30 May 1866, the *Arkwright* started out from Liverpool with 450 passengers crowding onto the ship. The next to leave England was the *Cornelius Grinnell*, which also left London on 30 May. However, this vessel only carried 26 passengers who were traveling to Utah. The last ship to leave England, the *St. Mark* proceeded from Liverpool on 6 June and carried 104 individuals adhering to the tenants of their religion. A total of 2,066 church members sailed these ships from England to New York City with the dream of reaching Utah.[10]

All three ships from continental Europe started their journey to New York City from Hamburg. As previously illustrated, the first to sail was the *Kenilworth*, which set forth on 25 May with 684 passengers. Next, the *Cavour* departed on 1 June with 369 converts. The *Humboldt* was the last vessel to leave Hamburg in 1866 carrying 328 LDS passengers. Of the nine crafts carrying converts, five of the ships were of U.S. registry, two were British, one was Norwegian, and one was German. The largest of the vessels was the *John Bright*, which weighed in at 1,444 tons, and the smallest was the Norwegian registered *Cavour* at 369 tons.[11] Unfortunately, the German ship *Humboldt* was lost at sea on its return trip across the Atlantic Ocean after dropping off its passengers in New York City.[12]

Those emigrating from Europe in 1866, left behind their homes, family, friends, language, and culture in exchange for what they believed would be a better life. Polygamy, land issues in the territory, the depth of the rift between gentiles and Latter-Day Saints living in Salt Lake City, and the trouble with the Native Americans that erupted into the Blackhawk War likely would have impacted each of the immigrants in 1866. Yet, they left everything for the chance to gather to their Zion. Perhaps the opinions of some travelers had been shaped by articles in the *Millennial Star*, which was the official Church publication for Europe. In an article dated 14 April 1866, the *Star* extolled the virtues of living in Utah Territory.

---

The lessons of self-denial, virtue, industry, and irresistible energy learned by the people of Utah, in consequence of the circumstances in which they have been placed, are necessary for the perfection of a great people.[13]

---

Thus, the mission of the new converts upon arrival in Utah was to become a great people through hard work and strict obedience to church leaders. Unfortunately for the immigrants, not all church members living in Utah Territory viewed the newcomers in a positive light. Referring to the newly arriving European settlers, one individual stated the following:

> All expect to be at the top of the tree at once, and they find themselves in the wrong box; no man gets on here by pushing; he begins at the lowest seat; a new hand is not trusted; he is first sent on a mission; then married, and then allowed to rise higher if he shows himself useful. [14]

Personal accounts describe some perils faced during the ocean voyage. Ann Gregory Marriott described the process of cleaning the area below deck. She wrote how after only six days at sea all travelers were called to stand on deck while the crew burned "tar and spread lime to purify the air."[15] Marriott describes seven other occasions during her time on the vessel where they were called on deck to purify the air.[16] Anyone who has smelled burning tar can appreciate how dreadful the odor must have been below deck if the ghastly smell of tar is an improvement over the existing stench. One reason for needing continual cleaning below deck was the spillage created by the constant rocking of the vessel. Caroline Hopkins Clark described a particularly rough day where the passengers "had to keep to our bed because we could not stand up. Sometimes we were almost up-right in bed. There was such confusion with the boxes and tins, many smashed all to pieces."[17] John Lunn writes even more graphically about what took place during rough weather, ". . . and the Saints, some of them were singing, some of them laughing at others having a good fall and spilling the contents of their slop pails and chamber servers and others their dinners of gruel and pea soup and other kinds of victuals."[18] Lunn also writes about another aspect of ocean sailing. The ship depended totally on the wind for movement. On one occasion Lunn wrote, "The wind ahead which causes much trouble in crossing backwards and forwards, but we are all trusting God."[19]

William Driver, who sailed on the *Caroline*, described passing through a gale which caused the ship to go off course ending up "within a few yards of the Isle of Wright." During the same storm, the vessel "lost a yard and sail, [and] several ropes snapped like thread." Fortunately, the crew and passengers escaped shipwreck.[20] Later in the voyage, Driver described his feelings regarding the loss of children at sea.

> Brother Cox's child was buried at 8 o'clock p.m. Willie, my dearest child was very ill all night until 7:30 a.m. when he was released from his suffering. God bless his dear soul. How he suffered. He came to death through Mr. Poulters cart breaking on St. Anns Hill, Wandsworth, Surrey, England. Oh, how I mourn this great affliction.[21]

The next day Driver wrote, "Afternoon saw my dear son sewn in canvas by first and second mates." The grief-stricken father buried his beloved son in the depths of the Atlantic Ocean at 7:00 p.m. that evening.[22] As the *American Congress* neared the coasts of Newfoundland, a thick fog enveloped the ship, and the vessel came precariously close to the rocky shoreline. According to passenger John Nicholson, the swift action of the captain was the only thing that saved the passengers and crew from being dashed in pieces on the rocks.[23]

Andrew Jenson sailed on the *Kenilworth* and described a particular time when the ship sailed into an Atlantic storm. "On June 26th, we encountered a terrific thunder and rain storm, on which occasions all the sails of the ship were taken down in double quick time, and the good old ship reeled like a drunken man and caused some alarm among the passengers."[24] Jenson also recounted the suicide of one member of the company who jumped overboard towards the end of the voyage. He also wrote that during the trip two babies were born, and seven marriages were recorded.[25] Charles P. Warnick wrote about the rationing of food and water that took place during the voyage of the *Cavour*. Each family was allotted one quart of water a day, and the water was of a "very poor quality."[26] A further understanding of the water supply offered to the travelers comes from a passenger on the ship *Humboldt*. Olof Jenson wrote how the drinking water for the journey was taken from the river Elbe and placed in wooden barrels. The barrels had been burned on the inside which made the water turn black. Jenson wrote a simple sentence describing his view of the provisions onboard the ship, "Pigs would object to the food and water, but we had to take it."[27] After experiencing sea sickness, putrid air in the holds below deck, storms, rationed food, births, deaths, and a host of other challenges, each ship finally arrived at the pre-appointed destination of New York City. The passengers could now disembark and enter into Castle Gardens, the location designated to process arriving immigrants. The next stop on their journey west would be Wyoming, Nebraska Territory.

Upon arrival in the United States the immigrating Saints met Thomas Taylor, who again had been called as the Church Emigration Agent, with the responsibility of getting the travelers from New York City to Wyoming, NT. Taylor, born in England, had immigrated to Utah in 1848-49. He eventually settled in Lehi, Utah, and became one of its leading citizens. He was actively involved in a mercantile business, founded the Lehi Dramatic Club, and served faithfully in the LDS Church.[28] Taylor served as the Church Emigration Agent between 1864 and 1866, and he acted in this position at great personal expense. Even Brigham Young recognized the sacrifice endured by Mr. Taylor, as evidenced in a letter sent by Young to Taylor's bishop in 1866. President Young requested that Taylor remain exempt from paying tithing because of losing $10,000 of his own money the previous year while assisting people to Utah.[29] Taylor's role as the emigration agent was to negotiate pricing with railroads and steamers to transport the year's immigrants to Wyoming, NT. During the immigration of 1866, Taylor selected an economical route that had the travelers take a steamer from New York City to New Haven, Connecticut. The next step was to take a train into Canada and then back across the United States border into Chicago. From Chicago another train took the immigrants to Quincy, Illinois.

After crossing the Mississippi River, the rail travel ended in St. Joseph, Missouri.[30] From there a steamer took the various groups to Wyoming, NT.[31]

The experiences of traveling across the country were detailed by several immigrants. William Grant noted, "The crowd of hundreds of whom we started with have gone right along not having such burdens as we have. We cannot keep up and so we are lost in the streets of New York."[32] William Driver described two specific challenges those traveling in his group experienced. "Wednesday 13th. Luggage train on fire. Brothers Bates, Pain, Tracey, Miller and others lost a great portion of their luggage . . . met a body of British troops on the scout for Fenians at St. Alexander."[33] Fenians were an Irish nationalist group that tried to invade Canada in 1866. Therefore, troops stationed on the border of the United States and Canada were on heightened alert.[34] Olof Jenson noted how his group traveled in cattle cars during a part of the railroad journey.[35] Another group that traveled in cattle cars were those who sailed on the ship *Cavour*. Cholera had broken out among the passengers, so the cattle cars provided an unlikely place to rest—in the middle of the filth.[36] It was still challenging traveling through Missouri, a state that had expelled the Mormons three decades earlier. Describing the scene of passing through Missouri, Andrew Jenson wrote, "In several of the larger towns, through which we passed, the inhabitants acted hostile towards us and made several demonstrations in the shape of insults and threats."[37] The zig-zag rail crossing from New York City to St. Joseph, Missouri was a tiresome journey of approximately two weeks. Following a brief stay in St. Joseph, steamers took the immigrants to the outfitting station for that immigration year, Wyoming, NT.

In 1866, the 1,266 Mormon emigrants from Continental Europe equaled almost nine percent of the overall total of 14,495 Scandinavians who migrated to America that year. Moreover, according to Andrew Jenson, the first ship to sail, *The Kenilworth*, carried 583 Danish passengers[38] which would account for a large percentage of the out-migration from Denmark during that year. Farming was listed as the occupation by 94 of the Scandinavians, followed by 47 claiming to be laborers. There were 217 occupations recorded. Farmers and laborers accounted for 65 percent of the total listed livelihoods. Tailors, shoemakers, weavers, carpenters, joiners, and blacksmiths tallied 46 of the workers who listed how they made their living.[39] Like the converts who left England in the spring and summer of 1866, many of the Scandinavian travelers were economically disadvantaged. Of interest, a total of 181 families traveled on the vessels from Hamburg and widows accounted for 67 of the total passengers.[40]

There were 521 British emigrants from the 1866 migration who declared an occupation. Laborer was the largest group under the heading of employment, totaling 176, or more than 33 percent of individuals listing a livelihood.[41] Miners constituted 89 people, or 17 percent. Thus, 50 percent of employed persons traveling to the United States in this small church exodus were either laborers or miners. Carpenters, cabinet makers, and bricklayers constituted 32 of the occupations. Shoemakers, boot makers, tailors, weavers, blacksmiths, locksmiths, and tinners rounded out the majority of those claiming some work skill. Of interest, five iron workers, one boilermaker, one iron molder, one gas fitter, one engine smith, one brass caster, one oilman, and one iron turner walked away from their industrial jobs for a chance at living among others who held the same belief system. Those traveling as families constituted 221 units, while 79 widows started the voyage to Utah.[42]

Some conclusions can be drawn from the make-up of the 3,332 individuals that constituted the immigration group that sailed from Europe in 1866. Similarities existed between those leaving from England and the groups that departed from Hamburg. First, a large majority appeared to move as families. This movement as families supports a conclusion that those who joined the Mormon faith joined by and large as families.[43] Second, 146 widows who were willing to relocate to a different country, climate, and culture far away from family and friends creates the distinct sense they were not satisfied with their current situation. Third, those who left Europe for Utah were among the poorer class of people. Laborers and miners constituted 42 percent of the occupations held by these voyagers. Whatever their family situation, occupation, or disposition, all the immigrants had one thing in common.

They each boarded a ship, watched the gangplank pull away, and ventured out on an ocean most had never before seen. The words of Charles P. Warnick, who immigrated in 1866, sheds light into what was in the hearts of many immigrants when he wrote, "But alas! How short-sighted are we human beings! How little we know what is before us."[44]

The desire to migrate to America was the preoccupation of the LDS faithful who lived in Scandinavia during the mid-nineteenth century. In the case of Denmark, church emigration accounted for 2,898 individuals or 77 percent of the total out-migration during the 1850s. In addition, during the 1860s, church migration totaled 4,942 people, or 38 percent of the entire number of emigrants from Denmark that left for the United States.[45] Several factors influenced the desire of individuals to leave their home country. Europe during the 1860s was consumed in war. Denmark experienced the Second Schleswig-Holstein War, and Germany, under Otto Von Bismarck, was involved in the Wars of German Unification that took place between 1864 and 1871. In the minds of LDS Church leadership, these conflicts were a precursor to the end of the world. Orson Pratt, an apostle of the church, used the *Millennial Star* to deliver his views of how the wars engulfing Europe were punishment for rejecting the message of the church. Pratt began his warning by declaring, "When the Almighty determines to punish nations for their sins, he not infrequently accomplishes his purposes through the medium of war."[46] Then, speaking specifically to Prussia, Pratt wrote, "As you have rejected the only message which will save you, or any other nation, God has rejected you, and your king and your nobles, and all who sit in high places; and the days will shortly come that you will cease to be a kingdom."[47] In a later editorial, Pratt stated that the "great army of the Lord" would be found in the "far off mountains of America," strongly suggesting the need to immigrate to Utah.[48]

The predominant reason the church immigrants left Europe was the new religion they espoused. For example, Andrew Jenson noted, "It seemed as no great sacrifice to us to leave our native land, relatives and friends to go to the gathering place of the saints."[49] Charles P. Warnick wrote, "We were thankful that we had thus been blessed of the Lord that we were able to go to Zion where we might live and worship with those of our faith."[50] All who left, sacrificed. William Grant described how he sold off all his household effects and pictures. He lived with a friend to save money and then denied he and his family "of all luxury and barely took the necessities of life."[51] Not all who started the journey continued. Several died during the ocean voyage. Some died during the rail journey. Indeed, for a few, the experience of leaving home was too brutal to advance any farther. One person went insane and tried to kill herself.[52] Others stopped at various points along the way and traveled no further.[53] Evidence indicates some immigrants left their homes in Europe because of poverty or to escape conscription into military service.[54] Disillusionment, heartache over leaving family and friends, sickness, discouragement, and fear stalked many of the participants of this migration. Nevertheless, the vast majority of the three thousand plus Europeans that started the long journey in 1866 continued moving forward. The next chapter of their arduous passage began at the outfitting station of Wyoming, NT.

## 11

# THE THOUSAND MILE TREK TO THE GREAT BASIN BEGINS

The trip across the Nebraska and Wyoming Territories to Salt Lake City took about two months to complete when oxen pulled the wagons. However, the trains of Thomas E. Ricks and Samuel White were pulled by mules, and they completed their journeys two weeks faster. Ann Gregory Marriott traveled with the Thomas E. Ricks' church train. Just as she had done while at the docks in Liverpool, England, Marriott described what it was like to finally leave Wyoming and begin the march on the trail.

> Packing up to move out. They are now putting mules in the wagons to make a start for Salt Lake Valley. About three o'clock as near as I can guess we started to walk, we trotted along some with one stick and some with two, others took pieces of boards, some had umbrerellas [sic] others had not, the sun was scorching hot."[1]

Ann listed the date of the train starting west as 4 July 1866.[2] Jacob Zollinger, a teamster on the Ricks' train noted his wagon had two families, which amounted to twelve people traveling together in one wagon. Zollinger also wrote, "All the wagons were loaded heavy." The heavily loaded wagons meant "all able-bodied people had to walk." Interestingly, Zollinger noticed that three men traveled with the train in a white top buggy. One of the men was the son of Joseph Smith, founder of the Church of Jesus Christ of Latter-day Saints.[3] The first of the ten down and back trains of 1866 was now on the trail west.

Charles Savage commented on daily life on the trail. Savage noted that at five o'clock a.m. a bugle sounded to wake the passengers up, at which time they would prepare their breakfast. At six o'clock, prayer was held which was followed by preparations to roll out. The wagon train would then travel until about twelve o'clock noon. At this time, dinner was prepared. At two o'clock, the train again moved out, traveling until camp was made around six o'clock. At this point, the night herders would drive the herd to a suitable feeding location. In the evening, a supper was prepared, prayers were held, and orders for the next day's travel were given by the captain. Following the captain's directions, guards were placed around the camp.[4]

Savage was a professional photographer, and he traveled with the down and back train, but he used his own specially fitted photography wagon. His desire was to photograph "a series of views on the overland route."[5] In an article written in 2008, John Carter noted that it was during this trip in 1866 that Savage took the only known views of "emigrants traveling through Nebraska's Platte Valley in covered wagons during the migration years."[6] Savage's photograph of the Roland Reed ranch provides visual evidence that the Ricks' church train followed the Nebraska City Cut-off Trail, as the Reed ranch bordered the crossing on Beaver Creek in present-day southern Seward County.[7] During his travels though Nebraska Territory, Savage also photographed Cheese Creek, Fort Kearny, O'Fallon's Bluff, a wagon train crossing the Platte River, and Chimney Rock. Savage described the difficulty of taking photographs on the plains.

---

Photographing in the circumstances under which we traveled, is *work*; what with the care of animals, and standing guard at nights, and having no time to spare, it was a scramble to photograph anything, and unless a man can travel with *art* companions he can do but little.[8]

---

The equipment needed to take photographs was bulky; the weather was often too hot for the chemicals to work effectively, and the others traveling on the down and back train were not interested in stopping so Savage could take pictures. However, he persevered in his efforts to chronicle the overland travel of 1866.

Captain Samuel White's train was the second to leave Wyoming, NT, and William Grant described how the beginning of the journey was for him. First, he noted the wagon he and his family traveled in was half full of freight, "so we were not comfortable in any way." Regarding his first day of travel Grant wrote, "We are now on our way over the plains. I had bad eyes and was three days almost blind. Had to walk holding on behind the wagon."[9] Grant was the trumpeter for the train, and one of his responsibilities was to call the people to prayer both morning and night. He and his wife traveled with their three small children. Occasionally, his wife would walk three to six miles a day, so he could ride in the wagon with the children.[10] Richard Litson noted that on the first day the train traveled for two-and-a-half hours and stopped to camp for the night. Litson indicated, "[they camped by a] beautiful house where there was water and wood." Litson also noted they passed several teams heading east on the trail.[11] He wrote about passing several graves "which marked the trail & bore a testimony of those who had passed ahead."[12]

The third train to leave Wyoming that year was under the direction of William Henry Chipman. B. H. Roberts, who later would sit in the leading councils of the church, described his feelings about beginning the journey on the trail. Roberts wrote, "There was a thrill in the departure for the long journey. All were rested up by the stay at the Missouri encampment, and all were eager for the march." He noted this particular company was one of the larger ones of the season and made an imposing procession of covered wagons.[13] Roberts also recorded that sleeping arrangements placed the women in the wagons, while the men and boys slept under or beside the wagons.[14] On 11 July 1866, Caroline Hopkins Clark wrote a one sentence entry, "Left Wyoming five miles and then we joined Captain Chipman's train."[15]

Captain Chipman kept a notebook where he recorded some revealing details of life on the trail. For instance, he records how much food he distributed to the pioneers traveling on the church train. In addition, he details the type of food the immigrants received for the trip to Zion. One particular page in his notebook revealed flour, bacon, molasses, sugar, and coffee were the products rationed to the travelers.[16] Chipman recorded five deaths that took place on the trail from Wyoming, Nebraska Territory to Salt Lake City. The ages of those who died on the trail varied from an eight-month-old baby girl to a 60-year-old woman.[17] Captain Chipman's notebook detailed cattle that died during the journey and noted where the deaths occurred. Entries such as Provo Canyon, Platte Bridge, and Sweet Water confirm where the incidents happened.[18] In addition, Chipman noted some animals simply gave out or were lost. At different points along the trail, Chipman made entries explaining the need to pay individuals for supplies or services. Corn for the herder's horses, oxen shoes, nails, and a herd bill at Kearney City to a Mr. Summerwell summarize some debts incurred during the travel west.[19] Chipman's journal demonstrates some challenges faced by the captains of the down and back trains.

The fourth wagon train to leave Wyoming, NT was under the direction of Captain John D. Holladay. Regarding the beginning of his journey to Utah, Charles Denny wrote, "Here I knew scarcely anybody, almost an entire stranger in a strange land. Yet I did not feel discouraged, but still desired to go on to the valleys of the mountains."[20] Denny noted the names some teamsters wrote on the covers of the wagons. The wagon Denny used during the march to Zion was named Weber Sal, other names were Pony Express, to Salt Lake City, Pike's Peak, or Bust by Golly, and, The Mountain Boy.[21] Denny wrote how he (and likely others in the group) would bathe and wash his shirt. "I would go into the water with it [the shirt] on, then after I had splashed about a while, and rubbed my shirt I would lay it on the bank to dry while I went into the water again, so you see I was clean myself and had a clean shirt to put on."[22] Holladay's train hauled coal oil, which was destined for the old tabernacle and the theatre in Salt Lake City. Furthermore, most of Holladay's wagons contained church freight in addition to the immigrants and their luggage.[23]

The next two trains to depart from Wyoming were captained by Daniel Thompson and Peter Nebeker, respectively. Justin Wixsom was selected as the chaplain for the Thompson train. In one of his entries, Wixsom revealed other services he had rendered on the pioneer trail. He wrote that during the crossing of the plains he served as a chaplain, doctor, drove the ox team and worked in every possible capacity to assist those in his wagon train. Wixsom also noted that one person apostatized and stopped her journey west while near Fort Kearny.[24] Two other travelers with Captain Thompson were Mary Wagstaff and her brother. They purchased their own wagon and supplies and simply traveled with the church train for protection.[25] Olof Jenson, who traveled with the Peter Nebeker train, described the crossing of the Platte River. He noted the river bottom was very uneven and five to six pair of oxen per wagon were needed to ford the river. He remembered one wagon box floating down the river some distance before it was rescued. After crossing the river, Jensen wrote, "We had to pause for a few days to dry our clothes." One other interesting bit of information shared by Jenson was that the travelers cooked their bread in Dutch Ovens and used buffalo chips for fuel.[26]

Joseph Rawlins and Andrew Scott captained the next two trains that left Wyoming. A passenger in Captain Rawlins train, Mary Ann Greenhalgh, noted how two families were assigned to the different wagons, but one of the mother's did not offer approval of the arrangements. This particular mother did not like the appearance of other immigrants, and she believed her children would catch some sort of disease from them.[27] Greenhalgh further described how the freight being hauled in one of the wagons consisted of "flat wooden boxes which just fit into the bottom of the wagon box and completely covered the floor." Contained in these boxes were materials for the Great Salt Lake Tabernacle organ.[28] One humorous incident occurred as the

Rawlins' train began the march to Utah. Eliza Harrison noted their wagon was overweight, so her father quickly removed the feather bed from the wagon. Whereupon, the mother promptly sat on the bed and refused to go any further. The wagon train left the mother sitting on the bed and started the journey west. Fortunately, after a short time, the father returned and loaded both the mother and the bed into the wagon.[29]

Andrew Jenson, who traveled with the Andrew Scott train, described his feelings as he left the small village of Wyoming. "Wednesday, August 8, 1866, will always remain a red-letter day in my recollection. At 10:00 o'clock in the forenoon, as passengers in Capt. Andrew H. Scott's train, we left Wyoming to cross the plains."[30] As noted earlier, Captain William H. Chipman detailed the type of food distributed to the immigrants. Jenson, who later became a noted church historian, recorded the number of rations issued. One-and-one-half pounds of flour and one pound of bacon per day were allowed for each person. He goes on to explain various situations that arose while preparing meals on the plains. The rain fell so hard at times that the pioneers were drenched to the skin, and the rain doused the fires used to cook. Alternatively, the wind would sometimes blow so savagely as to envelop the camp in a cloud of dust.[31]

The ninth train to leave the banks of the Missouri River was captained by Horton D. Haight and was unique among the other church trains of 1866 in that the main function of this particular wagon train was to bring freight to Utah. John Clark Dowdle, a teamster serving on the train, was appointed to receive and load 167 thousand pounds of telegraph wire, insulators and other needed products for the establishment of Deseret State Telegraph. The telegraph line was to run from St. Charles in current day southeastern Idaho to St. George located in the southern portion of present-day Utah.[32] Dowdle noted the freight was unloaded from the steamer and placed in the wagons preparatory for the trip west. Due to the weight and volume of the wire, this train took only four families (mostly friends of the teamsters).

As the train was preparing to depart, William E. McClellan, a prominent member of the church from its early days, applied a *writ of attachment* to the telegraph wire which forced the train to remain in Otoe County until a suit brought against Brigham Young, Heber C. Kimball, and others could be tried in court. McClellan sought money for a situation that had occurred many years earlier when the church was headquartered in Kirtland, Ohio.[33] According to Dowdle's account, a trial was held and the *writ of attachment* was lifted, which allowed the train loaded with thousands of pounds of telegraph wire to begin its trip to Utah. Dowdle noted, the attachment and subsequent trial caused a one-month delay for the departure of Holladay Church Train.[34] The last train to leave the western banks of the Missouri River in 1866 was led by Abner Lowry from Sanpete County in Utah Territory. John Nielson, one of the passengers on this train, noted how he walked the entire distance to Utah, even though he celebrated his eighth birthday on the trail.[35] Those with excess luggage either left the items behind or paid an extra fee. The journey to Zion was now underway.

## 12

# TRAVELS ACROSS NEBRASKA, WYOMING AND ON TO ZION

Fort Kearny was the blending point of the Nebraska City Cut-off Trail, the Ox-Bow Trail, and the Oregon California Trail. Even though a peace treaty had been signed at Fort Laramie in June, each wagon train needed special permission from the military at Fort Kearny to continue moving west. The records of the fort during the migration of 1866 detail each wagon train as they passed the fortification. The amount of traffic passing the fort is staggering. Several days during the months of May, June, July, and August, four and five wagon trains passed by each day. Each wagon train was listed, with their destination, the number of wagons, men, guns, and revolvers. Captain Samuel D. White was granted permission to travel west on 21 July 1866. He was followed by W. H. Chitman (Chipman), J. D. Holladay, D. Thompson, Joseph Rollins (Rawlins), D. H. Haight, Peter Nebeker, and Abner Lowry. According to the post records, Abner Lowry's wagon train consisted of 62 wagons and men, 58 guns and 68 revolvers. Captain Lowry passed the fort on 26 August, which was thirteen days following his departure from Wyoming, NT.[1]

From the fort, the church trains would travel further west and locate a suitable location to ford the Platte River. The difficulties of fording the Platte were chronicled by several of the pioneers. Caroline Hopkins

Clark wrote, "Today we crossed the Platte River. It was very deep. In places it took the wagons up to the covers. We all got over safe, but wet our clothes."[2] William Grant described his crossing as follows: ". . . and all able-bodied persons were called on to walk across the river and in places four foot deep. As I could not swim I dreaded the journey of a mile across the river . . . we all crossed in safety."[3] Ann Gregory Marriot noted that prior to crossing the Platte, a young child died and was buried beside the river. She and her sister were one of the last groups to cross the river that day and made it over after the sunset.[4] Teamster Jacob Zollinger noted, "When we came to the Platte River, which was about one third of a mile wide, we had to put four pair of mules on a wagon in order to ford the stream."[5] After crossing the Platte River, the church trains gained access to either the Oregon California Trail, or the original Mormon Trail for the balance of the trip to Utah Territory.

The pioneers continued the long grueling journey to Utah. Caroline Hopkins Clark noted that the William Chipman train passed Chimney Rock several days after crossing the Platte. On 14 August, the wagon train passed Fort Laramie, Wyoming, and the soldiers stopped the train to "see what firearms we had. They told us the Indians had killed a hundred or more and robbed them." [6] The Native Americans did drive away ninety-one head of cattle during an evening meal, but the livestock were located ten days later and brought back to the train. On 1 September, the wagon train reached South Pass, and she noted the weather was "very severe." South Pass is where the pioneers crossed the Continental Divide and the travelers now understood, in a very real sense, they were inching closer to their destination. The rivers now flowed toward the Pacific Ocean instead of the Atlantic. Clark also provided a brief description of the pioneer's diet on the trail. Men caught fish in the various streams, and they also shot wild game. Additionally, wild currants and gooseberries were used to make puddings. Pancakes and bran dumplings were sometimes prepared to provide a change in diet. Referring to her life on the trail, Clark penned these words, "So, altogether, we get along very well."[7]

Jacob Zollinger indicated that sometimes his train traveled between 20 and 30 miles a day, and the only river that was not forded was the

Green River in Wyoming. During long climbs up steep terrain, the animals would be doubled up for the ascent. Zollinger wrote that Captain Ricks would hunt for game almost every day, and he typically returned with two to four animals. The available meat would be divided among the pioneers, but the teamsters always received their portion first. The train eventually crossed the Sweetwater and the Little and Big Sandy Rivers. The last stream the company crossed before reaching Fort Bridger was called Ham's Fork. By this point in the journey, the mules began to "get poor, even though we had grain to feed them most of the way." [8] The daily routine of walking mile after mile was wearing down both people and animals, but fortunately the end of the journey was near.

William Grant detailed two interesting episodes that took place on the latter portions of the trek. One particular day, Grant had stayed behind the train after he had located some currants, gooseberries, and other wild fruit. He was surrounded by a group of Native Americans who begged for tobacco. Grant showed them his clean teeth and said he did not use tobacco. He was left unharmed, but the incident taught him a valuable lesson about never leaving the protection of the wagon train. The second incident happened because the Samuel White train was three to four days behind the Thomas Ricks train. Grant noted the train that was ahead of them "killed and drove off the game—and we had but little."[9] This was a very specific example of the advantage of being first on the trail.

B. H. Roberts wrote that night drives were occasionally undertaken to reach certain streams for the benefit of trailing teams. Roberts called the night drives a terror. At the end of one of the night drives, the company camped by the side of a very large number of tepees. According to Roberts, the train was now in the area occupied by Sioux, Cheyenne, and Arapahos. Roberts, like so many others had been infected with lice. The teamsters on the train took care of the lice issue by taking sheep shears and clipping Roberts' head until nothing more could be snipped. He was now totally bald. Early the next morning, Roberts encountered a group of Native Americans sitting in a circle, passing around a peace pipe. One of the Native

Americans looked at Roberts's cleanly shaven head, slapped the top of young Roberts' head with great force and yelled no scalp![10] Roberts failed to see the humor in the verbal exchange. Shortly after crossing the South Pass, Roberts said rations of food were drastically reduced, because the train had slowed down following an incident with a group of Native Americans. For several days, the pioneers subsisted on sage hens, rabbits, mountain hares, and a few antelope. The camp was completely void of bread rations, and there was very little wild game in the area. Fortunately, Arza Hinckley's relief train bound from Salt Lake City encountered the Chipman Train and provided needed food rations.[11]

Charles Denny described a challenging night on the trail. Denny traveled on the John Holladay train, which carried freight to the Salt Lake Valley. The church train had been traveling many days when Charles described a particular night as follows:

---

> In the afternoon it commenced to rain, and continued to do so up till dark, it was now bedtime, but I had no place to lay my head, the wagon, then containing 10 persons, was too crowded, and the ground was soaking wet, and I had but a knotted quilt for bedclothes, I laid down under a wagon for a short time but was soon sopping wet, I could do nothing else but walk around all night in the rain, and I thought the morning would never come.[12]

---

The rain stopped at six o'clock the next morning, and Denny gathered buffalo chips and cattle dung to make a fire. He dried himself as best he could under the circumstances. The next day Denny, along with the other passengers on the wagon train, continued the long mind-numbing walk to their Zion. Pioneering left little choice, but to move forward every single day. Being drenched in an all-night downpour, or feeling the pangs of hunger from the lack of food did not qualify as a justification to stop the journey to the Great Basin. Even death stopped the wagon trains for only a short time. Once the individual was interred and final respects were paid, the wagon train continued the long trek west.

Andrew Jenson left vivid descriptions of experiences on the trail. The lack of food, constantly stalked the pioneers—particularly as the journey wound down. As the pioneers began climbing in altitude their hunger increased, but the food rations dwindled. Jenson noted that Captain Andrew Scott had cached stocks of food at various locations along the trail, but stocks had been stolen. Additionally, on 19 September, as the company drew near South Pass, a severe snowstorm hit the travelers. It had snowed the previous night, and the weather turned bitterly cold. Jenson described the night as the coldest and most unpleasant day on the whole journey.[13] As a result of the storm, cattle froze to death, and the immigrants could not start fires, because the fuel to start fires was covered by the snow. Fortunately, before the situation became disastrous, the teamsters started a huge campfire for the pioneers to warm themselves. Towards noon the teamsters hitched up the half-frozen cattle, and the train traveled for a few miles to a more sheltered location, and the company made an encampment. The snow continued to fall during the entire episode.[14]

William Driver kept an excellent diary containing regular accounts of situations faced on the trail. On 18 September, after over two months on the trail, Driver recorded a typical day of travel in the higher elevations. Mr. Driver and his fellow travelers were now only five days from their destination. This day's entry contains several elements each traveler faced daily in their walk to Zion. Walking in a windy, dusty environment, using sage brush for fuel, having little water to drink, observing the death of a fellow traveler, and contending with restless children were all part of this one day. Driver wrote about feeling sick, how barren the country appeared, how the wind and blowing dust made traveling miserable.[15]

The photographer, Charles Savage described in detail the landscape of the land the trains passed through. His particular train crossed the Platte River at Fremont Springs and traveled on the south side of the North Platte River where they found antelope, deer, prairie fowl, and sage hens. Savage noted that landmarks such as Ash Hollow, Scott's

Bluff, Castle Rock, and Chimney Rock offered welcome relief from the day-to-day grind of walking. Fort Laramie provided access to a succession of scenes of great interest and beauty. After crossing over the North Platte River Bridge, the weary travelers passed Independence Rock and Devil's Gate, eventually reaching the South Pass which was the dividing ridge for the entire trip. From South Pass the pioneers viewed the snow-capped mountains of the Intermountain West and they were within 100 miles of Fort Bridger, Wyoming Territory.[16] The travel distance from Fort Bridger to the Salt Lake valley was about 113 miles. However, the last portion of the trail looped through mountain passes and winding trails which reduced the number of miles the teams could travel in a day. After passing Fort Bridger, some teamsters began telling stories around the evening campfires about how Johnston's Army was repulsed a decade earlier and the invasion of Utah Territory was stopped.[17]

In July 1866, due to the late departure of some wagon trains from Wyoming, NT, Brigham Young called on Arza Erastus Hinckley to take a mule train and seek out those who might be struggling on the trail. Hinckley left with a small wagon train pulled by mules and headed out to locate those who needed assistance. Hinckley located the cholera train of Captain Abner Lowry (referenced later) about 400 miles east of the Great Basin, and they provided much needed relief to the struggling travelers. Hinckley also loaded the orphans into the rescuer's wagons and took them back to Salt Lake City.[18] The Hinckley rescue wagon team also aided Captain William Chipman's train after a group of Native Americans stampeded their cattle and stole 100 oxen. Captain Hinckley's train provided 40 sacks of flour for the ill-fated Chipman group. As detailed earlier, B. H. Roberts noted, this act of mercy saved the pioneers from absolute starvation.[19]

The pioneers of 1866 were protected by the military against incursions from Native Americans. However, because those who originally settled the land were being driven from their homes and settlers were flooding the pioneer trails, conflict between the two parties was inevitable. As noted, Captain Chipman lost almost 100 cattle as the Native Americans stampeded the herd during a noon encampment.[20] John Jenkins a teamster for the Horton D. Haight Church Train indicated the wagons were held up by the military at Fort Kearny. They were allowed to proceed only by traveling with another train. Twenty-five miles further west Jenkins was driving the lead wagon and came upon a man stretched across the road who had been killed by the Native Americans. After driving a few miles further west, the train came upon eleven more men who had been killed. Twelve wagons were burned, and a woman and two children were carried away.[21] Ann Gregory Marriot described a time when "three Indians and one squaw came to see us." Marriot indicated the visitors were "quite friendly" and camped for the night. Nothing of note happened during the night.[22] For the most part, the church member pioneers of 1866 had a peaceful coexistence with the Native Americans while traveling on the trails to Utah Territory.

The end of the trail in Salt Lake City elicited enthusiastic responses from the men and women who had left their homes in Europe. They had traveled by sailing vessel to New York City, boarded trains and steamboats to Wyoming, NT, and walked the final thousand miles to reach their Zion in the Utah Territory. Andrew Jenson and some friends climbed a bluff near the city and years later described his feelings.

---

> From that point of vantage, I enjoyed my first view of Great Salt Lake City. The city appeared grand and beautiful, as it nestled in the full blaze of the afternoon sun. Together with my companions, I shouted for joy as we felt that our fondest hopes and anticipations had been realized.[23]

---

Robert Aveson recalled the following:

---

> Well do we remember when we reached the end of our long journey, and we were taken to the old tithing yard, how we felt to rejoice that our lives had been spared to reach the land of Zion, where we were

free to worship the Lord according to the dictates of our conscience.[24]

---

Charles Denny expressed his thoughts as follows: "I shall never forget my feelings as I looked upon the City of Salt Lake from the bench at the mouth of Parley's Canyon, it seemed so beautiful to me."[25] The most animated portrayal from one of the pioneers entering the valley came from William Grant. As he caught his first glimpse of Salt Lake City, Grant noted, "We passed through Echo Canyon and Parley's Park, emigration Canyon, and then the beautiful city of Salt Lake burst to our views. Joy. Joy. Here was to us a Paradise indeed, five miles brought us to the heart of the city and we were delirious with delight."[26] With the exception of Captain Lowry's church train, the long, seemingly endless journey was now completed and the Mormon pioneers of 1866 had finally reached their Zion. Sadly, the last wagon train to leave Wyoming, NT suffered extensively during their trek west. Their remarkable story follows.

## 13
# THE CHOLERA TRAIN FROM SANPETE COUNTY

The Scandinavian emigrants of 1866 traveled on several down and back church trains. Some accompanied Captain Joseph Rawlins' ox train, another group left Wyoming, NT with Captain Peter Nebeker, and a third group made the trek west with Captain Andrew Scott. Unfortunately, due to their late arrival at the outfitting station, the group of Saints who sailed on the ship *Cavour* traveled with the Abner Lowry church train after only two days of rest from their arduous ocean and cross-country travels. Lowry's wagons had waited a long time for the last group of Saints to arrive, and due to the lateness of the season, the determination was made to begin the travel west quickly. The wagons began moving west on 13 August 1866. Not all travelers on the Abner Lowry Church Train had immigrated to the United States in 1866. One example comes from a short account written by Johanna Kristena Jensen Anderson. Johanna, her father, mother, and four other siblings left Denmark in 1865 to immigrate to Utah. The family made the journey as far as Wyoming, Nebraska Territory before they ran out of money. Her father (and the family) resided in the Wyoming, NT area until the 1866 immigration. Anderson indicated, "Many saints remained until they could accumulate enough money to proceed to Utah."[1]

Andrew Jenson, a Scandinavian emigrant and one who traveled with

Captain Andrew Scott's ox team in 1866, wrote the following about the cholera train from Sanpete County in his book *History of the Scandinavian Mission*:

> If the details of the journey across the Plains of this company were written, it would probably present one of the most pitiable and heart-rending chapters in the history of the Church, but it is perhaps better to close the episode and not revive the memory of something so touching and sorrowful. At some future day, undoubtedly, more details will be published about the experience of that ill-fated company, and in the great hereafter those who laid down their lives on the way will have the opportunity to give an accurate and truthful account of their suffering.[2]

Andrew Jenson's strong feelings regarding the sufferings experienced by those who traveled on the cholera train of 1866 in no way diminishes the afflictions of the ill-fated Martin Willie handcart companies ten years earlier, nor of the thousands of individuals who suffered pain and death while crossing the plains to the western United States. However, his statement reflects the admiration Mr. Jenson held for this relatively small group of immigrants who suffered greatly in their effort to reach their Zion.

Cholera significantly impacted the nineteenth century church. The first symptom to strike victims would be odorless, clear diarrhea. The afflicted person could lose over ten percent of his or her body weight in just a few hours. Next, vomiting and intestinal and muscle cramps could also overwhelm the tormented individual. As the disease progressed, extreme thirst, rapid heartbeat, weakness, dizziness, and fainting would manifest themselves. The kidneys would stop producing urine, and the person's heartbeat would become irregular. The symptom that would initiate impending death was an elevated fever.[3] Sanitation was an issue on board sailing ships and during the walking trek to Utah. Rats, bilge water, sea sickness, and overcrowding were faced by those who traveled across the Atlantic. Overland travel found dirty dusty conditions during daily travel and as meals were prepared. Food would be cooked over an open fire, using buffalo dung, fixed with filthy hands and utensils, which would be tainted with contaminated water.[4] As the wagon trains moved to higher, cooler altitude, the symptoms of cholera seemed to dissipate.

Understanding how sickness ravaged the people who traveled on the *Cavour* and during the rail travel across the country offers insight into their situation when they arrived at Wyoming, NT. Magnus Cederstrom, who traveled on the *Cavour*, wrote about how cholera claimed many lives during the ocean voyage and rail travel from New York City to Independence, Missouri. Evidence indicates Cederstrom wrote about the events as they happened—not years later than was the case with many who migrated in 1866. Magnus begins his account at the start of the ocean voyage. The first recorded death occurred after the *Cavour* had been underway for ten days. On 10 June 1866, Anna Christian Hansen, a 64-year-old widow, passed away after an eight-day illness. Eleven days later Sjelan Larsson, age one-and-one-half years, died after a lengthy illness. On 1 July Lissa Larsson died after a long sickness. The 26th of July witnessed the death of Rasmus Martensen, who was just over four-and-one-half years of age. Shortly after reaching the shores of the United States, Hans Hansen, age 26 years old, died after five weeks of illness. Following the docking of the *Cavour* in New York City, five sick people were taken to the hospital.[5]

The rail journey across the United States to St. Joseph, Missouri witnessed the deaths of thirteen people, and several individuals were stricken with the deadly disease of cholera. Anna Helena Warnick died before the travelers reached Chicago, Illinois. Upon arriving at Chicago, cholera swept through the traveling group, with many becoming sick. Sadly, Anna Malena Berbom [Bernbom] died during the afternoon, but she could not be buried until the train reached Quincy, Illinois. Christen Hansen was left in Chicago because he was too ill to travel. After crossing the Mississippi River at Quincy, Erasmus Pederson was so sick with cholera that he was left behind. Tuesday, 7 August, the widow Anna Christine Larson died at the age of 38. The train arrived at St. Joseph, Missouri, at nine o'clock in the evening and by eleven o'clock a two-year-old boy, Johan Gustaf Warneck of Sweden, succumbed to the dreaded disease that was stalking the immigrants. On 8 August, an act of kindness was shown the travelers by a group of women who came from the city with all kinds of mild foods to restore the sick. In addition, a doctor came of his own free will to administer to the needs of the sick. At eleven o'clock that evening, Nils Ohlson died. Death continued to claim additional travelers among those who desired to gather to Zion. Anna Henrickson, Carl Peder Ringquist, Christina Christjanson, Anna Sorensen, the Widow Hansen from Holland, and three more individuals succumbed to the deadly illness.[6] From St. Joseph, the intrepid group boarded a steamer to travel to Wyoming, NT. During the journey up the Missouri River, four people were buried the first day, and five were buried on the second day. The paddle wheeler arrived at Wyoming, 11 August 1866.[7]

Abner Lowry, the Captain of the Sanpete down and back church train, led a group of immigrants who had suffered through a challenging ocean voyage, a cross-country voyage by rail, and now must face the prospects of a 1,100 mile walk across the states of current day Nebraska and Wyoming, before entering Utah and the Salt Lake Valley. The lateness of the arrival and the issue of weather at higher altitudes necessitated the wagons must begin rolling west at the earliest possible opportunity. Having lived in the Utah valleys since 1847, Lowry was aware of the harshness of weather conditions in the mountains of Wyoming and Utah, and he understood that a late departure could spell disaster for the immigrating Saints from Scandinavia. Captain Lowry brought strong qualities to his role as the leader of this particular down and back train. Along with his father, Abner was one of the original settlers called by Brigham Young in 1849 to colonize an area that would be called Manti. Other settlements were formed and eventually Sanpete County was organized. Lowry, who was born on 12 October 1831, passed through many of the early church persecutions and in 1846 removed to Winter Quarters. Lowry served in the Provo War, the Walker War, and the Black Hawk War. He relocated to a small town named Moroni where he served as town mayor and as a county selectman for fourteen years. Abner married Betsey L. Bradley in 1852, and together they raised ten children.[8] Abner Lowry was uniquely qualified to lead a distressed group of immigrants from Scandinavia across an untamed wilderness for the sought-after home among other believers.

Cholera struck many of those traveling with the Abner Lowry church train. Regarding the epidemic that ravaged the camp, John Nielson penned these words, "For a time there was never a day [that] went by without someone having to leave a loved one in a lonely grave on the plains."[9] Echoing the sentiments of Nielson, Charles Anderson wrote,

> I never heard how many but at least one third, perhaps more died. One family from Denmark of thirteen all died but one, another from Sweden of five, only one remained, who arrived in Salt Lake City. I was sick across the Atlantic, through the states, and did not gain strength until the cool weather on the latter part of the journey across the plains.[10]

Another description of the suffering experienced by those traveling on this church train comes from Anders Peter Warnick. He vividly describes the process of burying the dead, "Some families had been entirely wiped out. There was sorrow and continued suffering in the depleted ranks. One noon all the men that were able were busy digging one large grave in which seven bodies were buried."[11] One name attached to this ill-fated train was the Ox Team Cholera Company of 1866. Captain Lowry was described as having a husky build, and he was very considerate of those in the company who were sick. Each evening Lowry would pitch his large tent, and his teamsters would help carry the sick to the tent at nightfall and back to their wagons the next morning.[12] Niels Rasmussen paid a deeply touching tribute to Abner Lowry with these words:

> His name will ever be held in affectionate remembrance by all the

survivors from that fearful journey, especially from those who recovered from their sickness through his untiring efforts in alleviating their suffering, which he did in so many instances very successfully.[13]

---

Melvin L. Bashore, retired Historic Sites Curator for the LDS Church History Department, compiled a list of all who died on the trail in 1866. According to Bashore's calculations, there were 50 estimated deaths from the Lowry Church Train during the trail journey to the Utah Territory.[14] Captain Lowry's account indicated the number of immigrants on the train totaled 248.[15] Therefore, the 50 probable deaths on the trail exemplify a 20 percent death rate within that particular company. This represents perhaps the highest percentage of deaths on the trail for church immigrants from 1847 to 1868. In addition, 1866 was the year with the highest overall mortality rate of just under seven percent. The total death rate, on the trails, for church pioneers from 1847 to 1868 averaged 3.41 percent from the years 1847 to 1868.[16] Most of the deaths from cholera for the Sanpete down and back church train occurred during the first nineteen days of the journey. From August 13 through August 31, 37 persons died on the trail. Death spared no age group; applying mortality percentages to those who traveled in 1866 is meant to deepen our understanding of their sacrifices —not diminish them. Eleven of those who passed away, during the first nineteen days, were five years of age or younger. Evidence from the Oregon California Trail Association indicates that over a 25 year span, up to 65,000 deaths occurred along the emigrant trails, and if evenly spaced along the length of the Oregon Trail (from Missouri to Oregon City) would be a grave about every 50 yards.[17] The Abner Lowry church train of 1866 suffered a death rate three times higher than the average of other wagon train parties during the mid-nineteenth-century western migration.

On the very first day of travel, five people were buried along the side of the trail or were interred at Wyoming, NT. Ane Marie Larson, Lars P. Larson, Kristine Anderson, Katrine Bolen, and Karen Anderson

Rasmussen were buried in shallow graves as the survivors continued their journey west—likely never to see the resting place of their loved ones again. Most of the burials along the trail were conducted without coffins, and the deceased were typically buried with only a sheet to protect their remains from the elements and predators. Dozens of unmarked grave sites resulted from deaths suffered during the long journey west by the members of Abner Lowry's train. On 15 August, three more individuals passed away. Karen Frandsen, Elizabeth Jensen, and Niels Jacob Sanderson all died. Captain Lowry traveled on the Nebraska City Cut-off Trail between Wyoming, NT and Fort Kearny, and based upon an average travel day of 15 miles; these three individuals likely would have met death near present-day Palmyra, Nebraska. The next day 16 August, Peter Petersen, Karen Christine Nielson, Sine Petersen, and Hans Peter Rasmussen all probably succumbed to the dreaded cholera. Two more deaths occurred the following day. Anders Gustaf Warnick, and a baby, Marie Josephine Nielson Frandsen, were quietly laid to rest beside the trail. It is likely that these persons passed away somewhere between Syracuse and Lincoln, Nebraska. Christine Frandsen and Parley Pratt Peterson died on 18 August and the following day Karen Jensen, Cissel Nielson Eskildsen and Maren Jorgensen Rasmussen met death from the ravages of cholera. Their remains might have been left between the present towns of Beaver Crossing and York, Nebraska. Cholera continued sweeping through the ill-fated wagon train. Six more deaths occurred over the next two days. Marie Andersen, Hans Jensen, August Nielsen, Niels Frandsen, Lars [or Jens] Christian Jensen, and Carl Ephraim Frandsen died along the trail perhaps somewhere near present-day Aurora, Nebraska. Death continued claiming innocent victims. Bodel Jakobsen, Ane Marie Nielson, Marie Hansen, Caroline Frandsen, Regina Bolette Frandsen, infant Warnick (one-day-old infant), and Rebekka Rasmussen all passed away between 22 August and 24 August 1866.[18] All of these tragic deaths took place before the wagon train reached Fort Kearny.

Abner Lowry notified Brigham Young on 1 September 1866 he was at Cottonwood, NT. His telegraph communication was short and to the point, "Passed here today. Sick all improving. Stock in good condition."[19] To verify Captain Lowry's point about the sick improving, six people had died between 26 August and 1 September. Birthe Hansen, Niels Anthon Hansen, Katrine Andersen, Ane Marie Peteren, Niels Peter William Hansen, and Anders Marius Smith Hansen all died along the trail between Aurora and Cottonwood.[20] Over the next seven weeks, nine people died before arriving in Zion. Lauritz Alma Nielson [or Larsen], Charlotta Bengtson [or Ericksen], Trine Hansen, Johannes Alma Sandersen, Charlotta Christina Warnick Arlekulen, Jorgen E. Jorgensen, Else Marie Olsen, Hans Daniel Hansen, and Karen Pedersen Madsen all lost their lives before reaching the Salt Lake Valley. The last person, Karen Pedersen Madsen died near the mouth of Echo Canyon just four days before Captain Lowry's church train entered Salt Lake City.[21] As the Sanpete train moved west, travel became more difficult, and the weather deteriorated.

Likely, the Lowry wagon train crossed the Platte River near Julesburg, Colorado. Verification of this comes from a telegraph Captain Lowry sent to Brigham Young on 10 September 1866 from Mud Springs, NT. Mud Springs lay on the old Pony Express and Stage wagon Road in western Nebraska.[22] Once again, Lowry's message was to the point, "Our teams are in good condition, but very little sickness in camp very cold and stormy."[23] Several interesting points are evident in this communication. First, as with almost all telegraphs sent from the down and back captains to Brigham Young, the condition of the livestock was almost always reported, even if nothing was shared regarding the condition of the passengers. The second issue that was beginning to impact the travelers was the changing weather. Five days later, on 15 September, Lowry telegraphed Brigham Young with the news he had arrived at Fort Laramie and the company was all in excellent health and the teams were in good condition.[24] Difficulties with the Native Americans persisted during the 1866 migration. On 19 August 1866, Deer Creek Station, which was about 90 miles west of Fort Laramie, was attacked by a band of Indians. Two men escaped, but the station was burned to the ground and telegraph wires were torn down. A telegraph operator from a nearby station traveled to Deer Creek, with 20 soldiers to repair the wire and assess the damages.[25] The Lowry group experienced one peaceful interaction with the native inhabitants of the area during the journey to Zion.

Captain Lowry's train would have passed by several landmarks that were known to the pioneers of nineteenth century. Courthouse Rock, Chimney Rock, and Scott's Bluff were well-known natural wonders this group of travelers passed. Vivid descriptions of the landscape these Saints were now passing through were provided by other travelers on the trail. The trail in western Nebraska was described as very sandy ground with few trees and the country being generally very parched. Rattle snakes were killed regularly. The trail around Scott's Bluff was described as a rough, rocky road.[26] Noted photographer and painter of the west, William Henry Jackson (a bullwhacker on an 1866 freight wagon train), described how the trail would now become much more challenging with steep climbs and precipitous drops. Mountains began looming in the background and the weather could be warm during the day but below freezing at night. The roads would be rocky and steep. For many miles, trees would be scarce. However, food in the form of jackrabbits and sage hens abounded, which allowed a change in meals.[27] Before arriving at Fort Laramie, the Lowry Church Train had been slowly moving west for five weeks. It would be approximately five more weeks before the entire group would arrive at Salt Lake City. Nine more days would pass before Abner Lowry communicated with Brigham Young about their progress from the banks of the Sweetwater River.

Finally, on 27 September, Captain Lowry's struggling train arrived at the Sweetwater River. On the same day, Arza Hinckley who was traveling back to Salt Lake City after picking up orphans and weak travelers from Captain Lowry's group (near the Platte River Bridge), was at Three Crossing on the Sweetwater River.[28] Lowry noted in his telegraph to Brigham Young that the oxen he had left at the Platte River Bridge, and three crossings had been "taken by Capt Chipman and others." He requested help in detaining those who had utilized his oxen, so he could have fresh livestock to complete the journey. Captain Lowry indicated he was able to locate only three of the twenty-five head that should have been available.[29] Lowry continued to move forward with his tired worn-out livestock. Three days later, Captain Lowry arrived at Three Crossings and told President Young the stock was doing tolerably well, but there were no nails to reshoe the oxen.[30] Cold weather and poor livestock were the key struggles facing Abner Lowry and those who traveled with the group from Sanpete County. On 3 October, Lowry arrived at South Pass. He was now crossing the Continental Divide, but significant challenges still lay ahead. His message to President Young contained just six words, "We camped here tonight. All well."[31] Captain Lowry sent his last message to President Young on 11 October 1866, from the Muddy Telegraph station. Poor weather, worn out stock, and exhausted travelers slowed the group down to a crawl. He indicated to Young that his travelers were doing well, but progress was slow.[32]

The distance from where Captain Lowry sent this last message to Salt Lake City was about 110 miles. The Big Muddy telegraph station was just west of Fort Bridger. Lowry had already passed off orphans and weak travelers to Arza Hinckley's rescue train, but it took eleven days for Lowry's group to travel the last agonizing 110 miles. That's an average of only ten miles per day. Yet, during the trek from Wyoming, NT to Fort Bridger the Lowry team averaged 15.6 travel miles per day. The situation that slowed the immigrants and the teamsters down during the last portion of the trail was the terrain and snow. William Henry Jackson, who traveled the last miles to Salt Lake City at approximately the same time as Captain Lowry's train, provides a vivid description of what it was like during the last agonizing days of the journey. Traveling with a fourteen-wagon freight train, Jackson described the journey:

---

> Mid-October suddenly became mid-winter. On Sunday the fourteenth, after two days of cold rain, snow began to fall. Next morning the storm increased, and the haul through Silver Creek Canyon became a terrible ordeal. Beneath two or three inches of snow lay mud; frozen in the morning when we started, soon it was beaten by hoofs and wheels into a stiff mush of hub-deep clay. One

wagon after another would crush sickeningly down into this stuff and stick there.³³

---

Like Captain Lowry's train, Jackson's continued to work forward against almost insurmountable odds. Jackson completed his description of the travel by sharing how the footwear he wore provided little protection against the elements. "One thin layer of leather was not much protection in a knee-deep mixture of mud, snow, and ice, or for running over a crusted snow drift, and by noon not even that one layer remained."³⁴

Captain Abner Lowry's beleaguered group traveled similar trails, experienced the same difficult terrain, and was challenged by the same storms of Jackson's fourteen-wagon freight train. Finally, on 22 October 1866, after a long tedious ocean voyage, a terrible ordeal of train and river boat travel from New York City to Wyoming, NT and a 1,100 mile walk across the deserts and mountains of a wild territory, Abner Lowry's down and back church train arrived in Salt Lake City.³⁵ The *Deseret News* announced, "Capt. Abner Lowry's train of 60 wagons and about 100 passengers got into the city on Monday, a little before noon. This is the last immigrant train of the season. They encountered some severe weather on the latter part of the trip; but the immigrants stood it very well."³⁶ Eight months earlier, on 10 February 1866, a call went out to all the District Conferences in Europe to send the names of individuals who expected to leave the continent for Zion in 1866.³⁷ Next, general instructions for immigration were published in the *Millennial Star* on 9 March 1866.³⁸ Brigham Young instructed bishops to call teamsters who were good men, who use good language and are of good habits; men will be fathers to the people, kind to the Saints, and to their team.³⁹

## 14

# ARZA HINCKLEY AND THE RESCUE TRAIN OF 1866

Arza Hinckley was a man well acquainted with overcoming tremendous odds and he faced many daunting situations during his lifetime. Arza was born in Canada 15 August 1826 and his father died when Arza was only five years old. His grandfather and grandmother raised him for many years. Arza's grandparents moved from Canada in the fall of 1837 after joining The Church of Jesus Christ of Latter-day Saints. The family settled in Missouri in 1838. Although only 12 years of age at the time, Arza remembered an event in Far West, Missouri, when a mob brought all the men into a public place and one by one at the point of a bayonet each man was told to deny their membership in the church, or sign over their property and leave the state. Those who would not leave the state were told they would be shot. Following the expulsion of the Mormons from Missouri, Arza and his family moved to Illinois where they lived near Springfield for two years. Arza and the family moved to Nauvoo in 1842. He indicated in his diary that he heard Joseph Smith preach many times and that his remarks were inspiring. In 1845, Arza worked on the Nauvoo Temple, which they were told to complete before heading west. Arza and his brother Ira went to Springfield in the fall of 1845 to prepare his grandparents for the move west. However, just before departing, it was determined their grandparents were too old and weak to endure long travel, so both Arza and Ira walked the 120 miles back to Nauvoo. Arza started west in the spring of 1846, driving a team for Joel Ricks, who was the father to Thomas E. Ricks. Thomas would interact with Arza on several occasions over the coming years—including as captain of a down and back church train in 1866.[1]

Arza settled near Kanesville, Iowa until he joined the Mormon Battalion. He was mustered into military service at Kanesville 16 July 1846, and on foot, he headed to Fort Leavenworth, Kansas which was approximately 200 miles away. From Fort Leavenworth, the battalion began the long trek to California—on or about 13 August. The sufferings of the men and women as they crossed the desert between Fort Leavenworth and Santa Fe, New Mexico were severe, and several deaths were recorded. Arza himself noted that at one point he walked 60 miles without water. The march to Santa Fe covered 900 miles and was accomplished in 61 days, or an average of roughly 15 miles a day—across some of the most intimidating topography in the United States. The battalion departed from Santa Fe on 19 October with only 54 days of rations. Shortly after leaving the village, they were placed on three-fourths rations. The roads (or trails) became very hilly and sandy. By 1 November, the group was reduced to half rations. At times, twenty men were used to push individual wagons over the almost impassable terrain. Eventually, Arza become sick and was obliged to march back to Santa Fe with 55 other sick and worn-out men. The men intended to winter in Santa Fe. However, the commanding officer at Santa Fe ordered the sick detachment to proceed to Pueblo—in present-day Colorado.[2]

Arza and the others who were sick left Santa Fe and traveled to Pueblo by following the Rio Grande River, and on 20 December 1846, they crossed the divide between the Rio Grande and Arkansas Rivers at an elevation of 10 thousand feet. At times, the snow was between two to four feet deep, and Arza's only protection from the elements was a wool hat, a hickory shirt, blue drilling pants, and a pair of shoes and socks. Arza further noted, "We found our shoes, socks, and feet frozen together in some instances." They reached Pueblo on 22 December. Arza wrote that he had traveled 2,925 miles in 1846.[3] The long winter in

Pueblo was spent hunting and trading with the Native Americans until each man had obtained a horse. Each man who wintered in Pueblo bartered for a horse. Thus, the infantry had turned into a cavalry. Arza recorded he made a pair of buckskin trousers by tanning them in soft soap. He cut them out and sewed them together with a buckskin thong. After getting the trousers wet, they shrunk to a perfect fit. Concerning the winter at Pueblo Arza wrote, "After 50 days recrute [sic], I weighed 126 lbs, as my muscles was the giest [sic] in the joints I was a living skeleton."[4] In the spring of 1847, the men of the Mormon Battalion, who had wintered in Pueblo, tried to connect with the Brigham Young's vanguard wagon train before the train reached the Salt Lake Valley. However, they missed connecting with Young's group and arrived at the Salt Lake Valley on 29 July 1847. Arza returned to Winter Quarters in the fall of 1847 and remained in that area for three years until he returned to the Salt Lake Valley. During his return to the Salt Lake Valley, Arza traveled with a freight wagon train. His brother Ira returned the same year, but he traveled in a different wagon train.[5]

For several years, Arza lived in the Salt Lake City area. He worked on the public works of the church, became a foreman under the direction of Daniel Wells, and was in charge of the church teams. He was also the personal teamster for Brigham Young, which offered Arza the opportunity to travel throughout church settlements. Hinckley estimated he drove five thousand miles visiting the settlements and acting as a bodyguard. During the time Arza served as a guard for Brigham Young, he took his turn standing watch at Brigham's home.[6] Concerning his duties with Brigham Young Arza noted, "I had charge of the gard [sic] at his office one night in a week for ten years, was in police of the city for seven years, a cavalraman [sic] in the Minit [sic] Men for 16 years."[7] In 1856, Arza assisted in the rescue of the ill-fated Martin Willie handcart companies. He, along with an estimated 368 others, joined a massive effort to help rescue the hundreds of pioneers who were stranded along the trail in Wyoming.[8] By 1861, Arza was distributing telegraph poles for the transcontinental line. In April 1862, he was called out to protect the same poles from Native Americans. When Daniel Wells left to fill a mission to England, Arza was called upon to look after Wells' business. In 1866, before leaving with the relief train for the church trains, Arza was called to serve as a commissary sergeant in a cavalry unit that went to southern Utah to fight in the Black Hawk War. In late July 1866, Arza headed east with a relief wagon train pulled by mules to meet and assist the western traveling church trains.[9]

As noted earlier, when Arza departed Salt Lake City with his rescue mule train, his first responsibility was to assist the William Henry Chipman Company who had lost over 100 head of cattle when they were about 382 miles out of Salt Lake City.[10] We learn a great deal about the composition of Hinckley's rescue train from his reports upon the return to Salt Lake City and from the telegrams he sent to President Young during his travels. On 5 September 1866, Hinckley telegraphed Young with the message that he had met Captain Chipman at the Big Sandy station and left 40 sacks of flour for the company. Hinckley sent the communication from Little Sandy.[11] On 6 September, Hinckley telegraphed President Young that he was now at South Pass and had met with Thomas Taylor at Dry Sandy. Taylor managed the migration of the immigrants from New York City to Wyoming, NT, and Mr. Taylor was doing fine.[12] The next day Hinckley sent another telegraph to Young indicating three remaining teams were on the western side of the Sweetwater Bridge, but Captain Lowry's company had not yet crossed the bridge. A portion of Hinckley's telegraph read, "Where is Captain Lowry?"[13] By 8 September, Hinckley's rescue train was at Three Crossings. At this point, Hinckley noted he had met with Captain Holladay's group and all was well with them. He also told Brigham Young that the men in his wagon train wanted to turn around and head back to the valley. They had not yet located Lowry's train, and "they had only started to meet Chipman." Hinckley's question for Young was direct and to the point, "Shall we go on or return?"[14] Arza Hinckley's rescue train continued east to meet with Captain Lowry.

On 11 September, Hinckley sent a telegraph to Brigham Young stating that Captain Nebeker and his train had passed the Sweetwater Station, and Hinckley wrote that several of Nebeker's company were sick with mountain fever. Hinckley also indicated that Nebeker's group had flour to last until the Bear River where he would be able to obtain 20 sacks of flour that should last until the end of the journey. Arza indicated he and his group would look to meet with the Lowry train at the Platte River Bridge near current day Casper, Wyoming, because their numbers were too small to pass the fort at Casper.[15] Hinckley's next communication was sent 15 September from the Platte River Bridge. Captain Hinckley had camped with Captain Scott's team at Fish Creek. According to the telegram the pioneers were doing well, but the livestock was looking bad. In addition, Hinckley camped with Captain Haight's train, and all on the train were doing well. Hinckley's team moved past the Platte River Bridge at Casper and continued east looking for Lowry's company.[16]

According to a telegraph sent on 21 September, Arza Hinckley had met Lowry's train just east of Casper, Wyoming, on 18 September and loaded 78 of the 200 individuals on the wagon train. That meant 78 of those who were traveling with Abner Lowry's church train were either orphans or too sick to continue the journey on the slow-moving ox train. Arza sent the telegraph from the Deer Creek Station, and he told President Young that the health of those on the Lowry's train was fair. Both trains encountered snow on the 19th and 20th of September.[17] Both Hinckley (with the extra passengers) and Lowry were now headed west towards Salt Lake City. Hinckley's last communication via telegraph came on 6 October from the Weber Station. His message was brief and to the point, "Passed here today camp at Head (sic) of Silver Creek tonight all night."[18] Arza Hinckley and ten of his 20 original wagons entered the Salt Lake Valley on 8 October 1866 with the ailing passengers he had taken from the Lowry wagon train.[19]

At the beginning of his eastward journey, Arza Hinckley traveled 21 days before he happened upon the Henry Chipman train. The rescue train trekked 31 days before meeting with Captain Holladay. Arza Hinckley traveled approximately 44 days to reach Abner Lowry's wagon train to retrieve those who were too weak to continue traveling alone. Moreover, Arza Hinckley's rescue train not only aided Henry Chipman's train with 40 sacks of flour and brought orphans and others safely to the valley, he accomplished much more. Hinckley also gave flour to Captain

Scott, Captain Holladay, and Captain Haight. Additionally, hobbits for the oxen and grain for livestock was also shared with the beleaguered church trains. Most of the grain for livestock was deposited at Ham's Fork. Several wards from the Salt Lake City and surrounding areas constituted the rescue train led by Hinckley. Brigham Young also supplied a four-mule team wagon with needed teamsters for the trip.[20] The efforts of Arza Hinckley, his teamsters, and those who gave so freely of their food and supplies saved hundreds from starvation or worse. Hinckley's rescue team should be remembered for their courage and determination in the service of others. Lives were saved, and starvation was averted through the efforts of these stalwart individuals.

According to Hinckley's freight report, his rescue train hauled freight to the Salt Lake Valley. The freight hauled by Hinckley's rescue train came from Captain Holladay's train. Teamsters from Ogden hauled one barrel of an unknown substance, two boxes of dry goods, and one sack of coffee. The wagon that carried this freight used eight mules for the journey. The teamsters for this wagon were Brigham Sharpe and Jos. Douglas. A team from Kaysville carried fifteen boxes of coal oil, two boxes of oysters, one box of castor oil, sugar, coffee, fancy soap and peppermint. This particular wagon also carried passengers. The team was made up of four mules. The teamster who supervised this wagon was Chas. Landon. A teamster, Levi M. Donalde, from Farmington hauled three cooking stoves, one parlor, and three sacks of peppers. This four-mule team also carried two passengers. The rescue wagon from the Salt Lake City 14th Ward hauled thirteen boxes of coal oil, a box of soap (not labeled as fancy), one large tin box for a passenger, and two pitchforks. This particular wagon was led by four mules, and Chas Lett was the teamster.[21]

When Arza Hinckley met the Lowry Train near Fort Caspar, it has been noted that he listed 78 individuals taken from the Lowry Train to take back to Salt Lake City. A record of those who were passengers with Arza Hinckley was made as a part of Hinckley's final report. As the names were written, a numerical running total was kept on the right-hand side of the page. At the bottom of the second page, the number 78 is shown in the lower right-hand side, which coincides with the number of passengers Hinckley picked up. Hinckley's list reveals the following names (original spelling retained). Maria Larsen, Nickoli Nielsen, Anna C. Larsen, Jens Olsen, Maria Madsen, Anne C. Thompson, Andw. Jonasen, Sven P. Nielson, Sis Keeting, Doratha Hansen, Inger Nielsen, Thos. C. Jensen, John E. Stone, Wm. M Farnsworth, Dorathia Larsen, Fred Olsen and Sister, Julian Matisen, Christn. Brown, Johan M. Rassumussen, Sis Brown, Sis Peacock, Sis Keep and child, Johan F. Andersen, Haming Madsen, Gustave Isaacson, Herman Kling, and Christian Christensen.[22] Only 29 people are listed by name on Hinckley's report, but additional individuals traveled with them on Hinckley's wagons.

Years later Andrew Jenson wrote the names of 40 persons who possibly arrived in Salt Lake City on the Hinckley rescue train. Of the names listed by Jenson, only ten match Arza Hinckley's list. Jenson wrote that these people were helped into the valley by mule train. According to Jenson's record, these individuals would have arrived in the valley on 8 October 1866. The spelling as shown in the journal history is retained. The individuals were listed as follows: Catherine Margrethe Jensen, with Nicholai N., Andreas Johnson, Marie, Inger and Jensine Jensen; Anne Christensen Thomsen, Marie Madsen and child; Nikolai Nielsen, Inger Nielson, Severin Nielsen; Hannah Nelsen, Johanne Mortensen, Johanne M. Rasmussen, Gustav Isaksen, Johan F. Andersen; William Farnsworth, Elizabeth Farnsworth; Fillis Peacock, Martha Peacock; Emma M. Lansaw; Thomas C., Karen M., Johanne, Chris. Julius, Niels Peter and Ane Mathilda Jensen; Marie, Christine M., Antomine and Joseph C. Petersen; Sarah Keep; Marie C., Nikoline C, Niels R., Johanne and Mariane C. Hansen; Sven P. and Marie C. Nielsen.[23] Both Hinckley's and Jenson's accounts are of value to gain an understanding of individual people who were rescued and provided a swifter journey over the last 400 miles to the valley.

On 19 January 1866, the Territorial Legislature approved an act to establish a toll road from "Great Salt Lake City to Wanship, Summit County." The Territorial Road Commissioner was allocated six thousand dollars to examine the route and construct a road that would be twenty feet wide where practical and divided into four sections with not more than one toll-gate at each section. The fourth section of the road started at Wanship for those traveling west to Salt Lake City. The Territorial Road Superintendent was granted eight months from the time the act for the new road was established to "put the present traveled road in good repair from Charles Decker's residence on Big Cañon creek, to Wanship in Summit County; to establish toll-gates, and demand and collect not to exceed the rates of [the] toll prescribed in the third section of this act."[24] Specific charges were established for those who used the road. "For any vehicle drawn by one or two animals, twenty-five cents; for each additional pair of animals fifteen cents; for cattle, loose horses or mules, fifty cents . . ." In addition, if any captain or teamster in charge of any train would camp on the road, or cause any delay would be subject to a five hundred dollar fine.[25] This road was used by both Abner Lowry and Arza Hinckley as they reached the final stages of their trek into the Salt Lake Valley. Arza Hinckley was charged a toll on 6 October 1866, at section four (Wanship) of $15.20 for ten wagons and one riding animal. Hinckley arrived with his ten wagons at Salt Lake City two days later.[26] On 18 October, 12 days after Hinckley, Abner Lowry arrived at the toll Wanship toll station. Lowry paid a toll for sixty wagons (plus three independent wagons), six riding animals and 30 head of loose livestock. Lowry and his beleaguered group struggled into the Salt Lake Valley on 22 October, a full four days after reaching Wanship.[27]

Arza Hinckley traveled hundreds of miles with his relief train to reach individuals who possibly would have been unable to reach Salt Lake City. He and those who traveled with him put their lives at risk to assist a group of people they had never met and served those they would not see again. On the lonely high plains of Wyoming, Arza and his brave band of heroes offered help to those who could not help themselves. They never sought recompense or accolades for their selfless efforts. Regarding this part of his life Arza's diary reads,

---

July late started out to meet Chipman train that had had some of their cattle stolen by the Indians, as Capt. of a mule train, but before starting had orders to go back to reap train as they ware [sic] late and would be caught by the Indians and cold weather. I went back to Larima ford and took a part of the Lowery loading. The Indians followed up to the Plat bridge, then turned over to the government heard & stole there [sic] animals, not leaving a saddle pona.[28]

---

Perhaps Joel Hinckley Bowen, a direct descendent of Arza Hinckley, captured Arza's life best with the following thought.

---

There is no way of estimating the number of lives saved by Arza E. Hinckley's unflagging efforts on his relief and rescue trips out on the emigrant trails of Wyoming and beyond, but he was a man for the times and filled a useful niche in the saga of the Mormon pioneers.[29]

---

This was the last time Arza was called on to travel the immigrant trails to seek out those who needed help. Arza's efforts, like so many others who lived common lives during this time in the church's history, enabled many people to reach their Zion, marry, raise a family, and pay forward the type of service they received from Arza Erastus Hinckley.

## 15

# WRAPPING UP

The call for gathering to Zion was as strong in the years of 1864 to 1866 as when first issued by Joseph Smith in 1830. Over the years, thousands answered the call to gather to a central location. These particular years' gathering comprised mainly those from Europe. Brigham Young's down and back wagon trains provided the means for more than 5,900 people to leave the western banks of the Missouri River and travel to their Zion in 1864 and 1866. In addition, the freight wagon trains and independent trains provided the opportunity for over 700 Saints to begin their final journey to Salt Lake City. The details of moving so many people such a great distance were staggering. While the Perpetual Emigration Fund helped many European Saints migrate to the United States, several paid their own way or were the beneficiaries of a donor. In addition to obtaining the needed funds, families disposed of real and personal property, concluded their employment, and determined that leaving their ancestral homes for an unknown country was in their best interests.

The church provided immigration agents both in Europe and the United States, supplied wagon trains for the trek to the Great Basin, and assisted with food rations for the time spent on the trails to Utah Territory. Amazingly, within the span of about seven months, the pioneers of 1864 to 1866 traveled by sailing ship from Europe, took trains to the shores of the Missouri River in the Nebraska Territory, then completed the 1,100 mile walk to the Utah Territory. Disease, hunger, storms at sea, dust on the trail, and elation upon arrival at their Zion were all a part of the experiences of this group of pioneers. This represents one of the great stories of the entire western migration of the mid-1800s. The Vanguard wagon train of 1847 and the immigrants of 1864 to 1866 held common themes. Most left family behind, and many were economically disadvantaged, but each participant in these migrations, which took place nearly two decades apart, held the same conviction in their hearts. Settling in the west, far away from civilization would provide the possibility to live in peace and practice the religion they had embraced.

However, there were significant differences between those who traveled in 1847 and the immigrants of the mid-1860s. For example, the original trek in 1847 required roughly 110 days to complete. The distance covered during the migration of this pioneer group totaled 1,031 miles.[1] By contrast, in 1866 the pioneers were transported from Wyoming, Nebraska Territory to Salt Lake City in 58 days by the Samuel White mule train—saving 52 days of travel time.[2] Those traveling in the initial wagon train of 1847 received little or no protection from the military during their trek west. Those who led the church trains in 1864 and 1866 utilized ranches along the trail to rest and feed both the people and livestock. In addition, the camping locations were often predetermined by the train's captains. The travelers of 1847 created their own rest locations as they traveled along the trail. After leaving Winter Quarters for the west, communication with the 1847 wagon train was limited, and could only be done with couriers. Immigrants leaving Wyoming, NT between 1864 and 1866 used the telegraph to communicate their positions along the route.

Those traveling in 1847 journeyed on the north side of the Platte River, while the pioneers of the mid-1860s primarily used the Nebraska City Cut-off Trail to reach Fort Kearny. Those participating in the original wagon train to the Salt Lake Valley were hand-picked by Brigham Young. The pioneers traveling during 1864, 1865, and 1866 were mostly European converts and were traveling to the location established by earlier settlers. There were no cities, towns or villages when the first train arrived in present day Utah, but many settlements existed when these later emigrants arrived. The vanguard train located, established, and settled the area that welcomed the travelers of the years included in this book. While the variations from the first train in 1847 to the last year trains that left the Missouri River were many, one fact remained unchanged. Those who participated traveled in covered wagons, faced the same weather conditions, and walked the majority of the distance to their Zion. Death was a constant companion to all pioneer travelers. Often the dead were buried in unmarked graves. Perhaps in an effort to remember those who had lost their lives on the trail, Richard Litson noted the names found on several graves. One inscription read, "H. Voigt, died 1865, Sept. 15, age 31 years." Another grave was inscribed with the following: "K. Milden died June 2, 1864, late of Preston, England." Further along the trail Litson passed several more graves, and he wrote their names. "Lawkin K. Stevens, aged 14 years; E. Hunter, died July 3, 1865; N. P. Wells, late of Biethan, Missouri, killed by Indians, aged 39 years." The last grave inscription noted by Litson read, "John Brain [G.aon], crossed shore, died August 23, 1844."[3] A review of the deaths that occurred on the trail during the pioneer migration of 1866 reveals 71 deaths out of an estimated total of 2,826 individuals (excluding Abner Lowry's cholera train).[4] By contrast, no deaths occurred during the 1847 vanguard wagon train exodus.[5]

## Individual Accounts from the year 1864

### Joseph W. Young

Joseph W. Young, who managed the western migration from Wyoming, NT in 1864, was called the "executive brain of the emigration of his people from the eastern frontiers to the Rocky Mountains" by author Edward Tullidge.[6] Tullidge backs up his claim by reviewing some of Joseph's accomplishments through the migration years. Joseph W. Young was the second son of Lorenzo Dow Young, brother of Brigham

Young. Joseph was one of the first companies to leave Nauvoo during the exodus from that city. He traveled across the plains in 1847 with Jedidiah M. Grant and spent the first winter in the Salt Lake valley. He served a mission in England for nearly three years before returning home. On his return home from his mission, he successfully brought to the valley a large company of British Saints. In the spring of 1857, he left as a missionary with a group of 70 men and 26 handcarts from Salt Lake City and pulled the carts across the plains to Florence, NT. During the Utah War, Joseph, along with other missionaries, were called back to Utah Territory. In early 1858, Joseph led a company of 32 missionaries back across the plains to Salt Lake City.[7]

In the spring of 1860, Joseph W. Young led an ox train of 29 wagons out of the Salt Lake valley to Florence, NT. The down and back journey was made in the same season. The wagon train left in the spring and returned 3 October 1860. The oxen that left in the spring returned in the fall and appeared to be as healthy as when the company left. This was the first time this experiment had been tried, which resulted in the formation of the famous down and back church trains of the early to mid1860s. Thousands of immigrants and tons of needed supplies and equipment for the Utah Territory came about as a direct result of Joseph W. Young's fearlessness.[8] In 1861, Joseph again headed east for the Missouri River; this time he directed one of the first down and back church trains. Young led this wagon train along with Ansil Perce Harmon and Heber Parley Kimball. The company arrived in Salt Lake City in September of that same year. This particular wagon train consisted of ninety wagons, machinery, merchandize, and immigrants.[9] Joseph died at Harrisburg, Washington, Utah Territory 6 June 1873, and was lamented by the whole community. He was truly one of the founders of Utah.[10]

### H. N. Hansen

Hans Niels Hansen left Denmark with his family to find their Zion in the valleys of Utah Territory. After his arrival, several events took place that caused he and his father to join the Josephite movement and eventually travel back east where he lived out his life in western Iowa. Hans wrote about his experiences later in his life, which included a brief overview of how he came to be associated with what he called the Reorganized Church. As noted earlier in this book, his passage from Denmark to the Salt Lake Valley was very challenging, and his situation did not improve after arriving in the valley. He described how he felt about those who led his company from Wyoming, NT to Salt Lake City. "Of course, our trip might have been more pleasant and comfortable had those in charge had a decent respect for humanity, but we had been treated not much better than dumb brutes." Shortly after arriving in the valley, Hans and his family met a gentleman who offered them work in Tooele County, which stood west of Salt Lake City. The offer almost seemed to be too good to be true—and unfortunately it was. The Hanson family understood the offer was for a house, employment for both Hans and his father during the winter, a team to work the land, and one-half of the harvest. Hans' father did not inquire about the condition of the home or how much he would receive for pay. The home they settled in was typical of so many in the area, being a little log cabin with a dirt roof. The mud used to fill in the space between logs contained holes large enough to put a hand through.[11] The pay turned out to be fifty cents a day for his father, and the winter was harsh which meant Hans received no work through that winter.[12]

During this time in Utah Territory, the people this family met did not meet their vision of Zion. Therefore, the family determined to make a fresh start in northern Utah Territory at Bear River which was about 10 miles from Brigham City. Arriving at the new location they saw the country was a fine country for stock with grass being in abundance. A man loaned the Hansen family seed to plant wheat; in exchange, they repaid him with a percentage of the harvest. They eventually built their first dugout cabin, which Hanson recalled "was the first habitation of our own that we had in Zion and fully as good as any we had lived in." In the winter of 1866 to 1867, news of the Reorganized Church or Josephites first reached their ears. Later, the family heard of a meeting being held on Sundays a few miles north of Brigham City. Hans, his father, and a fellow named Ole Carlsen attended the meeting. After attending meetings two or three times, Hans and his dad were baptized into the church.[13] Soon after joining the Josephites, the family moved east, eventually settling in Iowa-eastern Nebraska, and were members of the Reorganized Church of Jesus Christ of Latter-day Saints.[14]

## Rescue during the year 1865

### Heber Robert McBride

One of the most compelling stories from the three years included in this book comes from a relatively unknown individual. His name was Heber Robert McBride, and he was one of the people to leave his home to assist in the rescue operations for the William S. S. Willes independent wagon train. Like so many others who had immigrated previous to the 1865 migration, he felt obligated to help those stranded on the trail to the Utah Territory. Fortunately, he kept a daily diary about his experiences on the trail, and mentioned a tragedy that happened to his father during the handcart migration of 1856. He and a friend left his home with only 24 hours' notice on 4 October 1865. When he and his companions left Ogden, Utah Territory, they had a total of four teams. Not knowing how far they needed to go to find the Willes train, they only took 10 days' worth of provisions and one change of clothing. His daily account reveals incidents of lost horses, alkali poisoning to some livestock, blinding snow, hurricane winds, and passing a company of Danes who were being helped to the valley by other rescuers.

On 25 October, McBride's group came across Thomas Taylor's rescue team. McBride noted Taylor was to wait for them at Echo Canyon and take charge of the group, but Taylor elected to continue traveling east and not wait for the company out of Ogden. One particular night the snow had accumulated to 16 inches deep in their camp. McBride was instructed to see if he could find the Platte River. He located the river and gave the signal to alert the others, so they could join him as they continued traveling east. His next sentence reads as follows: "I gave the signal and wated [sic] till the wagons came down. Then we went down about 12 miles to the Plat [sic] River to the place where my Father was buried in October 1856."[15] Incredibly, Heber, his father, mother, and three siblings participated in the ill-fated handcart trek of that year. Now nine years later he and his rescue team are nearing the very spot where his father froze to death! Heber expressed his feelings about that terrible incident in 1856 as follows:

> I went to look for Father and at last I found him under a wagon with snow all over him and he was stiff and dead. I felt as though my heart would burst. I sat down beside him on the snow and took hold of one of his hands and cried oh Father, Father. There we was away out on the Plains with hardly anything to eat and Father dead and mother sick and a widow with 5 small children and not hardly able to live from day to another; after I had my cry out I went back to the tent and told Mother; now to try and write to tell the feelings of Mother and the other children is out of the question; now we were not all the family that was called upon to mourn the loss of a Father this morning for there was 13 men died in camp; the men that was able to do anything cleaned of [sic] the snow and made a fire and thawed out the ground and dug a big hole and buried them all in one grave, some side by side and on top of one another any way to get them covered for I can asure [sic] you that the men had no heart to do any more than they had to.[16]

Furthermore, regarding his father's death, McBride wrote the following in a letter, written in 1923. "I went in the morning and found my father ded [sic] and frozen stif [sic] covered in snow" Heber wrote that he and his sister prayed many times, during this ordeal, that they could die so "we could get out of our misery."[17] McBride and the rescue team continued to travel east, locating a group from the Willes train 26 October. Sadly, because the group left Ogden with a limited supply of food, there was very little for the stranded immigrants to eat. Roughly 70 old men, women, and children were loaded into wagons and the rescue team began heading west, with a promise that another rescue train would be approaching soon with needed food. On their return trip, they crossed paths with a freight wagon train and obtained a small amount of food. Finally, on 3 November the group met a rescue team and obtained much needed food and grain. The rescue party arrived in Salt Lake City shortly after noon 11 November 1865.[18]

## The year 1866

**Charles Savage**

Charles Savage participated in the western migration of 1866. Although Savage did not begin his journey to Salt Lake City from Europe, his accomplishments provide an opportunity through photography to experience the trail west unlike any of the previous nineteen years. As was noted earlier in the book, Savage took photographs while the Thomas Ricks Church Train traveled to Salt Lake City. The church emigrant camp at Wyoming, crossing of the Platte River, and a picture of Fort Kearny are three of the priceless pictures Savage took during his trek west. The picture of Wyoming, NT was possibly taken before the wagon train began heading west, and the crossing of the Platte River likely took place at Fremont Springs (near present day Hershey, Nebraska).[19] To make the journey west, Savage had a wagon specially fitted out for photography. Savage recorded that the wagon was "about nine feet long and six feet high in the darkroom, leaving three feet of space in front for carrying a seat and provisions." Savage's specially fitted wagon was extremely heavy and would get very hot in the summer, because the sides were made of sheet iron. Savage shipped his wagon from Philadelphia to St. Joseph, Missouri by rail, and then he hauled the wagon from St. Joseph to Nebraska City, NT. From Nebraska City, Savage moved to the small village of Wyoming to begin the journey west.[20] The photograph of Fort Kearny was taken during gale-force winds, and Savage was not pleased with the results.[21] Evidence indicates that Savage took hundreds of pictures on his travel west in 1866, but sadly only a few are extant today.[22] Nevertheless, Savage's efforts at providing a visual record of the trail from Wyoming,

NT to Salt Lake City, Utah Territory offer a pictorial account unmatched by others prior to 1866.

## B. H. Roberts

Two members of the immigration of 1866 who became well known among the members of the Church of Jesus Christ of Latter-day Saints were Brigham H. Roberts and Andrew Jenson. Both men were prolific writers and spent much time chronicling the early history of the LDS Church. Without their efforts, many of the early events in church history might have been lost. Brigham H. Roberts' best-known work regarding LDS Church history is contained in *A Comprehensive History of the Church of Jesus Christ of Latter-day Saints*, which was published in 1930. In addition, Roberts wrote about David Whitmer, one of eleven people who testified he had viewed the plates from which *The Book of Mormon* originated. He also wrote about Joseph Smith, first President of the LDS Church and John Taylor, third President of the church. Eighteen books are credited to Roberts during his long writing career, which spanned for almost five decades.[23] Roberts served for much of his adult life in the First Council of the Seventy, one of the ruling bodies of the church. Mr. Roberts was elected to Congress in 1898 by the people of Utah. His election in Utah led to a massive nationwide effort to keep Roberts from serving in Congress due to his practice of polygamy. He was denied his seat in the House of Representatives on 25 January 1900.[24]

## Andrew Jenson

Andrew Jenson's first efforts at recounting history began in the mid-1870s when he translated the *History of Joseph Smith* into the Danish-Norwegian language. He performed the translation and distribution of this work using his own funds, as the church offered no assistance for his work. Jenson underwrote the costs of many of his early works.[25] In 1891, Jenson was appointed a historian for the church and in 1898 he became the Assistant Church Historian.[26] He traveled the world collecting information relating to the establishment of the church. He logged more than 300 thousand miles during his lifetime—accomplished via train, ship, wagon and walking. Twice he went around the world. He served ten missions for the Church, and during one three-year mission gave 1,000 speeches. Historian Louis Reinwand estimates Jenson delivered more than 6,000 addresses during a forty-two-year period. Jenson's writing includes both faith building experiences and events that were averse to the church.[27] The collections and writings of Andrew Jenson offer a look into early church history unmatched in scope and volume by any other early LDS historian. Amazingly, this was accomplished by a man with little formal education.

**Robert Aveson**

Appreciating the important contributions of the specific individuals offers an opportunity to celebrate their accomplishments. However, it was the thousands of ordinary individuals who gathered to their Zion from Europe that help make this book meaningful. One such person, Robert Aveson, emigrated from England during the 1866 migration. His story, like thousands of others who left their homes for Zion, provides the backbone of the European migration of 1866. Robert was born in Bradford, Yorkshire, England 22 August 1847. In 1860, Robert was indentured to a printer which was to run for seven consecutive years. In 1862, Robert was attracted to the Church of Jesus Christ of Latter-day Saints. Mr. Aveson indicated that once he became convinced The Church of Jesus Christ of Latter-day Saints was the one he wanted to associate with "the spirit of gathering came strongly upon us, and we felt desirous of immigrating at some future day to the land of Zion."[28] However, due to his mother's disapproval of the religion and his desire to obey his mother he was forbidden from associating with the church until the spring of 1866. Even though Robert was forbidden from meeting with the local congregation, he secretly disobeyed his mother and met with the group regularly. Concerning how his conscience was afflicting him during this time Robert later wrote, "Disobedience to my mother's wishes was ever a sore affliction."[29]

Even though he knew his indenture was still in force (he still had three years to serve), Robert's desire to gather to Utah caused him to begin saving for the journey. Interestingly, in 1866 his mother received a letter from relatives living in America who were desirous that she move there to live with them. However, with the apprenticeship still facing Robert, his mother determined the family should remain in England. She was unaware that Robert had been saving to immigrate to Utah for three and one-half years.[30] In the spring of 1866, Robert had saved enough money to pay for his ocean voyage and rail travel to Wyoming, NT. Accordingly, Robert was baptized 24 March 1866 without his parent's approval or knowledge. Shortly, he made arrangements to travel on the ship *American Congress*, which was set to leave London on the 23rd of May. Following his plans, Robert left his home to reach London before the ship sailed to America. Under false pretenses, he left his family and set out for London. Robert and a traveling companion, Richard Sedgwick, boarded a steamer to reach London. Richard was one of Robert's closest friends, and Richard had also become associated with the American religion. After reaching London and taking care of some last-minute arrangements, Robert and Richard boarded the ship *American Congress* and prepared to sail to the United States. As they were preparing to eat breakfast on the day of their departure, both young men were arrested for escaping from their apprenticeship.[31]

Both Robert and Richard were confined to jail for a short period, but were eventually taken back to their homes. A trial was held, and the two boys were given the choice of serving out their indenture in jail, or working for their employers. Both young men chose the second alternative. Robert reflected that he knew he had broken the law by leaving his apprenticeship, but had his parents been more favorable towards him and the church he would not have left home until his indenture was completed. Robert made a second attempt to leave home, which also ended in his return. Shortly after being sent back home, he tried a third time to leave for Zion. This escape was successful and Robert boarded the steamer *Virginia*, which only took sixteen days to complete the journey to New York City. Robert arrived at New York on 13 July and planned to travel to Wyoming, NT. While in New York City, Robert met with T.B.H. Stenhouse and H. P. Folsom. He was offered a job on the spot to work for Mr. Stenhouse for the *Salt Lake Daily Telegraph*. The agreement between Robert and the two gentlemen resulted in money for his fare across the plains, and they agreed to pay Robert twelve dollars a week for one year and thirteen dollars a week for the second year of employment. Robert Aveson arrived at Wyoming, NT 29 July, and he traveled with Captain Joseph Rawlins' church train to Salt Lake City.[32] Robert arrived in Salt Lake City early in October.

The Saints of 1864, 1865, and 1866 traveled to the Utah Territory as a show of faith to the religion they espoused. They were a part of more than three hundred emigrant, freight, and handcart companies that gathered to the Salt Lake Valley from 1847 to 1868.[33] The crucial component of the church migrations during the mid-nineteenth century, including those who traveled in the mid-1860s, was that it constituted one of the most substantial religious migrations in United States history. Tens of thousands of individuals left their homes, families, jobs, and countries to practice their religion. Although not all stayed, the vast majority of pioneers committed themselves to remaining in the valley of the Great Salt Lake and surrounding areas. The experiences on sailing vessels, a rail journey from New York City and the 1,100 mile walk from the Missouri River to the Utah Territory are invaluable. The struggles, pains and triumphs of the amazing group of individuals who undertook this journey constitute the heart of this book. Those who traveled to their Zion in Utah Territory during the years 1864, 1865 and1866 left a rich legacy. Their journey lasted six to seven months and covered six thousand miles. Their sacrifices for the cause they espoused represent a noteworthy piece of American history.

# ACKNOWLEDGMENTS

I thank Brigham Young University for providing the opportunity to complete an undergraduate degree four decades after I first entered that school. I am deeply indebted to the University of Nebraska Kearny (UNK) and the amazing professors at that institution of higher learning. Although my enrollment was online, each instructor took an active interest in helping me develop essential research and writing skills. In addition, those working at the Church History Library in Salt Lake City, Utah and the employees who worked at the Nebraska State Historical Society Reference Room in Lincoln, Nebraska directed me to needed documents, met with me one-on-one when needed, and were instrumental in helping me complete this project.

In the spring of 2012, my wife and I met Gail Holmes and Terry Latey at the Mormon Trail Center at Historic Winter Quarters in Omaha, Nebraska. During the short discussion, Gail introduced us to Wyoming, Nebraska Territory and an obscure trail named The Nebraska City Cut-off Trail. This meeting in Omaha provided the basis for a thesis and this book. In all likelihood, I would not have written either the thesis or this book. Dr. Mark Ellis provided crucial direction regarding the writing of my thesis during my time at UNK. Jim Johnson, who owns the land where the village of Wyoming once stood, spent many hours in interviews and driving my wife and me around the farm. Michael Landon and Emily Crompton, of the Church History Library spent innumerable hours working with me. Michael was particularly helpful with the thesis, and Emily provided needed direction with the book. Furthermore, Stacey Smekofske worked tirelessly editing the original manuscript to the completed work. Her input and direction helped me through many editing processes.

I extend a special thank you to every unnamed person who helped me with research, writing, and editing. Each one of you has influenced me in a positive manner, and I am grateful for your influence. Finally, I thank Marilyn, our children and grandchildren for their unceasing support.

# APPENDIX

Wyoming, Nebraska Territory Outfitting Station 1864–1866

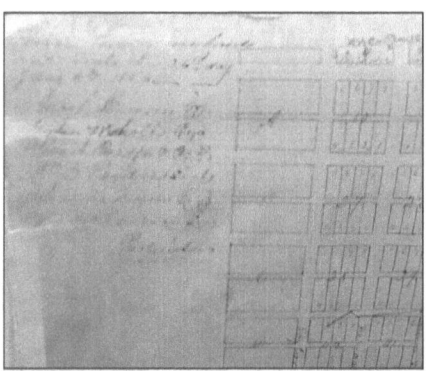

Portion of original Plat of Wyoming, Nebraska Territory, 26 July 1856. Jacob Dawson, Stephen F. Nuckolls, Allen A. Bradford, William E. Pardee, John H. Maxon and William McLennan are listed in this faded document. Plat located at the Nebraska City Courthouse, Nebraska City, Nebraska.

192 | *Appendix*

Plat of Wyoming, Otoe County, Nebraska Territory, Church History Library, SLC, Utah

Wyoming Townsite, view looking north, photograph by author 2012

Appendix | 193

Town site of Wyoming, Nebraska Territory looking east, photograph by author 2014

Site of levee for the village of Wyoming, Nebraska Territory, looking south, Photograph by author 2012

Current dirt road from levee leading up to the town site of Wyoming, Nebraska Territory photograph by author 2012

Site of the actual cemetery about 1½ miles outside of the old town site. This view looks east toward the Missouri River. Photograph by author 2012.

Appendix | 195

Historical marker sponsored by the John Watts Berrett Family Genealogical Organization, October 1998, with the cooperation of the Jim and Harold Johnson families, property owners. Only known remnants of remaining tombstones from Wyoming cemetery.

## A Photographic Journey of pioneer migrations to Utah

Mormon encampment near Wyoming, Nebraska Territory, 1866 Photo by Charles R. Savage, (HN-RG3351-31)

Ruts at Spring Creek Prairie Audubon Center, near Lincoln, Nebraska Photo by Erick Wadsworth March 2012

Cheese Creek Ranch, 1866. Photo attributed to Charles R. Savage (HN RG2469-03)

Appendix | 197

1866 picture of Roland Reed Ranch, Photograph attributed to Charles R. Savage. (HN RG2469-05)

Beaver Creek crossing, near present day Beaver Creek, Nebraska. Photo by Erick Wadsworth March 2013.

Swales on the opposite side of Beaver Creek crossing.
Photo by Erick Wadsworth March 2013.

1866 photograph of Fort Kearny, Nebraska Territory, attributed to Charles R. Savage. (HN RG2102:1 – 3)

Appendix | 199

O'Fallon's Bluff, 1866. Photograph by Charles R. Savage. (HN RG2154:8 – 27)

Wagon train fording the South Platte River near present day Hershey, Nebraska, 1866. Photograph by Charles R. Savage. (HN RG3351 – 32)

200 | *Appendix*

Chimney Rock, 1866. Photograph by Charles R. Savage. (HN RG3319:1-45)

Wagon Ruts near Guernsey, Wyoming, photo by Erick Wadsworth, July 2014

Appendix | 201

Emigrants in Echo Canyon, near present day Salt Lake City, Utah. 1866 (HN RG1227 – 04 – 01)

# NOTES

## 1. The Gathering Begins

1. Lucy Mack Smith, *The History of Joseph Smith by His Mother*, (American Fork: Covenant Communications, Inc., 2000), 34
2. Ibid, 63
3. Craig Ray, "Joseph Smith's History Confirmed," http://www.fairmormon.org/wp-content/uploads/2011/12/ray-joseph-smiths-history-confirmed.pdf, <accessed 27 December 2014>
4. George Brown Tindall and David Emory Shi, *America: a Narrative History*, (New York: W.W. Norton & Company, 1999), 543
5. Ibid
6. Joseph Smith, *History of the Church of Jesus Christ of Latter-day Saints*, 7 volumes, (Salt Lake City: The Deseret Book Company, 1973), 1: 3-4
7. Karen Lynn Davidson, David J. Whittaker, Mark Ashurst-McGee, Richard L. Jensen, editors, *The Joseph Smith Papers, Histories, Volume 1: Joseph Smith Histories, 1832-1844*, (Salt Lake City: The Church Historian's Press, 2012), 11-13
8. Smith, *History of the Church of Jesus Christ of Latter-day Saints*, 5
9. Ibid, 5-6
10. Ibid, 7
11. Ibid, 11
12. Ibid, 15
13. Ibid, 18
14. *The Joseph Smith Papers, Histories, Volume 1*, 551
15. Smith, *The History of Joseph Smith by His Mother*, 142
16. Joseph Fielding Smith, *Essentials in Church History*, (Deseret Book Company for The Church of Jesus Christ of Latter Day Saints, 1979), 79
17. *The Joseph Smith Papers, Histories, Volume 1*, 365n141
18. Ibid, 327n132
19. Smith, *History of the Church of Jesus Christ*, 1:40
20. Ibid, 1: 79
21. *The Joseph Smith Papers, Histories, Volume 1*, 337n137
22. Smith, *History of the Church of Jesus Christ*, 1: 145
23. *Doctrine and Covenants*, (Salt Lake City: The Church of Jesus Christ of Latter-day Saints, 1981), 62
24. Ibid
25. Ibid, 64
26. Smith, *History of the Church of Jesus Christ*, 1: 188
27. Ibid, 196
28. Davis Bitton, "The Waning of Mormon Kirtland," BYU Studies, 12, no. 4, (1972), 1 https://byustudies.byu.edu/content/waning-mormon-kirtland, <accessed 10 January 2015>

29. Dean C Jessee, Ronald K. Esplin, Richard Lyman Bushman, *The Joseph Smith Papers: Journals, Volume 1: 1832-1839*, (Salt Lake City: The Church Historian's Press, 2008), 227
30. Bitton, "The Waning of Mormon Kirtland," 1
31. T. Edgar Lyon, "Independence, Missouri, and the Mormons, 1827-1833," BYU Studies, Vol. 13: No. 1 (1972), 4
32. Ibid, 4-5
33. Smith, *Essentials in Church History*, 164
34. Karen Lynn Davidson, Richard L. Jensen, David J. Whittaker, editors, *The Joseph Smith Papers, Histories Volume 2: Assigned Histories, 1831-1847*, (Salt Lake City: The Church Historian's Press, 2012), 93n285
35. Ibid, 93n286
36. Ibid
37. Leonard J. Arrington, *Brigham Young: American Moses*, (Chicago: University of Illinois Press, 1986), 68
38. Smith, *The History of Joseph Smith by His Mother*, 259
39. *The Joseph Smith Papers, Histories, Volume 1*: 498n25
40. *The Joseph Smith Papers, Journals, Volume 1: 1832 – 1839*, 334
41. Ibid
42. Smith, *History of the Church of Jesus Christ of Latter-day Saints*, 7 volumes, , 3, 268
43. Smith, *Essentials in Church History*, 221
44. Dennis Rowley, "Nauvoo: A River Town," BYU Studies Quarterly, Vol. 18: No. 2, (1978), 1
45. Susan Easton Black, "How Large was the Population of Nauvoo," BYU Studies Quarterly, Vol. 35: No. 2 (1995), 92- 93
46. William Mulder, "Nauvoo Observed," BYU Studies Quarterly, Vol. 32: No. 1, (1992), 96
47. Smith, *Essentials in Church History*, 281-282
48. Ibid, 489
49. Edgar T. Lyon, "Doctrinal Development of the Church during the Nauvoo Sojourn, BYU Studies Quarterly, Vol. 15: No. 4, (1975)," 436
50. E. Dale LeBaron, "Benjamin Franklin Johnson in Nauvoo: Friend, Confident, and Defender of the Prophet," BYU Studies Quarterly, Vol. 37: No. 1 – 2, (1992), 184
51. Lyndon W. Cook, "William Law, Nauvoo Dissenter," BYU Studies Quarterly, Vol. 22: No. 1 (1982), 49
52. Ibid, 68
53. Smith, *History of the Church of Jesus Christ of Latter-day Saints*, , 6: 448
54. Kenneth W. Godfrey, "The Road to Carthage Led West," BYU Studies Quarterly, Vol. 8: No. 2, (1968), 209-210
55. Smith, *History of the Church of Jesus Christ of Latter-day Saints*, 6: 519-527
56. Ibid, 6: 555
57. Ibid, 561-562
58. Smith, *Essentials in Church History*, 314
59. Smith, *History of the Church of Jesus Christ of Latter-day Saints*, 6: 605
60. Ibid, 617-619
61. Arrington, *Brigham Young: American Moses*, 111
62. D. Michael Quinn, "The Mormon Succession Crisis of 1844," BYU Studies Quarterly, Vol.16: No. 2 (1976), 189-190

63. Ibid, 209
64. Ibid, 211-212
65. Ibid, 192
66. Ibid, 228-230
67. Arrington, *Brigham Young: American Moses*, 118-119
68. Quinn, "The Mormon Succession Crisis of 1844," 232fn136
69. William G. Hartley, Glenn Rawson, Dennis Lyman, Bryant Bush, editors, *History of the Saints*, William Hartley, "Exodus from Nauvoo," (American Fork: Covenant Communications, Inc., 2012), 18-19
70. Arrington, *Brigham Young: American Moses*, 127
71. Hartley, *History of the Saints*, William Hartley, "Exodus from Nauvoo," 19
72. Ibid, 21
73. Ibid, 24-25
74. Ibid, 28-29
75. Ibid, 29
76. Journal History of the Church, 1846 January-July, https://catalog.churchofjesuschrist.org/assets?id=dd163195-554a-403e-bc9f-7299b106c7d2&crate=0&index=281 , image 282, <accessed 7 March 2015>
77. Ibid, image 283
78. William Hartley, Glenn Rawson, Dennis Lyman, and Bryant Bush, editors, *History of the Saints: the Great Mormon Exodus and the Establishment of Zion*, Sherman L. Fleek, "The Mormon Battalion: a Unique Military Unit," 34
79. Ibid, 38
80. Ibid, 39
81. Michael N. Landon, Brandon J. Metcalf, *The Remarkable Journey of the Mormon Battalion*, (American Fork: Covenant Communications, Inc. 2012)
82. Ibid, 97

## 2. Winter Quarters, Growth, Troubles, Down and Back Trains

1. William W. Slaughter, Michael Landon, *Trail of Hope: The Story of the Mormon Trail*, (Salt Lake City: Shadow Mountain, 1997), 36
2. Ibid, 44
3. Journal History of the Church, 1846 6 September 1846 – 11 September 1846, , image 177, https://catalog.churchofjesuschrist.org/assets?id=c8703fa3-c68c-495e-aadc-63c50f024f41&crate=0&index=176, <accessed 13 March 2015>
4. Ibid
5. Richard E. Bennett, "Winter Quarters," *Ensign*, The Church of Jesus Christ of Latter-day Saints, September 1997, unpaginated, https://www.lds.org/study/ensign/1997/09/winter-quarters-church-headquarters-1846-1848?lang=eng <accessed 2 May 2019>
6. Ibid, unpaginated
7. Ibid, unpaginated
8. Ibid, unpaginated
9. Ibid, unpaginated

10. William G. Hartley, Glenn Rawson, Dennis Lyman, Bryant Bush, editors, *History of the Saints*, "The Great Mormon Exodus and the Establishment of Zion," (American Fork: Covenant Communications, Inc., 2012), 63
11. Maurine Carr Ward, *Winter Quarters: The 1846-1848 Life Writings of Mary Haskin Parker Richards*, (Logan: Utah State University Press, 1996), 29
12. Ibid, 100-101
13. Richard E. Bennett, "Finalizing Plans for the Trek West: Deliberations at Winter Quarters 1846-1847," BYU Studies Quarterly, Vol. 24: No. 3, (1984), 303
14. Ibid, 303-304
15. Ibid, 305-308
16. Ibid, 311
17. *Doctrine and Covenants*, (Salt Lake City: The Church of Jesus Christ of Latter-day Saints, 1981), 282
18. Ibid, 283
19. Ibid
20. Bennett, "Finalizing Plans for the Trek West" 311-312
21. Stanley B. Kimball, "Mormon Trail Network in Nebraska, 1846-1868: A New Look," 3-4, https://byustudies.byu.edu/content/mormon-trail-network-nebraska-1846-1868-new-look, <accessed 7 April 2013>
22. B. H. Roberts, *A Comprehensive History of the Church of Jesus Christ of Latter-day Saints*, 6 volumes, (Salt Lake City: Deseret Book, 1950), 3:161-162
23. Ronald O. Barney, editor, *The Mormon Vanguard Brigade of 1847, Norton Jacob's Record*, (Logan: Utah State University Press, 2005), 117fn98
24. Ibid, 118
25. Will Bagley, *South Pass: Gateway to a Continent*, (Norman: University of Oklahoma Press, 2014), 21
26. Ibid, 129-130
27. Barney, editor, *The Mormon Vanguard Brigade of 1847*, 190fn173
28. Leonard J. Arrington, *Brigham Young: American Moses*, (Chicago: University of Illinois Press, 1985), 142
29. Barney, editor, *The Mormon Vanguard Brigade of 1847*, 193fn4
30. Ibid, 192
31. Ibid, 216fn94
32. Ibid, 217fn101
33. Ibid, 219fn108
34. Leonard J. Arrington, *Great Basin Kingdom: an Economic History of the Latter-day Saints, 1830-1900*, (Cambridge: Harvard University Press, 1958), 47
35. Ibid, 49
36. Barney, editor, *The Mormon Vanguard Brigade of 1847*, 234
37. Ibid
38. Ibid, 247
39. Rawson, Lyman, Bush, edited by William G. Harley, *History of the Saints: the Great Mormon Exodus*, 105
40. Mormon Pioneer Overland Travel, "The Church of Jesus Christ of Latter-Day Saints,"https://history.churchofjesuschrist.org/overlandtravel/companies, <accessed 12 March 2013>
41. Ronald W. Walker, "The Affair of the 'Runaways': Utah's First Encounter with the Federal Officers," *Journal of Mormon History*, Vol. 39, No. 4, (Fall, 2013), 2-3

42. Ibid, 3
43. Ibid, 12
44. Hartley, *History of the Saints: the Great Mormon Exodus and the Establishment of Zion*, 137
45. Ibid, 138
46. Barney, editor, *The Mormon Vanguard Brigade of 1847*, 285fn55
47. Arrington, *Brigham Young: American Moses*, 172
48. Ibid
49. Arrington, *Great Basin Kingdom: an Economic History of the Latter-day Saints*, 58
50. Ibid, 59 – 62
51. Arrington, *Brigham Young: American Moses*, 173
52. Glen M. Leonard, "Seeking an Inheritance: Mormon Mobility, Urbanity, and Community," *The Journal of Mormon History*, Vol. 40, No. 2, (Spring 2014), 21
53. Ibid, 27
54. Ibid, 30
55. Leonard J. Arrington, "Religion and Economics in Mormon History," BYU Studies Quarterly, Vol. 3: No. 3-4 (1961), 7
56. Stanley B. Kimball, *Heber C. Kimball, Mormon Patriarch and Pioneer*, (Chicago: University of Illinois Press, 1981), 191, https://archive.org/details/PresidentHeberC.KimballsJournal/page/n231, <accessed 6 May 2019>
57. Ibid, 195fn3
58. Richard L. Jensen, Utah History Encyclopedia , https://www.uen.org/utah_history_encyclopedia/p/PERPETUAL_EMIGRATING_FUND_COMPANY.shtml, <accessed 6 May 2019>
59. Territory of Utah (1856), Resolutions, Acts and Memorials passed at the Fifth Annual Session of the Legislative Assembly of the Territory of Utah, convened at Fillmore City, Dec. 11, 1855, 39-41,https://books.google.com/books?id=sgBFAQAAMAAJ&pg=PA30&lpg=PA30&dq=Territorial+session+utah+12+January+1856&source=bl&ots=AZtulJ_q-T&sig=ACfU3U21vyDOxwR6-76JUFvY3XlfOEoyQA&hl=en&sa=X&ved=2ahUKEwjHy5Gm5qLhAhUk5IMKHW15Bn0Q6AEwCHoECAkQAQ#v=onepage&q=Territorial%20session%20utah%2012%20January%201856&f=false, <accessed 12 Dec. 2012>
60. Compiled and edited at Brigham Young University, *Journal of Discourses Delivered by President Brigham Young, His Two Councilors, the Twelve Apostles*, 26 Vol., (Salt Lake City, Utah, 1967) Vol. I, 325-326
61. William E. Lass, *From the Missouri to the Great Salt Lake: An Account of Overland Freighting*, (Lincoln: Nebraska State Historical Society, 1972), 57
62. *Journal of Discourses*, Vol. V, 233-234
63. Lass, *From the Missouri to the Great Salt Lake*, 70
64. Leonard J. Arrington and Davis Bitton, *Saints Without Halos*, (Salt Lake City: Signature Books, 1981), 35-38, http://signaturebookslibrary.org/?p=5178, <accessed 24 November 2012>
65. Ronald W. Walker, Richard Turley Jr., Glen M. Leonard, *Massacre at Mountain Meadows*, (New York: Oxford University Press, 2008), 230
66. Robert H. Briggs, "A Seething Cauldron of Controversy: The First Trial of John P. Lee, 1875, " *Journal of Mormon History*, Vol. 39: No. 1 (Winter 2013), 15
67. Walker, Turley, Leonard, *Massacre at Mountain Meadow*, 228-229
68. News Release, The Church of Jesus Christ of Latter-day Saints, Elder Henry B. Eyring's remarks at the Mountain Meadows Massacre Sesquicentennial, 11

September 2007, Washington County , Utah, http://www.mormonnewsroom.org/article/150th-anniversary-of-mountain-meadows-massacre, <accessed 19 April 2015>
69. *Journal of Discourses Vol.*8, 192
70. Ibid, 192-193
71. Roberts, editor, *A Comprehensive History of The Church of Jesus Christ of Latter-day Saints*, Vol. 5, p. 107
72. "Circular to Bishop Edward Hunter, and the Bishops throughout the territory," (Salt Lake City: 1861), 2-3, http://archive.org/details/circulartobishop00unse . <accessed 15 September 2012>
73. Ibid, 6
74. Ibid, 6-7
75. John K. Hulmston, "Mormon Immigration in the 1860s: The Story of Church Trains," *Utah Historical Quarterly*, Vol. 58, No. 1 (Winter, 1990), 48
76. William G. Hartley, "The Great Florence Fitout of 1861," BYU Studies, 371, https://byustudies.byu.edu/content/great-florence-fitout-1861, <accessed 20 August 2012>
77. William G. Hartley, Down-and-Back Wagon Trains: Travelers on the Mormon Trail in 1861, *Overland Journal*, (Winter 1993), 11: 4, p23
78. Hulmston, The Story of Church Trains, , 58:1, p. 48
79. Brigham Young office files, 1832-1878 (bulk 1844-1877); Letterbooks, 1844-1877; Letterbook, v.7, 1860 April 19-1866 January 8; Church History Library, Image 335-336, http://catalog.lds.org/assets/867b28d5-f5ea-44bb-b228-516179bc010a/0/336, <accessed 8 May 2019>
80. Manuscript Histories of the Church in the United States: Manuscript History of Call's Landing, Nevada, 1860 – 1870. Church History Library, The Church of Jesus Christ of Latter-day Saints, Salt Lake City, Utah.https://catalog.churchofjesuschrist.org/assets?id=eb55a779-9da5-4aae-abc6-89b9d1aed1d4&crate=0&index=6, <accessed 5 January 2019>

## 3. Wyoming, Nebraska Territory selected as an Outfitting Station 1864

1. Pound, Louise, "The Nebraska Legend of Weeping Water," *Western Folklore*, Vol. 6, No. 4 (October, 1947), 314
2. Climate in Otoe County, Nebraska, "Sperling's Best Places," http://www.bestplaces.net/climate/county/nebraska/otoe, <accessed 16 December 2013>
3. Jacob Dawson household, 1860 U. S. Census, Wyoming, Otoe, Nebraska Territory; Roll: M653_665; Page: 375; Image: 578; Family History Library Film: 803665; www.ancestry.com , <accessed 14 June 2012>
4. Raymond E. Dale, *Otoe County Pioneers, a Biographical Dictionary, Part III, D – F,* (Lincoln: Lincoln, Nebraska, 1961-1965), 691, Restricted Genealogy Section, 929.27 D, Morton-James Public Library, Nebraska City, Nebraska
5. Winter Quarters Project, "Dawsonburg," https://winterquarters.byu.edu/Settlements/FremontCounty.aspx , <accessed 28 October 2012>
6. Jacob Dawson household, 1850 U. S. Census, Fremont, Iowa; Roll: M432_184; Page: 149A; Image: 41; www.ancestry.com , <accessed 19 October 2012>

7. Book A Record of Deeds for Otoe County, N. T., April 5, 1855: 482, Otoe County Courthouse, Division of Deeds, Nebraska City, Nebraska
8. Ibid
9. Ibid
10. E. H. Cowles, "Otoe County in Early Days," 38, (1885), *Transactions and Reports, Nebraska State Historical Society*, Paper 38, http://digitalcommons.unl.edu/nebhisttrans/38, <accessed 12 November 2012>
11. "Letter of S. F. Nuckolls," 34, (1885), *Transactions and Reports, Nebraska State Historical Society*, Paper 55, http://digitalcommons.unl.edu/nebhisttrans//55 , <accessed 12 November 2012>
12. NEGenWeb Project, "The Nebraska and Midwest Genealogical Record, 1856, Otoe County, 25, http://www.usgennet.org/usa/ne/topic/resources/OLLibrary/Journals/NMGR/Vol16/nmgrp005.html, <accessed 2 August 2019>
13. Helen Roberta Williams, "Old Wyoming," *Nebraska History Magazine*, Vol. XVII, No. 2, (April-June, 1936), 81
14. Numerical Index of Deeds for Otoe County, N. T., Wyoming (original), 1855: 1-81, Otoe County Courthouse, Division of Deeds, Nebraska City, Nebraska
15. Record Book 3, Otoe County Nebraska Territory, 16-19, Otoe County Courthouse, Division of Deeds, Nebraska City, Nebraska
16. 1860 U. S. Federal Census: Wyoming, Otoe, Nebraska Territory, Roll: M653_665; Page: 377; Image: 580; Family History Library Film: 803665, www.ancestry.com , <accessed 20 July 2011>
17. "Population of Nebraska Incorporated Places, 1860 to 1920," http://www.neded.org/files/research/stathand/bsect5a.htm , <accessed 24 December 2012>
18. *The Wyoming Post*, Wyoming, Otoe County, Nebraska Territory, Vol. 1, No. 1, April 3, 1858, page 1, column 2, Film, 071 W998p, (Nebraska State Historical Society Library: Lincoln, Nebraska)
19. *The Wyoming Post*, page 2, column 1, Vol. 1, No. 2, April 10, 1858
20. *The Wyoming Post*, , Vol. 1, No. 1, page 4, column 4, April 3, 1858
21. *The Wyoming Post*, page 2, column 1, Vol. 1, No. 2, April 10, 1858
22. Ibid, Page 3, column 6
23. *The Wyoming Post*, page 1, column 1, Vol. 1, No. 3, April 17, 1858
24. Ibid
25. Ibid, page 1, column 2
26. Ibid, page 2, column 6
27. *The Wyoming Post*, page 3, column 1, Vol. 1, No. 6, May 8, 1858
28. Ibid, page 2, column 5
29. *The Wyoming Post*, page 3, column 1, Vol. 1, No. 6, May 15, 1858
30. *The Wyoming Post*, page 2, column 3, Vol. 1, No. 6, May 29, 1858
31. Historical Marker: sponsored by the John Watts Barrett Family Genealogical Organization, October 1998, with the cooperation of the Jim and Harold Johnson families, property owners.
32. Interview with Jim Johnson, by Erick Wadsworth, 4 December 2012. Video image of interview held in 2012 by Wadsworth. Mr. Johnson owns the land where Wyoming, Nebraska and the Wyoming cemetery once stood.
33. "2 Old Trees Only Signs of Early State Cemetery," undated clipping from unidentified newspaper, in possession of Erick Wadsworth, 29 December 2012, (2056 Sandcrest Loop, Nampa, Idaho 83686)

34. Williams, "Old Wyoming," 89
35. "In Old Wyoming," *Nebraska City News*, unpaginated, December 19, 1929, Wyoming Vertical File, misc. holdings, ID# 57929, Genealogy Section, Morton James Public Library, Nebraska City, Nebraska
36. "Recalls Old Wyoming Days," August 6, 1934, from unidentified newspaper in the Wyoming Vertical File, misc. holdings, ID# 57929, Genealogy Section, Morton James Public Library, Nebraska City, Nebraska
37. Joseph W. Young papers: Certificates of appointment, 1849 – 1864. Church History Library, The Church of Jesus Christ of Latter-day Saints, Salt Lake City, Utah, Reel 1, Box 2, Folder 9
38. Craig S. Smith, "Wyoming, Nebraska Territory: Joseph W. Young and the Mormon Emigration of 1864," 33 BYU Studies 39, No. 1 (2000), http://contentdm.lib.byu.edu/cdm/compoundobject/collection/byustudies/id/4258/rec/2 , <accessed 15 August 2012>
39. Ibid, 36
40. Andrew Jenson , "Manuscript History of Wyoming, Nebraska [1860-1870]," (Archives MS d 4029 Bx 3, fd 2, CHL, Salt Lake City, Utah), unpaginated
41. Brigham Young office files, 1832-1878, (bulk 1844-1877); General Correspondence, Outgoing, 1840-1876; 1864; Church History Library, https://catalog.lds.org/assets/f7501284-69cd-4218-a68f-e6eea1e0fad0/0/1, <accessed 28 February 2019>
42. Brigham Young office files, 1832-1878 (bulk 1844-1877); General Correspondence, Incoming, 1840-1877; Letters from Young Family Members, 1841-1877; Sons of Brigham Young, 1855-1877; Joseph A. Young, 1864-1865;Joseph A. Young letter, Church History Library, https://catalog.churchofjesuschrist.org/assets?id=0ab64086-07d8-438f-b2cd-7a3f776e7512&crate=0&index=1,<accessed 28 February 2019>
43. Brigham Young office files, https://catalog.lds.org/assets?id=a2a452ab-29d4-4450-a7b6-6cbc9ba62136&crate=0&index=1, <accessed 21 June 2019>
44. Ibid, https://catalog.lds.org/assets?id=b9d5625c-d783-4c49-8993-0a13ebdaa40a&crate=0&index=0, <accessed 21 June 2019>
45. Andrew Jenson , "Emigration from Wyoming," *Nebraska History Magazine*, Vol. XVII, No. 2, (April-June, 1936), 113-115
46. Ibid, 114
47. Ibid, 117
48. Ibid
49. Smith, "Wyoming, Nebraska Territory" p 36
50. Ibid.
51. Joseph W. Young papers: Letterpress copy book, 1864 – 1868, Church History Library, https://catalog.lds.org/assets?id=a9546a30-6ad6-48c3-82d3-208af6898102&crate=0&index=37 , <accessed 28 February 2019>
52. Ibid
53. Ibid
54. Ibid
55. Andrew Jenson , Jenson , "Emigration from Wyoming," 115
56. Joseph W. Young papers: Letterpress copy book, 1864 – 1868
57. "Ghost Towns Remain," undated clipping from unidentified newspaper, in possession of Erick Wadsworth, 29 December 2012, (2056 Sandcrest Loop, Nampa, Idaho 83686)
58. "Mormon Historian Visits Old Wyoming Landing Site," *The Nebraska Daily News-Press*,

unpaginated, 20 July 1934, Wyoming Vertical File, misc. holdings, ID# 57929, Genealogy Section, Morton James Public Library, Nebraska City, Nebraska

## 4. The Nebraska City Cut-off Trail

1. William E. Lass, *From the Missouri to the Great Salt Lake: an Account of Overland Freighting*, (Nebraska State Historical Society, 1972), 60-65
2. Alexander Majors, *Seventy Years on the Frontier; Alexander Majors Memoirs of a Lifetime on the Border*, (Chicago and New York, Rand, McNally & Company, 1893), p. 76
3. Ibid, p. 76 – 77
4. Ibid, p. 77
5. Charles Boyd Mapes, "The Nebraska City-Fort Kearny Cut-off as a Factor In the Early Development of Nebraska and the West," (1931), *Dissertations, Thesis & Research, Department of History*. 30-31 http://digitalcommons.unl.edu/cgi/viewcontent.cgi?article=1019&context=historydiss. <accessed 15 December 2015>
6. William E. Lass, *From the Missouri to the Great Salt Lake*, p. 90
7. Ibid
8. A Strait Road, *Peoples Press*, Nebraska City, NT, 30 March 1860, Page 2, Column 2
9. Charles Boyd Mapes, "The Nebraska City-Fort Kearny Cut-off, p. 35
10. Ibid
11. A Strait Road, *Peoples Press*,
12. The Nearest Point, *Peoples Press*, Nebraska City, NT, 27 April 1860, page 2, column 2
13. Merrill J. Mattes, *The Great Platte River Road: The Covered Wagon Mainline Via Fort Kearny to Fort Laramie*, (Lincoln: University of Nebraska Press, 1969) 166
14. Mr. Major's Business at Nebraska City, *Nebraska City News*, Nebraska City, NT, page 2, column 2
15. Nebraska City Board of Trade. Fifth Annual Report: Business for 1865, *The Nebraska City News*, 31 March 1866, page2, column 2
16. Ibid
17. Sheldon Reviews History of Kearney Cutoff Trail, *Republican Register*, Aurora, Nebraska, page 1, 6 Columns 1 – 4
18. Mapes, "The Nebraska City-Fort Kearny Cut-off," 50
19. Ibid, 50-51
20. Ibid, 52-53
21. John H. Waterman, *General History of Seward County, Nebraska*, (Beaver Crossing: John H. Waterman, 1916), 32-33
22. *York Nebraska News Times*, page 6, columns 1-3, 15 June 1979, copy located at the Plainsman Museum, Aurora, Nebraska
23. "Hamilton County," compiled by the Hamilton County Historical Society, 1936, unpaginated, copy located at the Plainsman Museum, Aurora, Nebraska
24. Mapes, "The Nebraska City-Fort Kearny Cut-off," 58-59
25. William E. Lass, "Nebraska City's Steam Wagon," *Nebraska History* 79 (1998): 24, William Lass' article writes in great detail about the steam wagon incident. Much of the information regarding the steam wagon comes from his excellent composition.
26. Ibid
27. Ibid
28. Ibid, 25 – 26

29. Ibid, 26
30. Ibid
31. Ibid, 27-28
32. Ibid, 28 – 29
33. Ibid, 30
34. *Laws and Joint Resolutions and Memorials, Passed at the Ninth Session of the Legislative Assembly of the Territory of Nebraska*, 1864, 267, https://babel.hathitrust.org/cgi/pt?id=ucl.a0005193388;view=1up;seq=275, <accessed 29 September 2018>
35. The Western Trade, *People's Press*, 3 July 1862, page. 2, column 3.
36. D. P. Rolfe, "Overland Freighting from Nebraska City,", written for the annual meeting of the Nebraska State Historical Society, January 10, 1900, by Hon. D. P. Rolfe, Nebraska City, 279-280
37. Ibid 281-282
38. Ibid, 285-286
39. Ibid, 287-288
40. James C. Olson, ed, "From Nebraska City to Montana, 1866: The Diary of Thomas Alfred Creigh, *"Nebraska History, 29* (1948):208 - 211
41. Ibid, 212 – 213
42. Ibid, 213 – 216
43. William Henry Jackson, *The Autobiography of William Henry Jackson*, (New York, G.P. Putnam's Sons), 1940, 107
44. Ibid, 111 – 116

## 5. The First Wagon Trains of 1864

1. Mormon Pioneer Overland Travel, "Chronological Company List," http://history.lds.org/overlandtravels/companydatelist, <accessed 10 March 2013>
2. Ron Anderson, "Immigration Summary of 1864," copy in possession of Erick Wadsworth, 2059 Sandcrest Loop, Nampa, ID 83686, Historian Ron Anderson prepared a well documented summary of the migration of 1864. Contained in the summary are routes taken by the various wagon trains, recaps of individual diaries and reminisces and archival locations of the records cited.
3. Conway B. Sonne, *Saints on the Seas: A Maritime History of Mormon Migration, 1830 – 1890*, Salt Lake City: University of Utah Press, 1963), 153
4. Stanley B. Kimball, "Sail and Rail Pioneers before 1869", BYU Studies (Vol. 35, No. 2, 1995) 9-10
5. Andrew Christian Nielson, *Autobiography of Andrew Christian Nielson*, (CHL, Salt Lake City, Utah), (Archives MS 2735 282), 4-6
6. Mary Roberts Roskelley, Reminisces, Liverpool to New York 21 May 1864 – 23 June 1864, Mormon Migration, https://mormonmigration.lib.byu.edu/mii/account/458?keywords=General+McClellan+1864&sweden=on&scandinavia=on&mii=on&netherlands=on&europe=on, <accessed 26 November 2018>
7. Mormon Pioneer Overland Travel
8. Andrew Jenson , "Manuscript History of Wyoming, Nebraska [1860-1870]," (Archives MS d 4029 Bx 3, fd 2, CHL, Salt Lake City, Utah), unpaginated
9. Mormon Pioneer Overland Travel, "Chronological Company List,"
10. Carma L. Sanberg, "Nellie Nash: (A pioneer Biography of Mrs. Ellen Elvira Parkinson

Wife of William Chandler Parkinson)" (1959). 7 *All Thesis and Dissertations. 5091*
11. Ibid, 8-9
12. Mormon Pioneer Overland Travel, "Chronological Company List,"
13. Ibid
14. Jensen, Andrew, "Latter-Day Saint Biographical Encyclopedia," Andrew Jensen History Company, (1901) 4 Volumes, 1: 304-305
15. J. M. Tanner, "A Biographical Sketch of John Riggs Murdock," (Salt Lake City: The Deseret News, 1909), 151-152
16. Will Bagley, Rick Grunder, "I Could Hardly Hold the Pen," *Overland Journal*, Vol. 27, No. 3, fall (2009) , 54
17. Ibid, 55
18. Ibid, 57
19. Ibid, 53
20. Ibid, 61
21. Ibid, 62
22. Ibid, fn36
23. Frank M. Gilcrest, Autobiography, in Personal Recollections of F.M. Gilcrest, 9 February 1908, (Archives MS 22344, CHL, Salt Lake City, Utah) 2 – 10
24. Ibid.
25. Ibid.
26. Ibid.
27. Mormon Pioneer Overland Travel, "Chronological Company List,"
28. Perpetual Emigrating Fund Company church trains accounts: Captains' accounts, 1862 – 1868, Captain William B. Preston Company (first ox train), manifests, 1864. Church History Library, The Church of Jesus Christ of Latter-day Saints, Salt Lake City, Utah, https://catalog.lds.org/record?id=5a2d8961-723e-4a15-8d35-0c296210f3f9&view=browse&subView=arrangement, <accessed 12 June 2018>
29. Perpetual Emigrating Fund Company church train accounts: Freight manifests, 1861 – 1868, Freight manifests, 1864, 1868. Church History Library, The Church of Jesus Christ of Latter-day Saints, Salt Lake City, Utah, https://catalog.lds.org/record?id=5a2d8961-723e-4a15-8d35-0c296210f3f9&view=browse&subView=arrangement, <accessed 23 June 2018>
30. Perpetual Emigrating Fund Company church trains accounts: Captains' accounts, 1862 – 1868, Captain William B. Preston Company
31. Jean A. Lukish, *Secret Brother: The Story of Solon Borglum, "Sculptor of the Prairie"* (Grand Island/Palmer, Nebraska, 2015), 176
32. Nils Flygare, Nils C. Flygare Papers, MSS 1496 Box 1 Folder 3, L. Tom Perry Special Collections, Harold B. Lee Library, Brigham Young University, Provo, Utah, 53-54
33. Ibid, 55
34. Letters translated by Edith Melgard Cox, History of Caroline Martine Anderson, first wife of Charles Keilgaard Hansen, (Archives MS 8889, Church History Library, Salt Lake City), 1
35. Ibid, 2
36. Letters translated by Edith Melgard Cox, History of Caroline Martine Anderson, first wife of Charles Keilgaard Hansen, (Archives MS 8889, Church History Library, Salt Lake City), 3
37. Ibid, 4
38. Ibid, 5

39. Ibid, 6
40. Ibid, 2
41. Ibid
42. Ibid

## 6. Additional Wagon Trains Head West During 1864

1. Mormon Pioneer Overland Travel, "Chronological Company List," See Joseph S. Rawlins Company (1864) https://history.lds.org/overlandtravel/companies/12537314572983645992/joseph-s-rawlins-company, <accessed 20 December 2018>
2. Kate B. Carter, compiler, "Our Pioneer Heritage," (Daughters of Utah Pioneers, Salt Lake City, 1965), 20 vol., 8: 36
3. Ibid, 37
4. Archie Leon Brown, Charlene L. Hathaway editors, *141 Years of Mormon Heritage: Rawsons, Browns, Angells-Pioneers*, 81-83 Mormon Pioneer Overland Travel, https://history.churchofjesuschrist.org/overlandtravel/sources/5850/brown-richard-daniels-jr-autobiography-in-archie-leon-brown-141-years-of-mormon-heritage-rawsons-browns-angells-pioneers-1973-82-83, <accessed 15 December 2018>
5. Ibid, 83
6. Gideon Allen Murdock, *Autobiography and journal, 1872-1923*, MS1773, fd.1, (Church History Library, Salt Lake City, Utah), unpaginated
7. Ibid
8. Perpetual Emigrating Fund Company church train accounts: Freight manifests, 1861 – 1868; Freight manifests, 1863-1864; Church History Library, https://catalog.lds.org/assets?id=820afd0d-26b4-4e72-8e1a-73446dc5f9d1&crate=0&index=0, <accessed 12 November 2018>
9. Perpetual Emigrating Fund Company church train accounts: Captain's accounts, 1862-1868, Captain William S. Warren Company (third ox train), manifests, 1864. Church History Library, https://catalog.lds.org/assets?id=9c22e7c1-9742-48f7-8f30-f3c2bdb8192d&crate=0&index=0, <accessed 12 November 2018>
10. Ibid
11. Orley Dwight Bliss, "Orley Dwight Bliss Autobiography and diary," MSS 615, Folder 3, (L. Tom Perry Special Collections, Harold B. Lee Library, Brigham Young University, Provo, Utah) unpaginated
12. David Hendee, "Plum Creek: A massacre that started a war," from an article written 10 August 2014, https://www.omaha.com/news/nebraska/plum-creek-a-massacre-that-started-a-war/article_e5afe5bd-08c2-5465-80a8-8c4947af43d3.html, <accessed 8 January 2019>
13. David Hendee, "Survivors account of massacre recalls the attack and her capture," from an article written 10 August 2014, https://www.omaha.com/news/nebraska/survivor-s-account-of-massacre-recalls-the-attack-and-her/article_cc1579cd-e6f4-5159-a8ef-ab26c8c0078a.html, <accessed 5 August 2018>
14. Ibid.
15. Awful Colliery Accident in Wales, *Deseret News*, Salt Lake City, Utah Territory, 1852-08-07, page 2, https://newspapers.lib.utah.edu/details?id=2578725&q=Thomas+Pritchard, <accessed 16 January 2019>

16. Welsh Coal Mines, Memorial page of colliery deaths from the year 1852, http://www.welshcoalmines.co.uk/fatalities/fatals.html, <accessed 16 January 2019>
17. British Mission Emigration Register, p. 122, Mormon Migration, https://mormonmigration.lib.byu.edu/mii/passenger/45760?keywords=General+McClellan+1864&mii=on&sweden=on&europe=on&netherlands=on&scandinavia=on, <accessed 16 January 2019>
18. Thomas Waters Cropper Autobiography, *Family History of Thomas Waters Cropper and Hannah Lucretia Rogers*, [1957], 22-26 , https://history.lds.org/overlandtravel/sources/6259/cropper-thomas-waters-autobiography-in-family-history-of-thomas-waters-cropper-and-hannah-lucretia-rogers-1957-22-26?lang=eng, <accessed 18 January 2019>
19. Ibid
20. J. W. P. Stannard, "The Journey Over the Plains," *Deseret News*, Salt Lake City, Utah, 1864-10-26, page 3, https://newspapers.lib.utah.edu/details?id=2598656, <accessed 18 January 2019>
21. Ibid.
22. Mormon Pioneer Overland Travel, "Chronological Company List," See John Smith Company, (1860), https://history.lds.org/overlandtravel/companies/272/john-smith-company-1860?lang=eng#description, <accessed 19 January 2019>
23. A Biographical Sketch of the Life of The Patriarch John Smith, Family Search, Salt Lake City, Utah, https://www.familysearch.org/photos/artifacts/3001754?p=3069661&returnLabel=John%20Smith%20(KWJZ-JXX)&returnUrl=https%3A%2F%2Fwww.familysearch.org%2Ftree%2Fperson%2Fmemories%2FKWJZ-JXX,<accessed 18 January 2019>
24. Mormon Pioneer Overland Travel, "Chronological Company List," See John Smith Company, (1864)
25. Brigham Young office files: General Letters, 1840-1877, Y, 1864, Church History Library, The Church of Jesus Christ of Latter-day Saints, Salt Lake City, Utah, https://catalog.lds.org/record?id=02e985d2-0e16-45c3-8891-986d21e20b37&compId=a5df0065-8d79-4d42-899b-255fe56d551b&view=browse&subView=arrangement , <accessed 19 January 2019>
26. Mormon Pioneer Overland Travel, "Chronological List," See John Smith Company (1864), Johnson, John Peter Rasmus, Diary, 1864 July—September, 11 p. https://history.churchofjesuschrist.org/overlandtravel/sources/6022/johnson-john-peter-rasmus-diary-1864-july-september-11-p, <accessed 15 December 2018>
27. Ibid.
28. Ibid.
29. Kate B. Carter, compiler, "Our Pioneer Heritage," 11: 277
30. Ibid, 278
31. Ibid.
32. Mormon Pioneer Overland Travel, "Chronological Company List," See Isaac Canfield Company, 1864
33. "Arrivals," *Salt Lake Daily Telegraph*, 6 October 1864, 3, Mormon Pioneer Overland Travel, https://history.lds.org/overlandtravel/sources/9687/arrivals-salt-lake-daily-telegraph-6-october-1864-3, <accessed 39 January 2019>
34. Perpetual Emigrating Fund Company church train accounts, 1861-1868; Captain's accounts, 1862-1868, Captain Isaac Canfield Company (fourth ox train), manifests,

1864; Church History Library, https://catalog.lds.org/assets?id=56beec76-d41a-4b46-a165-ee490a3f4a62&crate=0&index=13, <accessed 20 December 2018>
35. Ibid.
36. An Account of a Mormon Family's Conversion to the Religion of the Latter Day Saints and of Their Trip From Denmark to Utah, Part I, 717, Brigham Young University Articles, http://files.lib.byu.edu/mormonmigration/articles/AnAccountOfAMormonFamiliysConversion_part1+2.pdf, <accessed 20 October 2018>
37. Ibid
38. Ibid, 718
39. Ibid, 725
40. Ibid, 726
41. Ibid, 766
42. Ibid, 767
43. Mormon Pioneer Overland Travel, "Chronological List," See William Hyde Company (1864), view Summary, https://history.lds.org/overlandtravel/companies/166/william-hyde-company?lang=eng#description, <accessed 2 February 2019>
44. Perpetual Emigrating Fund Company church train accounts, 1861-1868; Freight Manifests, 1861-1868; Freight manifests, 1863-1864; Church History Library, https://catalog.lds.org/assets?id=820afd0d-26b4-4e72-8e1a-73446dc5f9d1&crate=0&index=111, <accessed 3 February 2019>
45. Hooper &Eldredge, *The Deseret News*, Salt Lake City, Utah Territory, 31 August 1864, page 7, column 1, https://newspapers.lib.utah.edu/details?id=2596095, <accessed 3 February 2019>
46. Ibid.
47. Historical Department journal history of the Church, 1896-2001; 1860-1869; 1864 July-December; Church History Library, https://catalog.lds.org/assets?id=72976e53-04a2-4a8e-985f-03149d21e3fd&crate=0&index=226, <accessed 4 February 2019>
48. Ibid
49. Ruby Snow Jensen, "Biography of Warren Snow (1818-1896), Family Search, The Church of Jesus Christ of Latter-Day Saints, https://www.familysearch.org/tree/person/memories/KWJW-7BS, <accessed 8 February 2019>
50. Perpetual Emigrating Fund Company church trains accounts, 1861-1868; Freight manifests, 1863-1864; Church History Library, https://catalog.lds.org/record?id=5a2d8961-723e-4a15-8d35-0c296210f3f9&compId=820afd0d-26b4-4e72-8e1a-73446dc5f9d1&view=browse&subView=arrangement, <accessed 8 February 2019>
51. Ibid
52. Ibid
53. Mormon Pioneer Overland Travel, "Chronological List," See Warren S. Snow Company (1864), view Summary, https://history.lds.org/overlandtravel/companies/166/william-hyde-company?lang=eng#description, <accessed 2 February 2019>
54. Perpetual Emigrating Fund Company church train accounts, 1861-1868; Freight manifests, 1863-1864; Church History Library Church History Library, https://catalog.lds.org/assets?id=820afd0d-26b4-4e72-8e1a-73446dc5f9d1&crate=0&index=119 <accessed 11 February 2019>
55. Carter, *Our Pioneer Heritage*, 8:57
56. Carter, *Our Pioneer Heritage*, 2:226
57. Ibid, 226-227

58. Jesse N. Smith, Autobiography and Journal, 1855 Oct – 1906, Mormon Pioneer Overland Travel, "Chronological List," See Warren S. Snow Company (1864), https://history.lds.org/overlandtravel/sources/5411/smith-jesse-n-autobiography-and-journal-1855-oct-1906-apr-212-18?lang=eng, <accessed 11 February 2019>
59. Biographical Events of Jens Christian Larsen Breinholt, Family Search, The Church of Jesus Christ of Latter-Day Saints, https://www.familysearch.org/photos/artifacts/4746001?p=13944870&returnLabel=Jens%20Christian%20Lauridsen%20Breinholt%20(KWZY-N4T)&returnUrl=https%3A%2F%2Fwww.familysearch.org%2Ftree%2Fperson%2Fmemories%2FKWZY-N4T, <accessed 12 February 2019>
60. Don Carlos Johnson, *A Brief History of Springville, Utah*, (Springville, Utah: William F. Gibson, 1900), 64 https://archive.org/details/briefhistoryofsp00john/page/64, <accessed 12 February 2019>
61. Perpetual Emigrating Fund Company church trains accounts 1861-1868, Freight Manifests, 1861-1868; Freight manifests, 1864, 1868; Church History Library, https://catalog.lds.org/assets?id=e416c8bd-c905-4565-b6aa-68c1455ed987&crate=0&index=111, <accessed 12 February 2019>
62. Carter, *Our Pioneer Heritage*, 3:278-283
63. Arrival of Merchandise, *The Deseret News*, Salt Lake City, Utah Territory, 7 September 1864, page 5, column 3, https://newspapers.lib.utah.edu/details?id=2596173, <accessed 13 February 2019>
64. Ibid, page 4, column 4

## 7. Migration to Zion 1865

1. John K. Hulmston, "Mormon Immigration in the 1860s: The Story of the Church Trains," *Utah Historical Quarterly* 58:1, winter, (1990): 45
2. Full Company List, Mormon Pioneer Overland Travel, "Chronological List," See departure dates for independent and freight wagon trains for the year 1865, https://history.lds.org/overlandtravel/companies?lang=eng, <accessed 19 February 2019>
3. Conway B. Sonne, *Saints on the High Seas, A Maritime History of Mormon Migration, 1830–1890*, (Salt Lake City: University of Utah Press, 1983), 153
4. Manuscript histories of Church in United States, circa 1919-1971, Manuscript history of Wyoming, Nebraska, 1860-1870; Church History Library, https://catalog.lds.org/assets/1549d9e9-1442-46cd-b68f-65aa5e1e316b/0/0, <accessed 23 February 2019>
5. Sonne, *Saints on the High Seas*, 153
6. Autobiography of Elizabeth McDermott Sims, "Mormon Migration," https://mormonmigration.lib.byu.edu/, <accessed 19 February 2019>
7. Ibid
8. Miner G. Atwood, *Diary of Miner G. Atwood*, "Mormon Migration," https://mormonmigration.lib.byu.edu/, <accessed 19 February 2019>
9. William H. Shearman, "America," *The Millennial Star*, Brigham Young University Digital Collections, Vol. 27; 397-399, https://contentdm.lib.byu.edu/digital/collection/MStar/id/8294/rec/28, <accessed 21 February 2019>
10. John Swenson, "Letter from John Swenson," *Mormon Migration*, https://mormonmigration.lib.byu.edu/mii/account/135?europe=on&sweden=on&

keywords=1865&mii=on&scandinavia=on&netherlands=on, <accessed 21 February 2019>

11. Peter A. Nielson, "Autobiographical Sketch of Peter A. Nielson," *Mormon Migration*, https://mormonmigration.lib.byu.edu/mii/account/133?europe=on&sweden=on&keywords=1865&mii=on&scandinavia=on&netherlands=on, <accessed 21 February 2019>

12. Kate B. Carter, compiler, *Our Pioneer Heritage*, 20 vol. (Salt Lake City, Utah: Daughters of Utah Pioneers, 1966), 9: 80

13. Liverpool to New York, "Ship's passenger manifest," *Mormon Migration*, https://mormonmigration.lib.byu.edu/mii/voyage/112, <accessed 22 February 2019>

14. Carter, *Our Pioneer Heritage*, 10: 111-112

15. John G. Holman for George Sims, "Correspondence," *The Deseret News*, 2 August 1865, 351, Utah Digital Newspapers, J. Willard Marriott Library, University of Utah, https://newspapers.lib.utah.edu/details?id=2598282, <accessed 22 February 2019>

16. Ibid

17. Ibid

18. Miner G. Atwood, Mormon Pioneer Overland Travel, "Miner G. Atwood Company (1865), https://history.lds.org/overlandtravel/companies/57/miner-g-atwood-company?lang=eng, <accessed 19 February 2019>

19. Historical Department journal history of the church,1896-2001; 1860-1869; 1865 July-December; Miner G. Atwood diary, 8 November 1865, Church History Library, https://catalog.churchofjesuschrist.org/assets/57a184a7-f690-4bf5-bba9-173e4439a1be/0/0, <accessed 22 February 2019>

20. Ibid

21. Ibid

22. Ibid

23. Ibid

24. A. W. D. [Albert Wesley Davis], "Adventures on the Plains," *Juvenile Instructor*, 15 December 1881, 278-279

25. *Our Pioneer Heritage*, 20 vol., 9: 51

26. Carter, *Our Pioneer Heritage*, 9: 67-70

27. Historical Department journal history of the church, 8 November 1865,

28. Carter, *Our Pioneer Heritage*, 9: 52

29. Albert Wesley Davis, [Autobiography],*Utah Genealogical and Historical Magazine*, Oct. 1926, 246

30. Carter, *Our Pioneer Heritage*, 9: 58

31. "Our Pioneers," *The Vernal Express*, Vernal, Utah, 9 June 1932, https://newspapers.lib.utah.edu/details?id=21417557, <accessed 25 February 2019>

32. Fredrickson, Lars, Biographical sketch of the Fredrickson family, in Mormon biographical sketches collection [ca. 1900-1975], reel 16, fd. 4, item 4, 2-3

33. Historical Department journal history of the church, 8 November 1865

34. Ibid

35. "Immigration," *The Deseret News*, 2 November 1865, https://newspapers.lib.utah.edu/details?id=2730797, <accessed 27 February 2019>

36. Manuscript histories of Church in United States, circa 1919-1971, Manuscript history of Wyoming, Nebraska,

37. Full Company List, Mormon Pioneer Overland Travel, "Chronological List," Henson Walker 1865

38. Manuscript histories of Church in United States, circa 1919-1971, Manuscript history of Wyoming, Nebraska
39. Immigration Lists, *The Deseret News*, 20 September 1865
40. Alston, Thomas [Autobiography], in Ray Lester Alston, comp. "Thomas Alston and Mary Ellen Holt Alston," [1975], 16-19 MS 270.1 A 464a, or Mormon Pioneer Overland Travel, https://history.churchofjesuschrist.org/overlandtravel/sources/6215/alston-thomas-autobiography-in-ray-lester-alston-comp-thomas-alston-and-mary-ellen-holt-alston-1975-16-19, <accessed 27 February 2019>
41. Ibid
42. Ibid
43. Richardson, Agnes Clementina Hefferan, Hefferan 1857-1941. Hefferan story, undated, Church History Library, MS 5815, pp. 12-15, Salt Lake City, Utah, or Mormon Pioneer Overland Travel, https://history.churchofjesuschrist.org/overlandtravel/sources/13854974450296125896-eng/richardson-agnes-clementina-hefferan-hefferan-story-12-15?firstName=William&surname=Hefferan, <accessed 27 February 2019>
44. Ibid
45. Ibid
46. William S. S. Willes Company (1865), Mormon Pioneer Overland Travel, https://history.lds.org/overlandtravel/companies/320/william-s-s-willes-company, <accessed 2 March 2019>
47. William Sidney Smith Willes Biography, Latter-day Saint Biographical Encyclopedia, volume 3,"Family Search," https://www.familysearch.org/photos/artifacts/1427163?p=20668900&returnLabel=William%20Sidney%20Smith%20Willes%20(KWJD, <accessed 2 March 2019>
48. Brigham Young, Office Files 1832-1878, (bulk 1844-1877); General Correspondence, Incoming, 1840-1877; General Letters, 1840-1877; Wh-Z, 1865; W.S. Willes letter; Church History Library, https://catalog.lds.org/assets?id=29e35922-c0a5-424c-b91a-0147d0ebd5a5&crate=0&index=0, <accessed 15 February 2019>
49. Thompson, Annie Maria Kershaw, "History of Annie Maria Kershaw Thompson" in Danny Jessop and Marla W. Jessop, comps. *Joseph Frederick Thompson Ancestry*, Mormon Pioneer Overland Travel, William S. S. Willes company 1865, https://history.churchofjesuschrist.org/overlandtravel/sources/11905/thompson-annie-maria-kershaw-history-of-annie-maria-kershaw-thompson-in-danny-jessop-and-marla-w-jessop-comps-joseph-frederick-thompson-ancestry-1996-38 , <accessed 2 March 2019>
50. Ibid
51. Carter, *Our Pioneer Heritage*, 10:111
52. Thompson, Annie Maria Kershaw, "History of Annie Maria Kershaw Thompson"
53. A Good Man Gone—A Deserving Family Destitute, *Semi-Weekly Telegraph*, 2 Nov. 1865, https://history.lds.org/overlandtravel/companies/320/william-s-s-willes-company, <accessed 2 March 2019>
54. The Immigration, *Semi-Weekly Telegraph*, 24 June 1865, Mormon Pioneer Overland Travel, https://history.churchofjesuschrist.org/overlandtravel/sources/9749/the-immigration-semi-weekly-telegraph-24-june-1865-3, <accessed 15 January 2019>
55. Help to the Immigration, *Semi-Weekly Telegraph*, 2 Nov. 1865, Mormon Pioneer Overland Travel, https://history.churchofjesuschrist.org/overlandtravel/sources/

9760/help-to-the-emigration-semi-weekly-telegraph-2-nov-1865-3, <accessed 17 January 2019>
56. The Immigration, *Deseret News*, 2 Nov. 1865, 28, Mormon Pioneer Overland Travel, https://history.churchofjesuschrist.org/overlandtravel/sources/9783/the-immigration-deseret-news-weekly-2-nov-1865-28, <accessed 12 January 2019>
57. Brigham Young Office files, 1832-1878 (bulk 1844-1877); Telegrams, 1861-1877; 1865; Thomas Taylor telegram; Church History Library, https://catalog.lds.org/assets?id=30967c98-11b5-46b2-8309-0f5856e72100&crate=0&index=0. <accessed 17 June 2019>
58. Brigham Young Office Files; Telegrams, Thomas Taylor telegram; https://catalog.lds.org/assets?id=0e5d581c-9408-4533-9e72-e75cd8be36b4&crate=0&index=0, <accessed 17 June 2019>
59. In, *Semi-Weekly Telegraph*, 16 Nov. 1865, 3, Mormon Pioneer Overland Travel, https://history.churchofjesuschrist.org/overlandtravel/sources/9769/in-semi-weekly-telegraph-16-nov-1865-3, <accessed 15 February 2019>
60. Immigration in, *Deseret News*, 23 Nov. 1865, 52, https://newspapers.lib.utah.edu/details?id=2730941, <accessed 22 February 2019>
61. Teams Returned, *Deseret News*, 16 Nov. 1865, 44, https://newspapers.lib.utah.edu/details?id=2730941, <accessed 22 February 2019>
62. Chipman's Arrival, *Semi-Weekly Telegraph*, 20 Nov. 1865, 2, Mormon Pioneer Overland Travel, https://history.churchofjesuschrist.org/overlandtravel/sources/9768/chipman-s-arrival-semi-weekly-telegraph-20-nov-1865-2. <accessed 23 February 2019>

## 8. Formation of the 1866 Down and Back Church Trains

1. Mormon Pioneer Overland Travel, "Alphabetical Company List," http://history.lds.org/overlandtravels/companynamelist , <accessed 23 March 2013>
2. Leonard J. Arrington, *Great Basin Kingdom: an Economic History of the Latter-day Saints, 1830-1890*, (Chicago: University of Illinois Press, 1958), 205
3. "Circular to Bishop Edward Hunter, and the Bishops throughout the territory," (Salt Lake City: 1861), 1, http://archive.org/details/circulartobishop00unse . <accessed 15 September 2012>
4. Susan Zollinger Beddes, *Life Histories of Some Ancestors of Bud David Zollinger*, (West Point, Utah: privately printed, 1994), 16. William Grant autobiography and diary, (archives, MS 1956; CHL, Salt Lake City Utah), 16.
5. "Circular to Bishop Edward Hunter, and the Bishops throughout the territory," 3-4
6. Ibid, 4
7. Ibid, 5
8. Perpetual Emigrating Fund Company Church trains accounts: Wards' accounts, 1861-1868, Account Book, 1866, 1868. Church History Library, https://catalog.lds.org/assets?id=0391933b-b37a-4c06-ba1b-67ca4cfdd0eb&crate=0&index=19, <accessed 1 November 2014>
9. Perpetual Emigrating Fund Company outfitting reports: Cache County outfit reports, 1866, Church History Library, https://catalog.lds.org/assets?id=bcab9456-856e-42cb-be14-d329d5b5bc37&crate=0&index=0, <accessed 15 April 2015>
10. Ibid
11. Perpetual Emigrating Fund Company Church trains accounts,1861-1868; ward

accounts, 1861-1868; Account book, 1866,1868; Church History Library, https://catalog.lds.org/assets?id=0391933b-b37a-4c06-ba1b-67ca4cfdd0eb&crate=0&index=21, <15 April 2015>
12. Perpetual Emigrating Fund Company outfitting reports, 1866; Outfit reports, 1866; Church History Library,, https://catalog.lds.org/assets?id=14d028e8-ffe5-4cb7-a19f-32095358b039&crate=0&index=2, <accessed 15 April 2015>
13. Ibid, Salt Lake City 7th ward report
14. Perpetual Emigrating Fund Company church train accounts, 1861-1868; Ward's accounts, 1861-1868; Account book, 1866,1868; Church History Library, https://catalog.lds.org/assets?id=0391933b-b37a-4c06-ba1b-67ca4cfdd0eb&crate=0&index=5, <accessed 3 May 2015>
15. Perpetual Emigrating Fund Company outfitting reports, 1866; Outfit reports, 1866; Church History Library, https://catalog.lds.org/assets?id=606fdf2f-7b4a-4e28-9265-ed27cf32cd6b&crate=0&index=11 , <accessed 3 May 2015>
16. Perpetual Emigrating Fund Company church trains accounts, 1861-1868; Wards' accounts, 1861-1868; Account book, 1866,1868; Church History Library, https://catalog.lds.org/assets?id=0391933b-b37a-4c06-ba1b-67ca4cfdd0eb&crate=0&index=11, <accessed 3 May 2015>
17. Ibid, Captain Thompson's Church Train
18. Perpetual Emigrating Fund Company Outfitting reports, Nephi ward, https://catalog.lds.org/assets?id=87ee198d-ee46-45ec-99f4-5bc8628b7520&crate=0&index=4   , <accessed 3 May 2015>
19. Ibid, St. George ward, https://catalog.lds.org/assets?id=87ee198d-ee46-45ec-99f4-5bc8628b7520&crate=0&index=30, <accessed 3 May 2015>
20. Perpetual Emigrating Fund church train accounts, wards' account book, Church History Library , Joseph Rawlins, https://catalog.lds.org/assets?id=0391933b-b37a-4c06-ba1b-67ca4cfdd0eb&crate=0&index=3, <accessed 3 May 2015>
21. Perpetual Emigrating Fund Company outfitting reports: Salt Lake City, 19th ward, https://catalog.lds.org/assets?id=26878191-6240-4f30-8ce2-06b0d60c954c&crate=0&index=22, <accessed 4 May 2015>
22. Perpetual Emigrating Fund Company outfitting reports, ward account book, Church History Library, Horton Haight, https://catalog.lds.org/assets?id=0391933b-b37a-4c06-ba1b-67ca4cfdd0eb&crate=0&index=15 , <accessed 3 May 2015>
23. Perpetual Emigrating Fund Company outfitting reports: Captain Horton D. Haight, https://catalog.lds.org/assets?id=63fb1aba-6158-48cb-90f2-cc0db8d40338&crate=0&index=5, <accessed 6 May 2015>
24. Perpetual Emigrating Fund church train accounts, wards' account book, 1866, 1868, Church History Library, Peter Nebeker, https://catalog.lds.org/assets?id=0391933b-b37a-4c06-ba1b-67ca4cfdd0eb&crate=0&index=9, <accessed 3 May 2015>
25. Ibid,     https://catalog.lds.org/assets?id=0b0ffe7f-e5b4-414c-b0e3-96e57f06cb7d&crate=0&index=2, <accessed 6 May 2015>
26. Ibid, Andrew Scott, https://catalog.lds.org/assets?id=0391933b-b37a-4c06-ba1b-67ca4cfdd0eb&crate=0&index=7, <accessed 3 May 2015>
27. Ibid, Captain A. H. Scott, https://catalog.lds.org/assets?id=a165f3f9-21fc-42fd-8a85-b6a9abf4b4f2&crate=0&index=19, <accessed 6 May 2015>
28. Ibid, Abner Lowry, https://catalog.lds.org/assets?id=0391933b-b37a-4c06-ba1b-67ca4cfdd0eb&crate=0&index=17, <accessed 3 May 2015>

29. Ibid, Abner Lowry, https://catalog.lds.org/assets?id=704c0b74-289e-4c7d-9e9f-f30506938850&crate=0&index=19, <accessed 7 May 2015>
30. Ibid, Captain Abner Lowry https://catalog.lds.org/assets?id=113df13e-01c6-4df6-93f9-2e176579addd&crate=0&index=13, <accessed 7 May 2015>

## 9. The Journey East

1. Andrew Jenson, "Manuscript History of Wyoming, Nebraska [1860-1870]," (Archives MS d 4029 Bx 3, fd 2, CHL, Salt Lake City, Utah), unpaginated
2. Ibid.
3. Charles P. Anderson, *Journal of Charles P. Anderson*, (Cleveland: Gilbert Publishing Company, 1975), 2 https://dcms.lds.org/delivery/DeliveryManagerServlet?dps_pid=IE935133&from=fhd , <accessed 15 august 2012>
4. Ibid
5. Brigham Young office files,1832-1878 (bulk 1844-1877); Telegrams, 1861-1877; B-Haight, 1866; Horton D. Haight telegram, Church History Library, https://catalog.lds.org/assets?id=92ee2ce0-fbae-4ab9-94a3-0a70efb12e6c&crate=0&index=0, <accessed 18 June 2019>
6. Brigham Young office files, 1832-1878 (bulk 1844-1877); Telegrams, Abner Lowry telegram, https://catalog.lds.org/assets?id=826e285f-45cc-48d0-ba43-017f6a16f29e&crate=0&index=0, <accessed 18 June 2019>
7. Moses Thatcher, "Thatcher, Moses, vol. 1, British Isles," (Vault MSS 248, 1866), 3, electronic reproduction, https://contentdm.lib.byu.edu/digital/collection/MMD/id/62352/rec/5, <accessed 23 March 2013>
8. Ibid, 5-6
9. Ibid, 9
10. Ibid, 10
11. Ibid, 11
12. Ibid, 14
13. Ibid, 18
14. Ibid, 19
15. Ibid, 20
16. Ibid, 21
17. Returns from U.S. Military Posts, 1800-1916, National Archives Microfilm Publications, Microfilm group 617, Roll 565, U.S. National Archives, Washington D.C.
18. J. W. Pickett, "Autobiography of J. W. Pickett, (Joel E. Ricks collection of biographies and histories, special collections archives, MSS 46 #87, Merrill-Cazier Library, Utah State University), unpaginated
19. Ibid
20. Ibid

## 10. Leaving the Homeland Behind

1. "Ann Gregory Marriott's Book of Remembrance," (Archives MS, 17064; Church History Library, LDS Church, 15 East North Temple, Salt Lake City, Utah), 1; as transcribed by Mrs. George Glade (Lorna) Shaw.

2. "British Mission Emigration Register," Book #1048, p 210, *Mormon Migration*, https://mormonmigration.lib.byu.edu/mii/passenger/25978?sweden=on&europe=on&keywords=1866&netherlands=on&scandinavia=on&mii=on, <accessed 4 August 2012>
3. "Marriott's Book of Remembrance,"1
4. Ibid
5. Kenneth L. Holmes, editor, *Covered wagon women: diaries & letters from the western trails, 1840-1890/* Vol. 9, 1864-1868, Church History Library, Salt Lake City Utah, 978 C873 v.9 1990. The story of Caroline Hopkins Clark is told under the title, "Liverpool to Utah in 1866 by sailing ship and prairie schooner
6. John Lunn Papers, "Circular and passenger contract," (Archives, MS9281 2; CHL, Salt Lake City, Utah),unpaginated
7. Emigration records, Scandinavian Mission (Denmark, Norway, Sweden) 1852-1920; FHL INTL Film [472897]
8. Andrew Jenson , *History of the Scandinavian Mission*, (Salt Lake City: Deseret News Press, 1927), 191
9. Hansen, Caroline Pederson [Reminiscences], *Our Pioneer Heritage*, compiled by Kate B. Carter, vol. 12 (Salt Lake City: Daughters of Utah Pioneers, 1969), 67
10. Conway B. Sonne, *Saints on the Seas; A Maritime History of Mormon Migration: 1830-1890*, (Salt Lake City: University of Utah Press, 1983), 153
11. Ibid
12. Ibid, 87
13. Advantages of Settling in Utah, *The Millennial Star*, 28:234-235, (April 14, 1866) https://contentdm.lib.byu.edu/digital/collection/MStar/id/11679, <accessed 3 Sep 2012>
14. Richard F. Burton, *The City of the Saints*, (London: Longman, Green, Longman and Roberts, 1862) 279, <accessed 18 September 2012>
15. "Marriott's Book of Remembrance," 3
16. Ibid, 3 – 9
17. Holmes, editor, *Covered wagon women: diaries & letters from the western trails*
18. "John Lunn Diary," (Archives MS 9281 1; CHL, Salt Lake City, Utah), 13 – 14
19. Ibid, 10
20. William Driver, "London to Salt Lake City in 1867 [(sic)]: The Diary of William Driver," Reprinted from New Mexico Historical Review (January 1942), 40
21. Ibid, 42
22. Ibid
23. John Nicholson, "Saved by Providence," *Juvenile Instructor* 16:2 (15 January 1881), 19
24. Andrew Jenson , *Autobiography of Andrew Jenson* , (Salt Lake City: Deseret News Press, 1938), 16
25. Ibid, 17
26. Charles Peter Warnick, [Autobiography], *Warnick Family History*, vol. 1, (M270.1W285w, CHL, Salt Lake City, Utah),233
27. Olof Jenson, "Autobiographical Sketch," (Archives MS, 11373, CHL, Salt Lake City, Utah), 2
28. Brent D. Corcoran, "My Father's Business: Thomas Taylor and Mormon Frontier Economic Enterprise," *Dialogue: A Journal of Mormon Thought*, Vol. 28, No. 1, (Spring, 1995), 106 www.dialoguejournal.com/wp-content/uploads/sbi/articles/Dialogue_V28N01_117.pdf , <accessed 8 October 2012>

29. Brigham Young, "Letter to Bishop David Evans," (Archives MS 3564 1; CHL, Salt Lake City, Utah), unpaginated
30. Fred E. Woods, "Mormon Transmigration through Quincy, Illinois, and Hannibal, Missouri," Mormon Historical Studies 2, (2001): 141 FN#10
31. "Marriott's Book of Remembrance," 14
32. William Grant, "Autobiography and diary," (Archives MS 1956, CHL, Salt Lake City, Utah), 15
33. Driver, "London to Salt Lake City in 1867 [(sic)]," 48
34. Brian Jenkins, *The Fenian Problem: Insurgency and Terrorism in a Liberal State, 1858-1874,"* (Montreal: McGill-Queen's University Press, 2008), 61-62
35. Jenson, "Autobiographical Sketch," 2
36. Warnick, [Autobiography], *Warnick Family History, vol. 1,* 233
37. Jenson , *Autobiography of Andrew Jenson* , 19
38. Jenson , *History of the Scandinavian Mission,* 191
39. Aurelia Clemons, extracted and translated, *Emigration from the Scandinavian Mission,* Family History Library, Salt Lake City, Utah, 948 W2ca, V. 1, unpaginated (photo copy of book pages in possession of the author)
40. Ibid
41. "Mormon Migration," https://mormonmigration.lib.byu.edu/search/?sweden=on&europe=on&keywords=1866&netherlands=on&scandinavia=on&mii=on, <accessed 16 August 2012> These conclusions were reached by accessing all the passenger manifests relating to this migration, which detailed occupations of those immigrating to the Utah Territory in 1866
42. Ibid
43. William Mulder, *The Mormon Migration from Scandinavia,* (Minneapolis: University of Minnesota Press, 1957), 106-107
44. Merrill N. Warnick, *Warnick Family History, Vol. 1,* (Provo: J. Grant Stevenson, 1967), 233     http://mormonmigration.lib.byu.edu/Search/showDetails/db:MM_MII/t:account/id:207/keywords:Warnick+%2B+Cavour , <accessed 5 October 2012>
45. Mulder, *The Mormon Migration from Scandinavia,* 104
46. Orson Pratt, "War," *Millennial Star 28* (June 30, 1866): 409 https://contentdm.lib.byu.edu/digital/collection/MStar/id/11821, <accessed 3 September 2012>
47. Ibid, 411
48. Orson Pratt, "Universality of Latter-Day Wars, *Millennial Star 28* (August 11, 1866): 497 http://contentdm.lib.byu.edu/cdm/compoundobject/collection/MStar/id/12150/rec/28, <accessed 12 September 2012>
49. Jenson, *Autobiography of Andrew Jenson,* Ibid, 12
50. Warnick, [Autobiography], *Warnick Family History, vol. 1,* 233-335
51. William Grant, "Autobiography and diary, 11
52. Gary James Bergera, editor, *The Autobiography of B.H. Roberts,* (Salt Lake City: Signature Books, 1990), 21
53. "Marriott's Book of Remembrance," 13
54. Zachary R. Jones, "War and Confusion in Babylon: Mormon Reaction to German Unification, 1864-80," *The Journal of Mormon History,* (Fall, 2011): 128

## 11. The Thousand Mile trek to the Great Basin Begins

1. "Ann Gregory Marriott's Book of Remembrance," (Archives MS, 17064; Church History Library, LDS Church, 15 East North Temple, Salt Lake City, Utah), 18; as transcribed by Mrs. George Glade (Lorna) Shaw
2. Ibid
3. Susan Zollinger Beddes, *Life Histories of Some Ancestors of Bud David Zollinger*, (West Point, Utah: privately printed, 1994) 17
4. Charles Roscoe Savage, "A Photographic Tour of nearly 9000 miles," (Archives, 973 S263p, pamphlet; Church History Library, LDS Church, 15 East North Temple, Salt Lake City, Utah), 314
5. Ibid, 313
6. John E. Carter, "The Platte River Road in 1866: Charles Savage's Visual Narrative," *Nebraska History Magazine*, Vol. 89, No. 3, Fall 2008, 140
7. Ibid, 138
8. Savage, "A Photographic Tour of nearly 9000 miles," 315
9. William Grant, "Autobiography and diary," (Archives MS 1956, CHL, Salt Lake City, Utah), 16-17
10. Ibid, 17
11. Mabel Turpin, "The Emigration of Richard Litson," (Archives, M274.41 T957e, pamphlet, CHL, Salt Lake City, Utah), unpaginated
12. Ibid
13. Gary James Bergera, editor, *The Autobiography of B. H. Roberts*, (Salt Lake City: Signature Books, 1990), 25
14. Ibid
15. Kenneth L. Holmes, editor, *Covered wagon women: diaries & letters from the western trails, 1840-1890/* Vol. 9, 1864-1868, Church History Library, Salt Lake City Utah, 978 C873 v.9 1990. The story of Caroline Hopkins Clark is told under the title, "Liverpool to Utah in 1866 by sailing ship and prairie schooner"
16. William H. Chipman, "William H. Chipman notebook," (Archives, MS 915, CHL, Salt Lake City, Utah), unpaginated
17. Ibid, unpaginated
18. Ibid, unpaginated
19. Ibid, unpaginated
20. Charles Denny, "Charles Denny reminiscences and diary," (Archives, MS 1820, CHL, Salt Lake City, Utah), 15
21. Ibid, 16
22. Ibid, 23
23. Ibid, 17
24. Justin Chauncey Wixsom, "Justin C. Wixom diaries," (Archives, MS 1559 3-4, CHL, Salt Lake City, Utah) unpaginated
25. Mary Crystal Wagstaff, "Mary C. Wagstaff autobiographical sketch," (Archives, MS 24103, CHL, Salt Lake City, Utah), 2
26. Olof Jenson, "Olof Jenson family papers," (Archives, MS11373, CHL, Salt Lake City, Utah), III
27. Elvera Campbell Green, *Tartan, Sage and History: The Story of Robert William Rowe*

226 | Notes

  Campbell and Sarah Newton, (Salt Lake City, Utah: Robert Rowe Campbell Family Organization, c1981), 53
28. Ibid
29. Eliza Toward Harrison James Autobiography. Mormon Pioneer Overland Travel, https://history.churchofjesuschrist.org/overlandtravel/sources/15560302519310668264-eng/james-eliza-toward-harrison-autobiography?firstName=Eliza%20Toward&surname=Harrison, <3 April 2012>
30. Andrew Jenson , *Autobiography of Andrew Jenson* , (Salt Lake City: Deseret News Press, 1938), 21
31. Ibid, 22
32. Kate B. Carter, compiler, "They Came in 1866," *Our Pioneer Heritage*, 20 Volumes, Daughters of the Utah Pioneers, 1966, 10: 10
33. John C. Dowdle, "John C. Dowdle autobiography and diaries, circa 1884-1908," (Archives, MS 1814, Church History Library, Salt Lake City, Utah), 18. CHL https://catalog.churchofjesuschrist.org/assets?id=13476b1c-83b1-4ca7-bba6-a05a10e9a1f2&crate=1&index=119, <accessed 26 September 2019>
34. Ibid
35. Carter, *Our Pioneer Heritage*, 7: 311

## 12. Travels Across Nebraska, Wyoming and on to Zion

1. Robert Gruber, Maizie Johnson, Willna Uebrick-Pacheli, Evelyn Wade, Linda Wehrmann, compilers, "Preliminary Inventory of the Records of United States Army Continental Commands, 1821-1920," Fort Kearny, Special Orders, 07/00/1865-01/00/1870, 2 volumes, arranged by year and thereafter numerically, National Archives, Washington, D.C.
2. Kenneth L. Holmes, editor, *Covered wagon women: diaries & letters from the western trails, 1840-1890/* Vol. 9, 1864-1868, Church History Library, Salt Lake City Utah, 978 C873 v.9 1990. The story of Caroline Hopkins Clark is told under the title, "Liverpool to Utah in 1866 by sailing ship and prairie schooner"
3. William Grant, "Autobiography and diary," (Archives MS 1956, CHL, Salt Lake City, Utah),17
4. "Ann Gregory Marriott's Book of Remembrance," (Archives MS, 17064; Church History Library, LDS Church, 15 East North Temple, Salt Lake City, Utah), 18; as transcribed by Mrs. George Glade (Lorna) Shaw , 22
5. Susan Zollinger Beddes, *Life Histories of Some Ancestors of Bud David Zollinger*, (West Point, Utah: privately printed, 1994), 16. William Grant autobiography and diary, (archives, MS 1956; CHL, Salt Lake City Utah), 17
6. Holmes, editor, *Covered wagon women: diaries & letters from the western trails, 1840-1890/* Vol. 9
7. Ibid
8. Susan Zollinger Beddes, *Life Histories of Some Ancestors of Bud David Zollinger*, 17
9. William Grant, "Autobiography and diary," 18
10. Gary James Bergera, editor, *The Autobiography of B. H. Roberts*, (Salt Lake City: Signature Books, 1990), 30
11. Ibid, 31
12. Charles Denny, "Charles Denny reminiscences and diary," (Archives, MS 1820, CHL,

Salt Lake City, Utah),21
13. Andrew Jenson , *Autobiography of Andrew Jenson* , (Salt Lake City: Deseret News Press, 1938), 24
14. Ibid
15. William Driver, "London to Salt Lake City in 1867 [(sic)]: The Diary of William Driver," Reprinted from New Mexico Historical Review (January 1942), 61 http://files.lib.byu.edu/mormonmigration/articles/LondonToSaltLakeCityIn1867.pdf, <accessed 16 October 2012>
16. Charles Roscoe Savage, "A Photographic Tour of nearly 9000 miles," (Archives, 973 S263p, pamphlet; Church History Library, LDS Church, 15 East North Temple, Salt Lake City, Utah),315
17. Gary James Bergera, *The Autobiography of B. H. Roberts*, (Salt Lake City: Signature Books, 1990), 39
18. Niels Rasmussen, Mormon Pioneer Overland Travel, 1847-1868," *Latter-day Saint Biographical Encyclopedia,* 1971, https://history.churchofjesuschrist.org/overlandtravel/sources/4722/rasmussen-niels-autobiographical-sketch-in-andrew-jenson-comp-latter-day-saint-biographical-encyclopedia-1971-1-597,<accessed 12 March 2012>
19. Joel Hinckley Bowen, *Pioneer Rescues of Arza Erastus Hinckley*, unpaginated, http://www.kendallglad.com/KendallGlad/Genealogy/Arza/Arza%20Erastus%20Hinckley%20-%20Pioneer%20Rescues%20-%20by%20Joel%20Hinckley%20Bowen.pdf, <accessed 20 June 2019>
20. Ibid
21. "John Jenkins Autobiographical sketch, 1933," 3-5, Pioneer Overland Travel, https://history.churchofjesuschrist.org/overlandtravel/sources/15092015018899398157-eng/jenkins-john-autobiographical-sketch-1933-3-5?firstName=John&surname=Jenkins, <accessed 20 January 2013>
22. "Ann Gregory Marriott's Book of Remembrance," 20
23. Andrew Jenson , *Autobiography of Andrew Jenson* , 25
24. Robert Aveson, "Ox-Team Pioneer Recalls Joys of Long Trek," https://history.churchofjesuschrist.org/overlandtravel/sources/70799531152633631610-eng/aveson-robert-ox-team-pioneer-recalls-joys-of-long-trek-in-journal-history-of-the-church-of-jesus-christ-of-latter-day-saints-22-july-1922?firstName=Robert&surname=Aveson, <accessed 20 January 2013>
25. Denny, "Charles Denny reminiscences and diary," 24
26. Grant, "Autobiography and diary," 19

## 13. The Cholera Train from Sanpete County

1. Johanna Kristena Jensen Anderson, 1853-1940, "Autobiography," (Archives MS 18603, Church History Library, Salt Lake City, Utah, 1930), unpaginated
2. Andrew Jenson, *History of the Scandinavian Mission*, (Salt Lake City: Deseret News Press, 1927), 194
3. Patricia Rushton, "Cholera and Its Impact on Nineteenth-Century Mormon Migration," BYU Studies Quarterly, Vol. 44, No. 2, (2005), 127-128
4. Ibid, 129
5. Magnus Cederstrom, "Diary of Magnus Cederstrom," Mormon Migration, http://

mormonmigration.lib.byu.edu/Search/showDetails/db:MM_MII/t:account/id:205/keywords:Cavour, <accessed 21 June 2014>
6. Ibid
7. Charles P. Anderson, *Journal of Charles P. Anderson*, (Cleveland: Gilbert Publishing Company, 1975), 2 https://dcms.lds.org/delivery/DeliveryManagerServlet?dps_pid=IE935133&from=fhd , <accessed 15 august 2012>
8. W. H. Lever, *History of Sanpete and Emery Counties, Utah*, (Salt Lake City: Tribune Job Printing Company, 1898), 421-422
9. Kate B. Carter, compiler, *Our Pioneer Heritage*, 20 Volumes (Salt Lake City: Daughters of Utah Pioneers, 1964) 7: 311
10. Charles P. Anderson, *Journal of Charles P. Anderson*, 2
11. Merrill Newell Warnick, *Warnick Family History*, (Provo: J. Grant Stevenson, 1967), 31
12. Carter, compiler, *Our Pioneer Heritage*, 7: 311
13. Andrew Jenson , "Latter-day Saint biographical encyclopedia: a compilation of biographical sketches of prominent men and women in The Church of Jesus Christ of Latter-day Saints," 4 volumes, (Salt Lake City: Western Epics, 1971) 1: 597
14. Melvin L. Bashore, "1866 Death List," compiled from various primary and secondary sources, this report lists the name, gender, date of death, source, and familial relationship to others on the wagon trains. In possession of Erick Wadsworth, 2059 Sandcrest Loop, Nampa, Idaho, 83686, 14 August 2013
15. Perpetual Emigrating Fund Company church trains accounts: Captains' accounts, 1862-1868, Captain Abner Lowry, accounts, 1866. Church History Library, The Church of Jesus Christ of Latter-day Saints, Salt Lake City, Utah
16. Mel Bashore, H. Dennis Tolley, "Mortality on the Mormon Trail, 1847-1868," BYU Studies Quarterly, Vol. 53: No. 4 (2014), 117-121
17. Oregon-California Trail Association, "Life and Death on the Oregon Trail," https://www.octa-trails.org/articles/life-and-death-on-the-oregon-trail/, <accessed 20 June 2019>
18. Melvin L. Bashore, "1866 Death List,"
19. Brigham Young office files, 1832-1878 (bulk 1844-1877); Telegrams, 1861-1877; L-R, 1866; Abner Lowry telegram; Church History Library, https://catalog.lds.org/assets?id=1ac88e10-231a-4c92-ae9d-7773ee217751&crate=0&index=0, <accessed 20 June>
20. Melvin L. Bashore, "1866 Death List,"
21. Ibid.
22. Paul and Helen Henderson, *Maps of Manifest Destiny*, (Gering: Legacy of the Plains Museum, 2004), 103
23. Brigham Young office files, 1832-1878 (bulk 1844-1877);Telegrams, 1861-1877, L-R, 1866; Abner Lowry telegram; Church History Library, https://catalog.lds.org/assets?id=018fc150-4a5c-4aca-86d2-7883a4b49f3c&crate=0&index=0, <accessed 21 June 2019>
24. Ibid
25. Journal History of the Church: 1860-1869. 19 August 1866, Church History Library, The Church of Jesus Christ of Latter-day Saints, Salt Lake City, Utah
26. William Driver, "London to Salt Lake City in 1867 [(sic)]: The Diary of William Driver," Reprinted from New Mexico Historical Review (January 1942), 57
27. William Henry Jackson, *Time Exposure, The Autobiography of William Henry Jackson*, (New York: G.P. Putnam's Sons, 1940), 126

28. Journal History of the Church: 1860-1869. 27 September 1866, Church History Library, The Church of Jesus Christ of Latter-day Saints, Salt Lake City, Utah
29. Ibid
30. Ibid, 30 September 1866
31. Ibid, 3 October 1866
32. Ibid, 11 October 1866
33. William Henry Jackson, *Time Exposure*, 135
34. Ibid, 136
35. Charles P. Anderson, *Journal of Charles P. Anderson*, 2
36. Journal History of the Church: 1860-1869. 22 October 1866
37. Ibid, 10 February 1866
38. Ibid, 9 March 1866
39. Ibid, 8 April 1866

## 14. Arza Hinckley and the Rescue Train of 1866

1. Joel Hinckley Bowen, "Arza Erastus Hinckley, 1826-1901" p1-2 http://www.kendall-glad.com/KendallGlad/Genealogy/Arza/Arza%20Erastus%20Hinckley%20-%201826%20-%201901%20by%20Joel%20Hinckley%20Bowen%20[Grandson].pdf , <accessed 5 October 2014>
2. Ibid, 2-5
3. Ibid, 5
4. Michael Hinckley, transcriber, "Biography of Arza Erastus Hinckley," p. 3, https://familysearch.org/patron/v2/TH-301-45405-135-69/dist.pdf?ctx=ArtCtxPublic, <accessed 5 October 2015>
5. Joel Hinckley Bowen, "Arza Erastus Hinckley, 1826-1901," p. 6
6. Michael Hinckley, transcriber, "Biography of Arza Erastus Hinckley," 3
7. Vida Adams, Blondel C. Porter, transcribers, "Diary of Arza Erastus Hinckley," 2, http://www.kendallglad.com/KendallGlad/Genealogy/Arza/Arza%20Erastus%20Hinckley%20-%20LDS%20historians%20library%20file%20-%20%20titled%20DIARY%20OF%20ARZA%20ERASTUS%20HINCKLEY.pdf , <accessed 6 October 2015>
8. Ibid, 1-2
9. Ibid
10. Joel Hinckley Bowen, "Arza Erastus Hinckley, 1826-1901," p. 9
11. Brigham Young office files: Telegrams, 1861-1877, Hi-Holladay, 1866. Church History Library, The Church of Jesus Christ of Latter-day Saints, Salt Lake City, Utah, https://catalog.lds.org/assets?id=5364266c-e18b-4e56-96e3-47c53e72f5e4&crate=0&index=0 , <accessed 23 May 2014>
12. Brigham Young office files: Telegrams, https://catalog.lds.org/assets?id=0148f561-ad27-44b3-95fb-e4d8b1d0b90f&crate=0&index=0, <accessed 21 June 2019>
13. Ibid, https://catalog.lds.org/assets?id=2c502e98-6df9-4496-9bd9-b1ae036a39c5&crate=0&index=0, <accessed 21 June 2019>
14. Ibid, https://catalog.lds.org/assets?id=6fe6a1b2-b5e9-49c1-ab5f-abc7c40e1f44&crate=0&index=0, <accessed 21 June 2019>
15. Ibid, https://catalog.lds.org/assets?id=6fe6a1b2-b5e9-49c1-ab5f-abc7c40e1f44&crate=0&index=0, <accessed 21 June 2019>

16. Ibid, https://catalog.lds.org/assets?id=f6dc2225-afb5-4705-8247-e57b168fef39&crate=0&index=0, <accessed 21 June 2019>
17. Ibid, https://catalog.lds.org/assets?id=5a4ccf7d-1019-498a-9576-d7b72ddf2de3&crate=0&index=0, <accessed 21 June 2019>
18. Ibid, https://catalog.lds.org/assets?id=dbfa7f3c-ea3e-4da3-b955-5cc9b8d63733&crate=0&index=0, <accessed 21 June 2019>
19. "Got Back," *Deseret New [Weekly]*, 10 Oct. 1866, p. 5, https://newspapers.lib.utah.edu/details?id=2598925, <accessed 21 June 2019>
20. Perpetual Emigrating Church-Team accounts: Freight manifests, 1861-1868, Captain Arza Hinckley (relief train) account, 1866. Church History Library , The Church of Jesus Christ of Latter-day Saints, Salt Lake City, Utah, https://catalog.lds.org/assets?id=4770d621-c1fa-4818-b62a-3841eafba2f6&crate=0&index=4 , <accessed 5 April 2014>
21. Ibid
22. Perpetual Emigrating Church-Team accounts: Captain's accounts, 1862-1868, Captain Arza Hinckley (relief train) account, 1866, https://catalog.lds.org/assets?id=b0468533-3c61-4684-aca0-fbc00afb6b08&crate=0&index=0, <accessed 21 June 2019>
23. Journal History of the Church: 1860-1869, 1866 July-December. October 22, 1866, Church History Library, The Church of Jesus Christ of Latter-day Saints, Salt Lake City, Utah.
24. (1866) Acts, Resolutions and Memorials, Passed at the Seventh Annual Sessions of the Legislative Assembly of the Territory of Utah, 1866, p. 223, J. Willard Marriott Library, The University of Utah, Salt Lake City, Utah, http://content.lib.utah.edu/cdm/compoundobject/collection/uthisstat/id/706, <accessed 12 May 2014>
25. Ibid
26. Perpetual Emigrating church-train accounts, Captain's accounts, 1862-1868, Captains' promissory notes, 1866, Church History Library, https://catalog.lds.org/assets?id=767880ef-36fc-4591-985f-54bb8f69770c&crate=0&index=0, <accessed 21 June 2019>
27. Ibid
28. Vida Adams, Blondel C. Porter, transcribers, "Diary of Arza Erastus Hinckley," p. 2
29. Joel Hinckley Bowen, "Arza Hinckley" http://www.kendallglad.com/KendallGlad/Genealogy/Arza/Arza%20Erastus%20Hinckley%20-%20Pioneer%20Rescues%20-%20by%20Joel%20Hinckley%20Bowen.pdf, <accessed 5 October 2014>

## 15. Wrapping Up

1. Mormon Pioneer Overland Travel, "Brigham Young Vanguard Company "(1847), https://history.churchofjesuschrist.org/overlandtravel/companies/1/brigham-young-vanguard-company, <accessed 21 June 2019>
2. Mormon Pioneer Overland Travel, "Chronological Company List," Samuel White Company, https://history.churchofjesuschrist.org/overlandtravel/companies , <accessed 10 March 2013>
3. Leo John Turpin, "The Immigration of Richard Litson," (Archives, M273.41T957e, no place, no publisher, no date), unpaginated
4. Melvin L. Bashore, "1866 Death List," compiled from various primary and secondary

sources, this report lists the name, gender, date of death, source, and familial relationship to others on the wagon trains. In possession of Erick Wadsworth, 2059 Sandcrest Loop, Nampa, Idaho, 83686, 14 August 2013

5. Mormon Pioneer Overland Travel, "Brigham Young Vanguard Company" http://history.lds.org/overlandtravels/companyPioneers?lang=eng&companyId=1, <accessed 24 December 2013>
6. Edward Tullidge, "Life of Brigham Young: Or, Utah and her founders," (New York, 1877) quote located in Supplement under Biographical sketches, p. 100
7. Ibid
8. B. H. Roberts, "A Comprehensive History of the Church of Jesus Christ of Latter-day Saints," 6 volumes, (Provo, Utah: Brigham Young University, 1965) 5:101
9. Arrived from the Plains, *Deseret News*, 25 Sep. 1861, 172 <accessed 4 March 2019>
10. Edward Tullidge, "Life of Brigham Young: Or, Utah and her founders," (New York: 1877),105
11. An Account of a Mormon Family's Conversion to the Religion of the Latter Day Saints and of Their Trip From Denmark to Utah, Part I, 717, Brigham Young University Articles, http://files.lib.byu.edu/mormonmigration/articles/AnAccountOfAMormonFamiliysConversion_part1+2.pdf, <accessed 20 October 2018>
   768-771
12. Ibid, 768-776
13. Ibid, 778-779
14. Edith Matteson and Jean Matteson, "Mormon Influence on Scandinavian Settlement in Nebraska, http://www.xmission.com/~nelsonb/nebraska.htm, <accessed 5 April 2011>
15. McBride, Heber Robert, Autobiography [ca. 1868], 28 – 46, Mormon Pioneer Overland Travel, locate Heber Robert McBride's story under "Edward Martin Company (1856) https://history.lds.org/overlandtravel/pioneers/19168/heber-robert-mc-bride, <accessed 2 March 2019.
16. McBride, Heber Robert 1843-1925,Heber Robert McBride autobiography, 12, https://catalog.lds.org/assets?id=b544d863-2cef-4a7a-9bce-d6764369ea35&crate=0&index=38, <accessed 21 June 2019>
17. Heber Robert McBride's Letter to His Daughter, Elizabeth Jane McBride Ririe, 1923, Family Search, https://www.familysearch.org/photos/artifacts/45194856?p=20617858&returnLabel=Heber%20Robert%20McBride%20(KWCJ-W21)&returnUrl=https%3A%2F%2Fwww.familysearch.org%2Ftree%2Fperson%2Fmemories%2FKWCJ-W21, <accessed 2 March 2019>
18. McBride, Heber Robert, Autobiography, 36-44,
19. John E. Carter, "Photographing Across the Plains: Charles R. Savage in 1866," *Nebraska History Magazine*, Vol. 71, No. 2, summer 1990, 60
20. Ibid, 61
21. Ibid
22. Ibid, 63
23. Books by B. H. Roberts, (sorted by popularity), https://www.gutenberg.org/ebooks/author/37629, <accessed 21 June 2019>
24. R. Douglas Brackenridge, *Journal of Mormon History*, Vol. 39, No. 1, (winter 2013), 145
25. Louis Reinwand, "Andrew Jenson , Latter-day Saint Historian," *Brigham Young University Studies*, Vol. 14:1, 4, file:///C:/Users/Wadsworth/Down-

loads/14.1reinwandandrew-25b70f1f-c775-4d0e-bb4f-b33d0d0c3f4b%20(5).pdf <accessed 12 October 2012>
26. Ibid, 11
27. Ibid, 13
28. Robert Aveson, "Leaving Home," Sedgwick Research Site, unpaginated, http://www.sedgwickresearch.com/sedgwick/leavinghome.htm <accessed 3 July 2015>
29. Ibid
30. Ibid
31. Ibid
32. Ibid
33. William Hartley, Glenn Rawson, Dennis Lyman, and Bryant Bush, editors, *History of the Saints*, (American Fork: Covenant Communications, Inc., 2012), 92

# BIBLIOGRAPHY

**Primary Sources**

1850 U. S. Census. Fremont, Iowa. Jacob Dawson household. Roll: M432_184, Page: 149A, Image: 41. 19 October 2012. https://www.ancestry.com/search/collections/1850usfed cenancestry/

1860 U. S. Census. Wyoming, Otoe, Nebraska Territory. Jacob Dawson household. Roll: Denny, Charles. "Charles Denny reminiscences and diary." MS1820. Church History Library.

1865 Nebraska Census. Lancaster County, Lancaster Township. 8. Nebraska Historical Society. Microfilm RG207. 14 June 2012. https://www.ancestry.com/search/collections/nestate census/

*Acts, Resolutions and Memorials, Passed at the Seventh Annual Sessions of the Legislative Assembly of the Territory of Utah, 1866.* J. Willard Marriott Library. 12 May 2014. http://content.lib.utah.edu/cdm/compoundobject/collection/uthisstat/id/706

Anderson, Johanna Kristena Jensen. "Johanna K. Jensen Anderson autobiography, circa 1930." MS 18603. Church History Library.

Barney, Lewis. "Lewis Barney autobiography and diary." MS 526. Church History Library. 6 April 2013. https://catalog.churchofjesuschrist.org/assets?id=48cfd200-f722-4aa4-93e4-90635b964d8f&crate=0&index=0

Bliss, Orley Dwight. "Orley Dwight Bliss Autobiography and diary." MSS 615, Folder 3. L. Tom Perry Special Collections. Harold B. Lee Library.

Book A Record of Deeds for Otoe County, N. T. April 5, 1855. Otoe County Courthouse, Division of Deeds. Nebraska City, Nebraska.

"Book of Record for the City of Wyoming." RG 515, SG 2, SI Research, RG312. Manuscript Division. Nebraska State Historical Society.

Brigham Young Office. Brigham Young office files 1832-1878 (bulk 1844-1877). Letterbooks, 1844-1877; Letterbook, v.7, 1860 April 19- 1866 January 8. CR 1234 1. Church History Library. 8 May 2019. https://catalog.churchofjesuschrist.org/assets?id=867b28d5-f5ea-44bb-b228-516179bc010a&crate=0&index=0

Brigham Young Office. "Joseph A. Young, 1864-1865." Brigham Young office files 1832-1878 (bulk 1844-1877); General Correspondence, Incoming, 1840-1877; Letters from Young Family Members, 1841-1877; Sons of Brigham Young, 1855-1877. CR 1234 1. Church History Library. 28 February 2019. https://catalog.churchofjesuschrist.org/record?id=02
    e985d2-0e16-45c3-8891-986d21e20b37&compId=0c9ed17b-ec6e-4b85-ab79-8ad6a616
    d523&view=browse&subView=arrangement

Brigham Young Office. "W.S. Willes letter." Brigham Young office files 1832-1878 (bulk 1844-1877); General Correspondence, Incoming, 1840-1877; General Letters, 1840-1877; Wh-Z, 1865. CR 1234 1. Church History Library. 28 February 2019. https://catalog.churchof

jesuschrist.org/assets?id=29e35922-c0a5-424c-b91a-0147d0ebd5a5&crate=0&index=0

Brigham Young Office. "Outgoing, 1840-1876; 1864." Brigham Young office files 1832-1878 (bulk 1844-1877); General Correspondence, Outgoing, 1840-1876; 1864. Church History Library. 28 February 2019. https://catalog.churchofjesuschrist.org/assets/f7501284-69cd-4218-a68f-e6eea1e0fad0/0/1.

Brigham Young Office. "Y, 1864." Brigham Young office files 1832-1878 (bulk 1844-1877); General Letters, 1840-1877. CR 1234 1. Church History Library. 19 January 2019. https://catalog.churchofjesuschrist.org/record?id=02e985d2-0e16-45c3-8891-986d21e
20b37&compId=a5df0065-8d79-4d42-899b-255fe56d551b&view=browse&subView=
arrangement

Brigham Young Office. "Telegrams, 1861-1877." Brigham Young office files 1832-1878 (bulk 1844-1877). CR 1234 1. Church History Library. 17 June 2019. https://catalog.churchof
jesuschrist.org/record?id=02e985d2-0e16-45c3-8891-986d21e20b37&compId=bc76767c
-887b-4de0-a334-
ef072b58dfcd&view=browse&subView=arrangement

Cederstrom, Magnus. "Diary of Magnus Cederstrom." USU_LIAHA MSS Box 2 Folder 7. Utah State University Special Collections and Archives. Transcribed excerpts can be found on the Saints by Sea website. 1 June 2014. https://saintsbysea.lib.byu.edu/mii/account/205

Chipman, William H. "William H. Chipman notebook." MS 915. Church History Library. 2 September 2019. https://catalog.churchofjesuschrist.org/assets?id=b68b6c17-a476-4c93-8191-d7bdd46e6fda&crate=0&index=0

*Circular. To Bishop Edward Hunter, and the Bishops throughout the territory.* Salt Lake City: 1861. 15 September 2012. http://archive.org/details/circulartobishop00unse

Clark, Caroline Hopkins. "Diary." MS 8306, Reel 1, Item 10. Church History Library.

Dowdle, John C. "John C. Dowdle autobiography and diaries, circa 1884-November 1896." MS 1814. Church History Library. 17 June 2019. https://catalog.churchofjesuschrist.org/assets?id=13476b1c-83b1-4ca7-bba6-a05a10e9a1f2&crate=1&index=119

European Mission emigration records, 1849-1925. "1863-1868," page 210. CR 271 25. Church History Library. 12 August 2012. https://catalog.churchofjesuschrist.org/assets?id=d8a1a2f8-623e-4857-ae6b-5c2f67e4d6d9&crate=0&index=208

Scandinavia, Mission Emigration Records, 1852-1920. FHL INTL Film [472897].

Flygare, Nils. Nils C. Flygare Papers. MSS 1496, Box 1, Folder 3. L. Tom Perry Special Collections. Harold B. Lee Library.

Gilcrest, Frank M. "Frank M. Gilcrest autobiography, 1908." MS 22344. Church History Library.

Grant, William. "William Grant autobiography and diary, 1882 May-1911 September." MS 1956, Church History Library.

Gruber, Robert, Maizie Johnson, Willna Uebrick-Pacheli, Evelyn Wade, Linda Wehrmann, compilers. "Preliminary Inventory of the Records of United States Army Continental Commands, 1821-1920." Fort Kearney, Special Orders, 07/00/1865-01/00/1870, 2 volumes, arranged by year and thereafter numerically. National Archives. Washington, D.C.

Hansen, Caroline Pederson. "Caroline Hansen autobiography, 1931," in Andrew J. and Caroline P. Hansen papers, 1883-1932. MS 4746. Church History Library. 14 December 2018. https://catalog.churchofjesuschrist.org/assets?id=66995651-e5fb-4cde-baec-afdd3f3c075f&crate=3&index=0

"Heber Robert McBride's Letter to His Daughter, Elizabeth Jane McBride Ririe, Written from Welling, Alberta, Canada in 1823." Transcribed. 2 March 2019. https://www.familysearch.org/photos/artifacts/45194856?p=20617858&returnLabel=Heber%20Robert%20McBride%20(KWCJ-W21)&returnUrl=https%3A%2F%2Fwww.familysearch.org%2Ftree%2Fperson%2Fmemories%2FKWCJ-W21

Hinkley, Arza Erastus. "Diary of Arza Erastus Hinckley." Transcribed by Vida Adams and Blondel C. Porter. 6 October 2015. http://www.kendallglad.com/KendallGlad/Genealogy/Arza/Arza%20Erastus%20Hinckley%20-%20LDS%20historians%20library%20file%20-%20%20titled%20DIARY%20OF%20ARZA%20ERASTUS%20HINCKLEY.pdf

"History of Caroline Martine Anderson, first wife of Charles Keilgaard Hansen, Circa 1917." Letters translated by Edith Melgard Cox. MS 8889. Church History Library.

Jenkins, John. "Autobiographical sketch, 1933." Transcription of pages 3-5 are available on the *Pioneer Database: 1847-1868*. 20 January 2012. https://history.churchofjesuschrist.org/overlandtravel/sources/15092015018899398157-eng/jenkins-john-autobiographical-sketch-1933-3-5?firstName=John&surname=Jenkins

Jenson, Olof. "Olof Jenson family papers, 1960." MS 11373. Church

History Library.

Joseph W. Young papers, 1849-1872. Certificates of appointment, 1849-1864. MS 1529. Church History Library. 28 February 2019. https://catalog.churchofjesuschrist.org/assets?id=dec9 a4b8-0002-4d1a-a5bd-c65b47909c87&crate=0&index=0

Joseph W. Young papers, 1849-1872. Letterpress copy book, 1864-1868. MS 1529. Church History Library. 28 February 2019. https://catalog.lds.org/assets?id=a9546a30-6ad6-48c3-82d3-208af6898102&crate=0&index=37

*Laws and Joint Resolutions and Memorials, Passed at the Ninth Session of the Legislative Assembly of the Territory of Nebraska.* Omaha: 1864. 267. 29 September 2018. https://babel.hathitrust.org/cgi/pt?id=ucl.a0005193388;view=1up;seq=275

"Letter of S. F. Nuckolls." *Transactions and Reports, Nebraska State Historical Society* (1885): 32-37.

Lunn, John. Papers, 1866. "Circular and passenger contract." MS 9281 2. Church History Library. 17 June 2019. https://catalog.churchofjesuschrist.org/assets?id=1d220557-2f72-41d6-9e22-85fe5d4eb475&crate=2&index=0

Manuscript histories of Church in United States, circa 1910-1971. Manuscript history of Call's Landing, Nevada, 1860-1870. Church History Library. 5 January 2019. https://catalog.churchofjesuschrist.org/assets?id=eb55a779-9da5-4aae-abc6-89b9d1aed1d4&crate=0&index=6.

Marriott, Ann Gregory. "Ann G. Marriott diary, 1866 April-September." Transcribed by Lorna M. Shaw. MS 17064. Church History Library.

Murdock, Gideon Allen. "Gideon A. Murdock autobiography and

journal, 1872-1923." MS 1773. Church History Library. 17 June 2019. https://catalog.churchofjesuschrist.org/
assets?id=7ecbfe08-9189-4267-917e-b99444031b64&crate=0&index=0

Nielson, Andrew Christian. "Andrew Christian Nielson autobiography, circa 1890." MS 2735 282. Church History Library.

"Numerical Index of Deeds for Otoe County, Wyoming, Nebraska Territory, 1855." Otoe County Courthouse, Division of Deeds. Nebraska City, Nebraska.

"Otoe County Commissioner Record," Book 1. Otoe County Courthouse. Nebraska City, Nebraska.

"Otoe County Commissioner Record," Book 3. Otoe County Courthouse. Nebraska City, Nebraska.

Perpetual Emigrating Fund Company church trains accounts, 1861-1868. Captains' accounts, 1862-1868; Captain William B. Preston Company (first ox train), manifests, 1864. MS 376 8. Church History Library. 12 June 2019. https://catalog.churchofjesus
christ.org/assets?id=3aaa647b-078a-4b73-b81a-9a8c39bfa2e3&crate=0&index=0

Perpetual Emigrating Fund Company church trains accounts, 1861-1868. Freight manifests, 1861-1868; Freight manifests, 1864, 1868. MS 376 8. Church History Library. 12 June 2019. https://catalog.churchofjesuschrist.org/assets?id=e416c8bd-c905-4565-b6aa-68c1455ed987&crate=0&index=0

Perpetual Emigrating Fund Company church trains accounts, 1861-1868. Captains' accounts, 1862-1868; Captain William B. Preston Company (first ox train), manifests, 1864. MS 376 8. Church History Library. 12 June 2019. https://catalog.churchofjesuschrist.org/

record?id=5a2d8961-723e-4a15-8d35-0c296210f3f9&compId=c07cbecf-285c-4d68-83cc-bb362352ad15&view=browse&subView=arrangement

Perpetual Emigrating Fund Company church trains accounts, 1861-1868. Freight manifests, 1864, 1868. MS 376 8. Church History Library. 12 June 2019. https://catalog.churchofjesuschrist.org/assets?id=e416c8bd-c905-4565-b6aa-68c1455ed987&crate=0&index=0

Perpetual Emigrating Fund Company church trains accounts, 1861-1868. Wards' accounts, 1861-1868. MS 376 8. Church History Library. 12 June 2019. https://catalog.churchofjesuschrist.org/record?id=5a2d8961-723e-4a15-8d35-0c296210f3f9&compId=57ad377b-ad9c-460f-baa1-3a294e78b15b&view=browse&subView=arrangement

Perpetual Emigrating Fund Company (1849-1887). Perpetual Emigrating Fund Company outfitting reports, 1866. MS 376 13. Church History Library. 15 April 2015. https://catalog.lds.org/record?id=d7efb3d2-2aef-4f8a-8cac-c5515a601dc5&view=browse&subView=arrangement

Pickett, J. W. "Autobiography of J. W. Pickett" in Joel E. Ricks Cache Valley history collection, 1847-1955. MSS 46, Box 3, Folder 87. Utah State University Special Collections and Archives.

*Resolutions, Acts and Memorials Passed at the Fifth Annual Session of the Legislative Assembly of the Territory of Utah, convened at Fillmore City, Dec. 11, 1855.* Salt Lake City: 1855, reprinted in 1920. 39-41.

Returns from U.S. Military Posts, 1800-1916. National Archives

Microfilm Publications, Microfilm group 617, Roll 565. National Archives. Washington, D.C.

Richardson, Agnes Clementina Hefferan. "Hefferan story, undated." MS 5815. Church History Library. Transcription of pages 12-15 available on the *Pioneer Database: 1847-1868*. 26 February 2019. https://history.churchofjesuschrist.org/overlandtravel/sources/13854974450296125896-eng/richardson-agnes-clementina-hefferan-hefferan-story-12-15?firstName=William&surname=Hefferan

Smith, Jesse N. "Jesse N. Smith autobiography and journal, 1855 Oct-June 1906." MS 1489. Church History Library. 11 February 2019. https://catalog.churchofjesuschrist.org/assets?id=c79a1a09-80ff-4509-9cbe-fd810a7d5fea&crate=0&index=0

Thatcher, Moses. "Thatcher, Moses, vol. 1, British Isles." Vault MSS 248. L. Tom Perry Special Collections. Harold B. Lee Library. Brigham Young University. 23 March 2013. https://contentdm.lib.byu.edu/digital/collection/MMD/id/62346/rec/5

Wagstaff, Mary Crystal. "Mary C. Wagstaff autobiographical sketch, circa 1916-1918." MS 24103. Church History Library.

Wixom, Justin Chauncey. "Justin C. Wixom diaries, 1863-1879." MS 27293 (Formerly MS 1559 3-4). Church History Library. 28 February 2019. https://catalog.churchofjesuschrist.org/record?id=a30a2e10-bebd-458c-b112-085f1cbf80d9&view=browse&sub View=arrangement

Young, Brigham. "Letter to Bishop David Evans." MS 3564 1. Church History Library.

**Newspapers and Periodicals**

"150th Anniversary of Mountain Meadows Massacre." *Church Newsroom*, September 11, 2007. 19 April 2015. https://newsroom.churchofjesuschrist.org/article/150th-anniversary-of-mountain-meadows-massacre

"Advantages of Settling in Utah." *The Latter-day Saints' Millennial Star* 28, April 14, 1866.

"A Good Man Gone—A Deserving Family Destitute." *Semi-Weekly Telegraph*, November 2, 1865. Transcript available on the *Pioneer Database*. 2 March 2019. https://history.churchofjesuschrist.org/overlandtravel/sources/9361

"Arrival of Merchandise." *The Deseret* News, September 7, 1864. 12 January 2019. https://newspapers.lib.utah.edu/details?id=2596173

"Arrivals." *Salt Lake Daily Telegraph*, October 6, 1864. Transcript available on the *Pioneer Database*. 12 January 2019. https://history.churchofjesuschrist.org/overlandtravel/sources/9687

"A Strait Road." *Peoples Press*, March 30, 1860, 2.

"Awful Colliery Accident in Wales." *Deseret News*, August 7, 1852. 16 January 2019. https://newspapers.lib.utah.edu/details?id=2578725&q

"Correspondence." Letter from John G. Holman to Brigham Young. *The Deseret News*, August 2, 1865. 22 February 2019. https://newspapers.lib.utah.edu/details?id=2598282

"Correspondence: America." Letter from William H. Shearman, C. B. Taylor, and W. S. S. Willes to President Young and Wells. *The Latter-day Saints' Millennial Star* 25, June 24, 1865. 21 February 2019. https://contentdm.lib.byu.edu/digital/collection/MStar/id/8294/rec/28

Davis, Albert Wesley. "Adventures on the Plains." *Juvenile Instructor*, 15 December 1881.

"General Notices: Hooper & Eldredge." *Deseret News*, August 31, 1864. 3 February 2019. https://newspapers.lib.utah.edu/details?id=2596095

"Ghost Towns Remain." Undated clipping from unidentified newspaper in the private possession of Erick Wadsworth.

"Got Back." *Deseret News*, October 10, 1866. 21 June 2019. https://newspapers.lib.utah.edu/details?id=2598925

"Help to the Immigration." *Semi-Weekly Telegraph*, 2 Nov. 1865. 071.9225 S471t v. 1-6 1864-1870. Church History Library. A transcription is available on the *Pioneer Database*. 17 January 2019. https://history.churchofjesuschrist.org/overlandtravel/sources/9760/help-to-the-emigration-semi-weekly-telegraph-2-nov-1865-3

Hendee, David. "Plum Creek: A massacre that started a war." *Omaha World-Herald*, 10 August 2014. 8 January 2019. https://www.omaha.com/news/nebraska/plum-creek-a-massacre-that-started-a-war/article_e5afe5bd-08c2-5465-80a8-8c4947af43d3.html

Hendee, David. "Survivors account of massacre recalls the attack and her capture." *Omaha World-Herald*, 10 August 2014. 5 August 2018. https://www.omaha.com/news/nebraska/survivor-s-account-of-massacre-recalls-the-attack-and-her/article_cc1579cd-e6f4-5159-a8ef-ab26c8c0078a.html

"The Immigration." *Deseret News*, November 2, 1865. 27 February 2019. https://newspapers.lib.utah.edu/details?id=2730797

"Immigration In." *Deseret News*, 23 November 23, 1865, 52. 22 February 2019. https://newspapers.lib.utah.edu/details?id=2730941

"Mormon Historian Visits Old Wyoming Landing Site." *The Nebraska Daily News-Press*, July 20, 1934.

"Mr. Major's Business at Nebraska City." *Nebraska City News*, 24 November 1860.

"Nebraska City Board of Trade. Fifth Annual Report: Business for 1865." *The Nebraska City News*, March 31, 1866.

Nicholson, John. "Saved by Providence." *Juvenile Instructor*, 15 January 1881.

"Our Pioneers." *The Vernal Express*, June 9, 1932. 25 February 2019. https://newspapers.lib.utah.edu/details?id=21417557

Pratt, Orson. "Universality of Latter-Day Wars." *The Latter-day Saints' Millennial Star* 28, August 11, 1866. 12 September 2012. https://contentdm.lib.byu.edu/digital/collection/MStar/id/11897

Pratt, Orson. "War." *The Latter-day Saints' Millennial Star* 28, June 30, 1866. 3 September 2012. https://contentdm.lib.byu.edu/digital/collection/MStar/id/11821

"Recalls Old Wyoming Days," August 6, 1934. From unidentified newspaper in the Wyoming Vertical File, misc. holdings, ID# 57929, Genealogy Section. Morton James Public Library.

"Sheldon Reviews History of Kearney Cutoff Trail." *Republican Register*, September 6, 1929.

Sims, Elizabeth McDermott. "Elizabeth M. Sims autobiography, 1912." MS 3202. Church History Library. Transcribed excerpts of her autobiography can be found on the Saints by Sea website. 19 February 2019. https://saintsbysea.lib.byu.edu/mii/account/871

Swenson, John. "Letter from John Swenson to President Wells." *The Latter-Day Saints' Millennial Star*, 15 July 1865. 21 February 2019. https://catalog.churchofjesuschrist.
    org/assets?id=7ff244a2-bd40-4ad2-9af3-df0a126f1ec0&crate=0&index=11

Stannard, J. W. P. "The Journey Over the Plains." *Deseret News*, October 26, 1864. 18 January 2019. https://newspapers.lib.utah.edu/details?id=2598656

"Teams Returned." *Deseret News*, November 16, 1865. 22 February 2019. https://newspapers.
    lib.utah.edu/details?id=2730896

"The Nearest Point." *Peoples Press*, April 27, 1860.

"The Western Trade." *People's Press*, July 3, 1862.

*The Wyoming Post* Vol. 1, No. 1, April 3, 1858. Film, 071 W998p. Nebraska State Historical Society Library.

"Two Old Trees Only Signs of Early State Cemetery." Undated clipping from unidentified newspaper in the private possession of Erick Wadsworth.

[Untitled Article]. *York Nebraska News Times*, June 15, 1979.

## Memoirs/Biographies

"10 September 1846." Historical Department journal history of the Church, 1896-2001 July; 1840-1849; 1846 August-December. CR 100 137. Church History Library. 4 February 2019. https://catalog.

246 | *Bibliography*

churchofjesuschrist.org/assets?id=c8703fa3-c68c-495e-aadc-63c50f024f41&crate=0&index=175

"26 October 1864." Historical Department journal history of the Church, 1896-2001; 1860-1869; 1864 July-December. CR 100 137. Church History Library. 4 February 2019. https://catalog.lds.org/assets?id=72976e53-04a2-4a8e-985f-3149d21e3fd&crate=0&index=226.

"8 November 1865." Miner G. Atwood diary excerpts in Historical Department journal history of the Church, 1896-2001 July; 1840-1849; 1846 August-December. CR 100 137. Church History Library. 22 February 2019. https://catalog.churchofjesuschrist.org/assets?id=57a184a7-f690-4bf5-bba9-173e4439a1be&crate=0&index=327

Alston, Ray L., compiler. "Thomas Alston and Mary Ellen Holt Alston." M270.1 A464a 1975. Church History Library. Transcription of pages 16-19 available on the Pioneer Database. 27 February 2019. https://history.churchofjesuschrist.org/overlandtravel/sources/6215/alston-thomas-autobiography-in-ray-lester-alston-comp-thomas-alston-and-mary-ellen-holt-alston-1975-16-19

Anderson, Charles P. *Journal of Charles P. Anderson* (Cleveland: Gilbert Publishing Company, 1975). 15 August 2012. https://www.familysearch.org/library/books/records/item/178597-redirection

Anderson, Ron. "Immigration Summary of 1864." Copy in the private possession of Erick Wadsworth.

Ashby, Robert L. *Family History of Thomas Waters Cropper and Hannah Lucretia Rogers.* 1957.

Atwood, Minor G. "Excerpts from the journal of Miner G. Atwood, 1861-1865." April 12, 1865. MS 11938. Church History Library. Also found in South Africa Mission manuscript history and historical reports, 1853-1977; Volume 1, 1852-1866; Part 2, 1855-1866; April 12, 1865: 12-25. LR 8452 2. Church History Library. A transcription is available on the Saints by Sea website. 19 February 2019. https://saintsbysea.lib. byu.edu/mii/account/869

Aveson, Robert. "Leaving Home." 3 July 2015. http://www. sedgwickresearch.com/sedgwick/
  leavinghome.htm

Aveson, Robert. "Ox-Team Pioneer Recalls Joys of Long Trek." Transcription available on the *Pioneer Database: 1847-1868*. 20 January 2013. https://history.churchofjesuschrist.org/
  overlandtravel/sources/70799531152633631610-eng/aveson-robert-ox-team-pioneer-recalls-joys-of-long-trek-in-journal-history-of-the-church-of-jesus-christ-of-latter-day-saints-22-july-1922?
  firstName=Robert&surname=Aveson

"Biographical Events of Jens Christian Larsen Breinholt." FamilySearch.org. 12 February 2019. https://www.familysearch.org/photos/artifacts/4746001?p=13944870&returnLabel=Jens%20Christian%20Lauridsen%20Breinholt%20(KWZY-N4T)&returnUrl=https%3A%2
  F%2Fwww.familysearch.org%2Ftree%2Fperson%2Fmemories%2FKWZY-N4T

"A Biographical Sketch of the Life of The Patriarch John Smith." FamilySearch.org. 18 January 2019. https://www.familysearch.org/photos/artifacts/3001754?p=3069661&returnLabel=
  John%20Smith%20(KWJZ-
JXX)&returnUrl=https%3A%2F%2Fwww.familysearch.org
  %2Ftree%2Fperson%2Fmemories%2FKWJZ-JXX

Bowen, Joel Hinckley. *Arza Erastus Hinckley*. 24 December 2013. http://www.kendallglad.com/
  KendallGlad/Genealogy/Arza/Arza%20Erastus%20Hinckley%20-

%201826%20-%201901%20by%20Joel%20Hinckley%20Bowen%20[Grandson].pdf

Bowen, Joel Hinckley. "Pioneer Rescues of Arza Erastus Hinckley." 20 June 2019. http://www.kendallglad.com/KendallGlad/Genealogy/Arza/Arza%20Erastus%20Hinckley%20-%20Pioneer%20Rescues%20-%20by%20Joel%20Hinckley%20Bowen.pdf

"Brigham Young Vanguard Company (1847)." *Pioneer Database: 1848-1868*. 21 June 2019. https://history.churchofjesuschrist.org/overlandtravel/companies/1/brigham-young-vanguard-company

Carter, Kate B. "Reminiscences of Mary Roberts Roskelley." *Our Pioneer Heritage*. 20 volumes. Salt Lake City: Daughters of Utah Pioneers, 1969. Transcription available on the Saints by Sea website. 26 November 2018. https://saintsbysea.lib.byu.edu/mii/account/458?keywords=General+McClellan+1864&sweden=on&scandinavia=on&mii=on&netherlands=on&europe=on

Davis, Albert Wesley. "Albert Wesley Davis." *Utah Genealogical and Historical Magazine* 27, no. 4 (October 1926): 241-246.

Denney, Charles. "Charles Denney reminiscences and diary." MS 1820. Church History Library.

*Emigration from the Scandinavian* Mission. Extracted and translated by Aurelia Clemons. 948 W2ca, V. 1. Family History Library.

"Full Company List." *Pioneer Database: 1848-1868*. 23 March 2013. https://history.churchof
jesuschrist.org/overlandtravel/companies

Fredrickson, Lars. "Biographical sketch of the Fredrickson family," in Mormon biographical sketches collection, ca. 1900-1975. MS 2050. Church History Library.

"Hamilton County." Compiled by the Hamilton County Historical Society. 1936. Plainsman Museum. Aurora, Nebraska.

Hansen, H. N. "An Account of a Mormon Family's conversion to the religion of the Latter Day Saints and of their trip from Denmark to Utah." Part I. The Annals of Iowa 41 (Summer 1971): 709-728. 20 October 2018. https://ir.uiowa.edu/cgi/viewcontent.cgi?article=11120 &context=annals-of-iowa

Hansen, H. N. "An Account of a Mormon Family's conversion to the religion of the Latter Day Saints and of their trip from Denmark to Utah." Part II. The Annals of Iowa 41 (Fall 1971): 765-799. 20 October 2018. https://ir.uiowa.edu/cgi/viewcontent.cgi?article=11123 &context=annals-of-iowa

Hinckley, Michael. Transcriber. "Biography of Arza Erastus Hinckley." 5 October 2015. https://familysearch.org/patron/v2/TH-301-45405-135-69/dist.pdf?ctx=ArtCtxPublic

Holmes, Kenneth L. Editor. *Covered Wagon Women: Diaries & Letters from the Western Trails, 1840-1890* Vol. 9, 1864-1868.

Jensen, Rub Snow. "Biography of Warren Snow (1818-1896)." *Bound to My Heart* a blog by "RT and M." http://margletan-familyhistory.blogspot.com/2014/01/biography-of-warren-stone-snow-1818-1896.html. A pdf copy of this source can be found on Familysearch.org. 8 February 2019. https://www.familysearch.org/photos/artifacts/3352 0747?p=24449091&returnLabel=Warren%20Stone%20S-now%20(KWJW-7BS)&return Url=https%3A%2F%2Fwww.familysearch.org%2Ftree%2Fperson%2Fmemories%2FKWJW-7BS

"Liverpool to New York, 10 May 1865-19 June 1865." Ship's passenger manifest. *Saints by Sea: Latter-Day Immigration to America*. 22 February 2019. https://saintsbysea.lib.byu.edu/

mii/voyage/112

Jenson, Andrew. "Niels Rasmussen." *Latter-day Saint Biographical Encyclopedia, Volume 1*. Salt Lake City: Andrew Jenson History Company and the Deseret News Company, 1901.

Jenson, Andrew. "Willes, William Sindey Smith." *Latter-day Saint Biographical Encyclopedia, Volume 3*. Salt Lake City: Andrew Jenson History Company and the Deseret News Company, 1901.

Jessop, Danny and Marla W. Jessop, compilers. "History of Annie Maria Kershaw Thompson." *Joseph Frederick Thompson Ancestry*. 1996. Transcription available on Pioneer Database: 1848-1868. 2 March 2019. https://history.churchofjesuschrist.org/overland travel/sources/11905/thompson-annie-maria-kershaw-history-of-annie-maria-kershaw-thompson-in-danny-jessop-and-marla-w-jessop-comps-joseph-frederick-thompson-ancestry-1996-38

Manuscript histories of Church in United States, circa 1910-1971; Manuscript history of Wyoming, Nebraska, 1860-1870. MS 4029. Church History Library. 23 February 2019. https://catalog.churchofjesuschrist.org/assets?id=1549d9e9-1442-46cd-b68f-65aa5e1e316b&crate=0&index=0

Manuscript histories of Church in United States, circa 1919-1971, Manuscript history of Wyoming, Nebraska, 1860-1870. MS 4029. Church History Library. 23 February 2019. https://catalog.lds.org/assets/1549d9e9-1442-46cd-b68f-65aa5e1e316b/0/0

McBride, Heber Robert. "Heber R. McBride autobiography." MS 810. Church History Library. 21 June 2019. https://catalog.churchofjesuschrist.org/assets?id=b544d863-2cef-4a7a-9bce-d6764369ea35&crate=0&index=0

"Miner G. Atwood Company (1865)." *Pioneer Database: 1847-1868*. 19

February 2019. https://history.lds.org/overlandtravel/companies/57/miner-g-atwood-company?lang=eng

Nielson, Peter A. "Autobiographical Sketch of Peter A. Nielson." The original source is housed at the Daughters of the Utah Pioneers Museum Library. Transcript found on the Saints by Sea website. 21 February 2019. https://saintsbysea.lib.byu.edu/mii/account/133?europe=on&sweden=on&keywords=1865&mii=on&scandinavia=on&netherlands=on.

Sandberg, Carma L. "Nellie Nash: (A pioneer Biography of Mrs. Ellen Elvira Parkinson Wife of William Chandler Parkinson)." M.A. thesis, Brigham Young University, 1959.

Savage, Charles Roscoe. "A Photographic Tour of nearly 9000 miles," *Philadelphia Photographer* 4 (1867): 288-289, 313-316. 973 S263p 1867?. Church History Library.

Turpin, Mabel and Leo Turpin. "The Emigration of Richard Litson." M273.41 T957e. Church History Library.

Welsh Coal Mines. Memorial page of colliery deaths from the year 1852, http://www.welshcoalmines.co.uk/fatalities/fatals.html. 16 January 2019.

"William S. S. Willes Company (1865)." *Pioneer Database: 1848-1868*. 2 March 2013. https://history.churchofjesuschrist.org/overlandtravel/companies/320/william-s-s-willes-company

**Books**

Arrington, Leonard J. *Brigham Young: American Moses*. Chicago: University of Illinois Press, 1985.

Arrington, Leonard J. *Great Basin Kingdom: An Economic History of the Latter-day Saints, 1830-1890*. Chicago: University of Illinois Press, 1958.

Arrington, Leonard J. and Davis Bitton. *Angels Without Halos.* Salt Lake City: Signature Books, 1981.

Arrington, Leonard J. and David Bitton. *The Mormon Experience: A History of the Latter-Day Saints.* Champaign: University of Illinois Press, 1992.

Bagley, Will. *South Pass: Gateway to a Continent.* Norman: University of Oklahoma Press, 2014.

Barney, Ronald O., editor. *The Mormon Vanguard Brigade of 1847, Norton Jacob's Record.* Logan: Utah State University Press, 2005.

Bashore, Melvin L. "1866 Death List." In private possession of the author.

Beddes, Susan Zollinger. *Life Histories of Some Ancestors of Bud David Zollinger.* West Point, Utah: privately printed, 1994.

Bergera, Gary James, editor. *The Autobiography of B. H. Roberts.* Salt Lake City: Signature Books, 1990.

Briggs, Asa. *The Age of Improvement, 1783-1867.* Great Britain: The Chaucer Press, 1978.

Brigham Young University, compiler. *Journal of Discourses Delivered by President Brigham Young, His Two Councilors, the Twelve Apostles. 26 Volumes, Vol. 1.* Salt Lake City, Utah, 1967.

Brigham Young University, compiler. *Journal of Discourses Delivered by President Brigham Young, His Two Councilors, the Twelve Apostles. 26 Volumes, Vol. 8.* Salt Lake City, Utah, 1967.

Brown, Archie Leon. *141 Years of Mormon Heritage: Rawsons, Browns, Angells-Pioneers.* Published privately: 1973.

Burton, Richard F. *The City of the Saints, and Across the Rocky Mountains to California.* New York: Harper & Brothers, Publishers, 1862.

Carter, Kate B. "They Came in 1866." *Our Pioneer Heritage* Vol. 10. Salt Lake City: Daughters of the Utah Pioneers, 1966.

Dale, Raymond E. *Otoe County Pioneers: A Biographical Dictionary.* Part III, D–F. Lincoln: 1961-1965.

Davidson, Karen Lynn, David J. Whittaker, Mark Ashurst-McGee, and Richard L. Jensen, editors. *The Joseph Smith Papers: Histories, Volume 1: Joseph Smith Histories, 1832-1844.* Salt Lake City: The Church Historian's Press, 2012.

Davidson, Karen Lynn, Richard L. Jensen, David J. Whittaker, editors. *The Joseph Smith Papers, Histories Volume 2: Assigned Histories, 1831-1847.* Salt Lake City: The Church Historian's Press, 2012.

*The Doctrine and Covenants of the Church of Jesus Christ of Latter-day Saints.* Salt Lake City: The Church of Jesus Christ of Latter-day Saints, 1981.

Green, Elvera Campbell. *Tartan, Sage and History: The Story of Robert William Rowe Campbell and Sarah Newton.* Salt Lake City: Robert Rowe Campbell Family Organization, 1981.

Hartley, William G., Glenn Rawson, Dennis Lyman, and Bryant Bush, editors. *History of the Saints.* American Fork: Covenant Communications, 2012.

Jackson, William Henry. *The Autobiography of William Henry Jackson.* New York: G.P. Putnam's Sons, 1940.

Jenson, Andrew. *Autobiography of Andrew Jenson.* Salt Lake City: Deseret News Press, 1938.

Jenson, Andrew. *History of the Scandinavian Mission*. Salt Lake City: Deseret News Press, 1927.

Jesse, Dean C., Ronald K. Esplin, and Richard Lyman Bushman, editors. *The Joseph Smith Papers: Revelations and Translations, Volume 1: Manuscript Revelation Books*. Salt Lake City: The Church Historian's Press, 2009.

Jesse, Dean C., Ronald K. Esplin, and Richard Lyman Bushman. *The Joseph Smith Papers: Journals, Volume 1: 1832-1839*. Salt Lake City: The Church Historian's Press, 2008.

Johnson, Don Carlos. *A Brief History of Springville, Utah*. Springville: William F. Gibson, 1900.

Kimball, Stanley B. *Heber C. Kimball, Mormon Patriarch and Pioneer*. Chicago: University of Illinois Press, 1981.

Landon, Michael N. and Brandon J. Metcalf. *The Remarkable Journey of the Mormon Battalion*. American Fork: Covenant Communications, Inc. 2012.

Lass, William E. *From the Missouri to the Great Salt Lake: An Account of Overland Freighting*. Lincoln: Nebraska State Historical Society, 1972.

Lever, W. H. *History of Sanpete and Emery Counties, Utah*. Salt Lake City: Tribune Job Printing Company, 1898.

Lukish, Jean A. *Secret Brother: The Story of Solon Borglum, "Sculptor of the Prairie"*. Grand Island/Palmer: Field Mouse Productions, 2015.

Majors, Alexander. *Seventy Years on the Frontier; Alexander Majors Memoirs of a Lifetime on the Border*. Chicago and New York: Rand, McNally & Company, 1893.

Mattes, Merrill J. *The Great Platte River Road: The Covered Wagon Mainline*

*Via Fort Kearny to Fort Laramie*. Lincoln: University of Nebraska Press, 1969.

Matteson, Edith and Jean Matteson. "Mormon Influence on Scandinavian Settlement in Nebraska." Originally published in *On Distant Shores: Proceedings of the Marcus Lee Hansen Immigration Conference, Aalborg, Denmark June 29-July 1, 1992* edited by Birgit Flemming Larsen, Henning Bender, and Karen Veinen. Aalborg: Danish Society, 1993. Transcription by Edith and Jean Matteson available on xmission.com. 5 April 2011. http://www.xmission.com/~nelsonb/nebraska.htm

Mapes, Charles Boyd. "The Nebraska City-Fort Kearny Cut-off as a Factor in the Early Development of Nebraska and the West." M.A. thesis. University of Nebraska, 1931

Millett, Allan R. and Peter Maslowski, editors. *For the Common Defense: A Military History of the United States of America*. New York: The Free Press, 1994.

Mulder, William. *The Mormon Migration from Scandinavia*. Minneapolis: University of Minnesota Press, 1957.

*Names of Persons and Sureties indebted to the Perpetual Emigrating Fund Company from 1850 to 1877 Inclusive*. Salt Lake City: Star Book and Job Printing, 1877.

Neff, Andrew Love. *History of Utah, 1847-1869*. Edited and annotated by Leland Hargrave Creer. Salt Lake City: The Deseret News Press, 1940.

Rawson, Glenn, Dennis Lyman, and Bryant Bush. Edited by William G. Hartley. *History of the Saints: The Great Mormon Exodus and the Establishment of Zion*. American Fork: Covenant Communications, 2012.

Roberts, B. H. *A Comprehensive History of the Church of Jesus Christ of Latter-day Saints, Volume 3*. Salt Lake City: Deseret Book, 1950.

Roberts, B. H. *A Comprehensive History of the Church of Jesus Christ of Latter-day Saints, Volume 5*. Salt Lake City: Deseret Book, 1950.

Rolfe, Deforest P. "Overland Freighting from Nebraska City." Proceedings and Collections of the Nebraska State Historical Society. Second Series. Volume 5. Lincoln: Jacob North & Co., Printers, 1902. 279-293.

Slaughter, William W. and Michael Landon. *Trail of Hope, The Story of the Mormon Trail*. Salt Lake City: Shadow Mountain, 1997.

Smith, Joseph. *History of the Church of Jesus Christ of Latter-day Saints, Volume 1*. Salt Lake City: The Deseret Book Company, 1973.

Smith, Joseph. *History of the Church of Jesus Christ of Latter-day Saints, Volume 3*. Salt Lake City: The Deseret Book Company, 1973.

Smith, Joseph. *History of the Church of Jesus Christ of Latter-day Saints, Volume 5*. Salt Lake City: The Deseret Book Company, 1973.

Smith, Joseph. *History of the Church of Jesus Christ of Latter-day Saints, Volume 6*. Salt Lake City: The Deseret Book Company, 1973.

Smith, Joseph Fielding. *Essentials in Church History*. Salt Lake City: Deseret News Press, 1922.

Smith, Lucy Mack. *The History of Joseph Smith by His Mother*. American Fork: Covenant Communications, Inc., 2000.

Sonne, Conway B. *Saints on the Seas: A Maritime History of Mormon Migration: 1830-1890*. Salt Lake City: University of Utah Press, 1983.

Tanner, J. M. *A Biographical Sketch of John Riggs Murdock*. Salt Lake City: The Deseret News, 1909.

Tindall, George Brown and David Emory Shi. *America: A Narrative History*. New York: W.W. Norton & Company, 1999.

Tullidge, Edward W. *History of Salt Lake City*. Salt Lake City: Star Printing Company, 1886.

Tullidge, Edward W. *Life of Brigham Young: Or, Utah and Her Founders*. New York: 1877.

Walker, Ronald W. Richard Turley, Jr., and Glen M. Leonard. *Massacre at Mountain Meadows*. New York: Oxford University Press, 2008.

Ward, Maurine Carr. *Winter Quarters: The 1846-1848 Life Writings of Mary Haskin Parker Richards*. Logan: Utah State University Press, 1996.

Warnick, Merrill Newell, complier. "Autobiography of Charles Peter Warnick" in *Warnick Family* History. Provo: J. Grant Stevenson, 1967. M270.1 W285w. Church History Library. Transcribed excerpts found on the Saints by Sea website. 5 October 2012. https://saintsbysea.lib.byu.edu/mii/account/207

Waterman, John H. *General History of Seward County, Nebraska*. Beaver Crossing: John H. Waterman, 1916.

## Articles

Arrington, Leonard J. "Religion and Economics in Mormon History." *BYU Studies* 3, no. 3/4 (1961): 1-14.

Bagley, Will and Rick Grunder. "I Could Hardly Hold the Pen." *Overland Journal* 27, no. 3 (Fall, 2009).

Bashore, Mel and H. Dennis Tolley. "Mortality on the Mormon Trail, 1847-1868." *BYU Studies* 53, no. 4 Article 9 (2014): 111-123.

Bennett, Richard E. "Finalizing Plans for the Trek West: Deliberations at Winter Quarters 1846-1847." *BYU Studies* 24, no. 3 Article 5 (1984): 301-320.

Bennett, Richard E. "Winter Quarters: Church Headquarters, 1846-1848." *Ensign*. September 1997.

Bitton, Davis. "The Waning of Mormon Kirtland." *BYU Studies* 12, no. 4 Article 9 (1972): 455-464.

Black, Susan Easton. "How Large was the Population of Nauvoo." *BYU Studies* 35, no. 2 Article 7 (1995): 91-94.

Brackenridge, R. Douglas. "'About the Worst Man in Utah': William R. Campbell and the Crusade Against Brigham H. Roberts, 1898-1900." *Journal of Mormon History* 39, no. 1 (Winter, 2013): 68-157.

Briggs, Robert H. "A Seething Cauldron of Controversy: The First Trial of John P. Lee, 1875." *Journal of Mormon History* 39, no. 1 (Winter 2013): 1-35.

Carter, John E. "The Platte River Road in 1866: Charles Savage's Visual Narrative." *Nebraska History Magazine* 89, no. 3 (Fall 2008): 132-141.

Carter, John E. "Photographing Across the Plains: Charles R. Savage in 1866." *Nebraska History Magazine* 71, no. 2 (Summer, 1990): 58-63.

Cook, Lyndon W. "William Law, Nauvoo Dissenter." *BYU Studies* 22, no. 1 Article 5 (1982): 47-72.

Corcoran, Brent D. "My Father's Business: Thomas Taylor and Mormon Frontier Economic Enterprise." *Dialogue: A Journal of Mormon Thought* 28, no. 1 (Spring, 1995): 105-141.

Cowherd, R.G. "The Politics of English Dissent, 1832-1848." *Church History* Vol. 23, No. 2 (June 1954).

Cowles, E. H. "Otoe County in Early Days." *Transactions and Reports, Nebraska State Historical* Society, Volume 1 (1885): 37-42.

Dale, Raymond E., editor. "Nebraska Census, 1856, Otoe County." *The Nebraska and Midwest Genealogical Record* 16, no. 3-4 (October 1938). Transcription available on NEGenWeb Project. http://www.usgennet.org/usa/ne/topic/resources/OLLibrary/Journals/NMGR/Vol16/nmgrp005.html#ca

Godfrey, Kenneth W. "The Road to Carthage Led West." *BYU Studies* 8, no. 2 (1968): 204-215.

Hartley, William G. "The Great Florence Fitout of 1861." *BYU Studies* 24, no. 3 (Summer 1984); 341-371.

Hartley, William G. "Down-and-Back Wagon Trains: Travelers on the Mormon Trail in 1861." *Overland Journal* 11, no. 4 (Winter 1993): 23-34.

Henderson, Paul and Helen Henderson. *Maps of Manifest Destiny.* Gering: Legacy of the Plains Museum, 2004.

Hulmston, John K. "Mormon Immigration in the 1860s: The Story of Church Trains." *Utah Historical Quarterly* 58, no. 1 (Winter, 1990): 32-48.

Jenson, Andrew. "Emigration from Wyoming." *Nebraska History Magazine* 27, no. 2 (April-June 1936).

Jensen, Richard L. "Perpetual Emigrating Fund Company." *Utah History Encyclopedia.* 6 May 2019. https://www.uen.org/utah_history_encyclopedia/p/PERPETUAL_EMIGRATING_FUND_COMPANY.shtml

Jones, Zachary R. "'War and Confusion in Babylon': Mormon Reaction to German Unification, 1864-80." *Journal of Mormon History* 37, no. 1 (Fall, 2011): 115-150.

Kimball, Stanley B. "Mormon Trail Network in Nebraska, 1846-1868: A New Look." *BYU Studies* 24, no. 3 (Summer 1984). 7 April 2013. https://byustudies.byu.edu/
    PDFLibrary/24.3KimballMormon-68c630a4-614b-46f9-a24e-af87bfeb236e.pdf

Kimball, Stanley B. "Sail and Rail Pioneers before 1869." *BYU Studies* 35, no. 2 Article 2 (1995): 6-42.

Larson, Gustave O. "The Story of the Perpetual Immigration Fund." *The Mississippi Valley Historical Review* 18, no. 2 (September 1931): 184-194.

Lass, William E. "Nebraska City's Steam Wagon." *Nebraska History* 79 (1998): 24-33.

LeBaron, Dale E. "Benjamin Franklin Johnson in Nauvoo: Friend, Confidant, and Defender of the Prophet." *BYU Studies* 37, no. 1 Article 13 (1992): 175-194.

Leonard, Glen M. "Seeking an Inheritance: Mormon Mobility, Urbanity, and Community." *The Journal of Mormon History* 40, no. 2 Article 1 (Spring 2014): 1-58.

"Life and Death on the Oregon Trail: Provisions for Birth and Letha Circumstances." *Oregon-California Trail Association*. 20 June 2019. https://www.octa-trails.org/articles/life-and-death-on-the-oregon-trail/

Lyon, Edger T. "Doctrinal Development of the Church during the Nauvoo Sojourn." *BYU Studies* 15, no. 4 Article 6 (1975): 435-446.

Lyon, Edger T. "Independence, Missouri, and the Mormons, 1827-1833." *BYU Studies* 13, no. 1 Article 4 (1972): 10-19.

Mulder, William. "Nauvoo Observed." *BYU Studies* 32, no. 1 (1992): 95-118.

Olson, James C., editor. "From Nebraska City to Montana, 1866: The Diary of Thomas Alfred Creigh." *Nebraska History* 29 (1948): 208-237.

Pound, Louise. "The Legend of Weeping Water." *Western Folklore* 6, no. 4 (October 1947): 305-316.

Quinn, Michael D. "The Mormon Succession Crisis of 1844." *BYU Studies* 16, no. 2 Article 2 (1976): 187-233.

Ray, Craig N. "Joseph Smith's History Confirmed." *FairMormon.org*. 27 December 2014. http://www.fairmormon.org/wp-content/uploads/2011/12/ray-joseph-smiths-history-confirmed.pdf

Reeve, Frank Driver. Editor. "London to Salt Lake City in 1867: The Diary of William Driver." *New Mexico Historical Review* 27, no. 2 (January 1942): 37-63. 16 February 2015. http://files.lib.byu.edu/mormonmigration/articles/LondonToSaltLakeCityIn1867.pdf

Reinwand, Louis. "Andrew Jenson, Latter-day Saint Historian." *BYU Studies* 14, no. 1 Article 4 (1974): 29-46.

Rowley, Dennis. "Nauvoo: A River Town." *BYU Studies* 18, no. 2 Article 12 (1978): 255-272.

Rushton, Patricia. "Cholera and Its Impact on Nineteenth-Century Mormon Migration." *BYU Studies* 44, no. 2 (2005): 123-144.

Smith, Craig S. "Wyoming, Nebraska Territory: Joseph W. Young and the Mormon Emigration of 1864." *BYU Studies* 39, no. 1 (2000): 30-51

Walker, Ronald W. "The Runaway Federal Officers." *Journal of Mormon History* 39, no. 4 (Fall, 2013): 1-43.

Williams, Helen Roberta. "Old Wyoming." *Nebraska History Magazine* 27, no. 2 (April-June 1936).

Woods, Fred E. "Two Side of a River: Mormon Transmigration through Quincy, Illinois, and Hannibal, Missouri." *Mormon Historical Studies* 2 (2001): 119-147.

**Miscellaneous**

Historical Marker: sponsored by the John Watts Berrett Family Genealogical Organization, October 1998, with the cooperation of the Jim and Harold Johnson families, property owners.

Interview with Jim Johnson, by Erick Wadsworth, 4 December 2012. Video image of interview held in 2012 in possession of the author.

Sperling's Best Places. "Climate in Otoe County Nebraska." 6 December 2013. http://www.bestplaces.net/climate/county/nebraska/otoe

"Population of Nebraska Incorporated Places, 1860 to 1920." *Nebraska Databook.* 24 December 2012. http://www.neded.org/files/research/stathand/bsect5a.htm

# INDEX

## A

Allen, James, 18
Alston, Ann, 103
Alston, Christopher, 80–81
Alston, Thomas, 112–13
*American Congress* (ship), 133, 136, 187
Andelin, Maria Lofdahl, 103
Andersen, Johan F., 174
Andersen, Katrine, 164
Andersen, Marie, 163
Anderson, Caroline Martine, 77–79
Anderson, Charles P., 127, 161
Anderson, Johanna Kristena Jensen, 157
Anderson, Kristine, 162
Arlekulen, Charlotta Christina Warnick, 164
Arnold, Orson, 111, 118
Atwood, Miner G., 101, 106–12, 113
Aveson, Robert, 155–56, 186–88

## B

Bagley, Will, 23
Barden, Jersha, 86
Barfoot, Joseph L., 115
Barrow and Co., 98
Bashore, Melvin L., 162
Battle Creek Massacre (1863), 129
Beckstead, Sidney, 70, 74
Beecher, Maureen, 21
*Belle Wood* (ship), 100, 101–2
*Belle Wood Gazette* (newspaper), 101–2
Bengtson/Ericksen, Charlotta, 164
Bennett, Richard, 21
Berbom, Anna Malena, 159
Biddleman, George, 42, 43
Birchfield, William, 41
births, during travel, 72, 80, 89, 113–14, 115, 136
Black, Samuel W., 53
Black Hawk War, 99, 125, 126, 160, 171
Bliss, Orley D., 83
Blue, Alfred, 56
Bolen, Katrine, 162
Book of Mormon, origins, 3–4
Boone, J. B., 43
Borglum, Jens Moller Haugaard, 76
Borglum, John Gutzon De Le Mothe, 76
Borglum, Solon De Le Mothe, 76
Bowen, Joel Hinckley, 176
Bradford, Allen A., 40, 189
Bradley, Betsey L., 160–61
Brannan, Samuel, 24
Breinholt, Jens Christian Lauersen, 97
*Bridgewater* (ship), 100, 103
Briggs, Thomas, 97–98
Brookfield, A. A., 43

Brown, Christn., 174
Brown, Joseph Renshaw, 56–59
Brown, Richard Daniels, Jr., 81
Brown, Sis, 174
*B. S. Kimball* (ship), 100, 102–3
Buchanan, James, 31
buffalo chips, 77, 80, 146, 152
Bugsley, Phillip, 124
Burnett, Ward B., 53

## C

California, 18–19, 24, 28
Call, Anson, 37
Canfield, Isaac A., 89–91
Cannon, George Q., 82, 117
Carlsen, Ole, 181
*Caroline* (ship), 133-134, 136
Carter, John, 143
cattle driving, 81–82, 105, 120–21
*Cavour* (ship), 134, 137–38, 157, 159
Cederstrom, Magnus, 159
Chase, John D., 66, 68–70
Chipman, William D., 118, 120, 122–23, 129–30, 144–45, 147, 150, 152, 154, 165, 171, 172
cholera epidemic, 127–28, 138, 154, 157–64
Christensen, Christian, 174
Christensen, Peter, 110
Christjanson, Christina, 160
Christoffersen, Niels, 97
Christofferson, Soren, 96–97

Church of Jesus Christ of Latter-day Saints
    Illinois evacuation, 16–18
    Illinois gathering, 10–13
    leadership crisis, 15–16

266 | Index

    Missouri gathering, 7–10
    Ohio gathering, 5–7
    organization, 4–5
    origins, 1–4
    Utah gathering. See Salt Lake Valley and Utah Territory

church trains. *See* down and back church trains
Clark, Caroline Hopkins, 132–33, 135, 145, 149–50
Clark, John B., 8
Clawson, Hiram B., 82, 96
Clayton, William, 23
coal mining, 85
Colorado River emigration, 36–37
*A Comprehensive History of the Church of Jesus Christ of Latter-day Saints* (Roberts), 185
Conner, Joseph, 129
Cooke, William F., 94
Cooke's Wagon Road, 18
Coombs, Fred, 89
Cordon, A., 124
*Cornelius Grinnell* (ship), 133
Corrill, John, 8
Council of Fifty, 21–22
Cowdery, Oliver, 4, 6
Cox, Frederick W., 115
Creigh, Thomas Alfred, 61–62
Cropper, Thomas Waters, 85–86
Crowther, Richard, 94
Cumming, Thomas, 31

D

Dallin, William, 97
Dangerfield, Daniel, 56
*David Hoadley* (ship), 100, 103
Davies, Anderson, 59

Davis, Albert Westley, 106–7, 108-111
Davis, Moses, 71-73
Davis, Phebe Ann Wooley, 71–73
Dawson, Editha Jane (Ross), 39
Dawson, Jacob, 39–44, 49
Dearborn, Henry C., 102–3

deaths
    from coal mining, 85
    during ocean crossings, 67, 100–1, 102, 136, 159
    during rail journeys, 159–60
    during riverboat journeys, 104
    statistics, 162
    during wagon train journeys, 70–74, 79, 83–84, 88, 89, 91, 92, 95–96, 107, 109–10, 115, 116–17, 145, 152–53, 161–64, 179
        in Winter Quarters, 20
        in Wyoming, NT, 106

Denney, Charles, 145–46, 152, 156
*Denver* (riverboat), 47, 63, 71, 104
*Deseret News* (newspaper), 76, 89, 92, 98, 111, 117–18, 167
disease. *See* sickness
Donalde, Levi M., 173
Douglas, Jos., 173
Dowdle, John Clark, 147, 148

down and back church trains
    1864 overview, 65–66
    1865 cessation of, 99
    1866 overview, 119–21
    deaths, 70–74, 79, 83–84, 91, 92, 95–96, 145, 152–53, 161–64, 179
    establishment of, 33–36
    food supplies, 35, 77, 81, 94–95, 121–25, 147, 150–51, 152, 171–73

268 | Index

    freight on, 70, 75–76, 82–83, 87, 89, 90, 92, 93–94, 96, 120–21, 147
    led by Canfield, 89–91
    led by Chipman, 120, 122–23, 129–30, 144–45, 149, 152, 154, 171, 172
    led by Haight, 120, 124, 147–48, 149, 155, 172, 173
    led by Holladay, 120, 123, 145–46, 148, 149, 152, 173
    led by Hyde, 91–93
    led by Lowry, 120, 125–26, 148, 151, 154, 157–58, 160–67, 171, 172, 175
    led by Murdock, 70–75
    led by Nebeker, 120, 124, 128–29, 146, 149, 157, 171–72
    led by Preston, 75–79
    led by Rawlins, 80–83, 120, 123, 146–47, 149, 157, 188
    led by Ricks, 120, 121, 128–29, 142–44, 153, 184
    led by Scott, 120, 125, 146–47, 153, 157, 172–73
    led by Snow, 91, 93–96
    led by Thompson, 120, 123, 146, 149
    led by Warren, 83–86
    led by White, 120, 121–22, 144, 149, 151
    relief and rescue trains, 111–12, 117–18, 152, 154, 165, 166, 170–76
    telegraph communication, 128, 147, 163–66
    *See also* independent wagon trains

Driver, William, 136, 138, 153

## E

*Echo* (ship), 67
Eldridge & Clawson (retail firm), 129
Ericksen/Bengtson, Charlotta, 164
Erickson, Andres, 110
Eskildsen, Cissel Nielson, 163

European pioneers

demographics, 138-139
funding for, 30, 77, 105, 177
ocean journeys, 67–68, 90, 100–4, 132–37
reasons for leaving homeland, 140–41
views of, 134–35, 138
*See also* down and back church trains

Eyre, Ann, 102
Eyring, Henry B., 32–33

## F

Farnsworth, Elizabeth, 174
Farnsworth, William, 174
Farnsworth, Wm. M, 174
Fenians, 138
Festesen, Catherine, 97
Fey, Anna Grosjohn, 44–45
Florence, Nebraska Territory, 35–36, 45, 46
Flygare, Nils, 78–79
Folsom, H. P., 187–88

food supplies
    in Salt Lake Valley, 24–25, 28
    on wagon train journeys, 35, 77, 81, 94–95, 111, 113, 114–15, 117–18, 121–25, 147, 150–51, 152, 171–73

Ford, Thomas, 14
Fort Kearny, 46, 47, 48, 51, 52, 53, 54, 55, 56, 59, 60, 62, 73, 74, 83, 88, 96, 107, 115, 116, 120, 129, 144, 146, 149, 155, 163, 184
Fort Laramie, 22, 62, 84, 91, 108–11, 128–130, 149, 150, 154, 164, 165
Fouse, John E., 55
Frandsen, Carl Ephraim, 163
Frandsen, Caroline, 163
Frandsen, Christine, 163

Frandsen, Karen, 163
Frandsen, Marie Josephine Nielson, 163
Frandsen, Niels, 163
Frandsen, Regina Bolette, 163
Fredrickson, Lars, 111

freighting
    on down and back trains, 70, 75–76, 82–83, 87, 89, 90, 92, 93–94, 96, 120–21, 147
        Nebraska City businesses, 51–53, 54–55, 59–64

freight wagon trains, 65–67, 88–89, 92, 96–98, 105
Fullmer, John S., 14

## G

Gass, Patrick, 38
*General McClellan* (ship), 67, 68, 85, 89
Gerber, John T., 92–93
Gilcrest, Frank, 74–75
Gilcrest, Mary Ann, 73–74
Gilcrest, Samuel, 73–74
gold rush, 18–19, 61-62
Grant, Jedidiah M., 180
Grant, William, 138, 141, 144, 150, 151, 156
[G.aon], John Brain, 179
Green, Thomas, 30
Greenhalgh, Mary Ann, 146
Grosjohn, Peter, 44
Grosjohn, Sarah, 44
Grundvig, Frants Christian, 109–10

## H

Hagell, John, 104
Haight, Horton D., 120, 124, 128, 147–48, 149, 155, 172, 173
Hammer, John, 112

Hammer, Joseph, 112
Hampton, B., 106
Hansen, Anders Marius Smith, 164
Hansen, Anna Christian, 159
Hansen, Birthe, 164
Hansen, Caroline Pederson, 133
Hansen, Charles Keilgaard, 77–79
Hansen, Christen, 159
Hansen, Doratha, 174
Hansen, Hans, 159
Hansen, Hans Daniel, 164
Hansen, Hans Niels, 89–91, 180–82
Hansen, Johanne, 174
Hansen, Mariane C., 174
Hansen, Marie, 163
Hansen, Marie C., 174
Hansen, Niels Anthon, 164
Hansen, Niels Peter William, 164
Hansen, Niels R., 174
Hansen, Nikoline C., 174
Hansen, Trine, 164
Harmon, Ansil Perce, 180
Harris, John, 56
Harrison, Eliza, 147
Hartley, William, 17
Harvey, Augustus, 53–54
Hathaway, Jane, 44
Hazell, William James, 102
health. *See* deaths; sickness
Hefferan, John Edwin, 102
Hefferan, William, 113–15
Henrickson, Anna, 160
Hill, William E., 59
Hinckley, Arza Erastus, 154, 155, 165, 166, 168–76
Hinckley, Ira, 168–70

*History of Joseph Smith* (Jenson), 185
*History of the Scandinavian Mission* (Jenson), 158
Holladay, John D., 120, 123, 128, 145–46, 148, 149, 152, 173
Holman, John G., 104, 112
Holmgren, Peter Oluf, 110–11
Hooper & Eldredge (retail firm), 70–71, 82-83, 89, 92, 98
Horne, Isabelle, 27
Horne, Thomas, 103
Hostmark, Frants and Jenssine, 109
*Hudson* (ship), 67
*Humboldt* (ship), 134, 137
Hunter, E., 179
Hunter, Edward, 46, 121–26
Hyde, Orson, 126
Hyde, William, 91–93

I

Illinois
   evacuation from, 16–19
   gathering in, 10–13

illness. *See* sickness

independent wagon trains
   1864 overview, 65–67
   deaths, 88, 89, 107, 109–10, 115, 116–17
   food supplies, 111, 113, 114–15, 117–18
   led by Atwood, 106–12, 113
   led by Chase, 68–70
   led by Smith, 86–89
   led by Walker, 106–7, 112–15
   led by Willes, 115–17, 118, 182, 183
   *See also* down and back church trains

Isaacson, Gustave, 174
Isaksen, Gustav, 174

**J**

Jackson, William Henry, 63–64, 165, 166–67
Jacobs, Norton, 25, 26
Jakobsen, Bodel, 163
James (apostle), 5
Jasperson, Hans, 85
Jenkins, John, 155
Jenkins, Thomas, 122
Jensen, Ane Mathilda, 174
Jensen, Catherine Margrethe, 174
Jensen, Chris. Julius, 174
Jensen, Elizabeth, 163
Jensen, Hans, 163
Jensen, Inger, 174
Jensen, Jensine, 174
Jensen, Johanne, 174
Jensen, Karen, 163
Jensen, Karen M., 174
Jensen, Lars/Jens Christian, 163
Jensen, Marie, 174
Jensen, Niels Peter, 174
Jensen, Peder, 97
Jensen, Thomas C., 174
Jensen, Thos. C., 174

Jenson, Andrew
    historical accounts, 157–58, 174, 187–86
    ocean and cross-country journey, 136–37, 138, 140, 147, 153, 155
        in Wyoming, NT, 46, 49–50

Jenson, Christian, 133

Jenson, Olof, 137, 138, 146
John (apostle), 5
*John Bright* (ship), 132–33, 134
Johnson, Andreas, 174
Johnson, Benjamin Franklin, 12
Johnson, John Peter Rasmus, 88
John the Baptist, 5
Jonasen, Andw., 174
Jones, Dan, 14
Jorgensen, Jorgen E., 164
justice system, 130

## K

Kane, Thomas L., 31–32
Kangaroo Courts, 130
Kay, John, 96
Keep, Sarah, 174
Keep, Sis, 174
Keeting, Sis, 174
*Kenilworth* (ship), 133, 134, 136, 138
Kerr, John Judge, 97, 105
Kershaw, George F. W., 101
Kimball, Heber C., 10, 19, 23, 27, 29, 45, 148
Kimball, Heber Parley, 180
Kimball & Lawrence (retail firm), 92, 97–98
Kirtland, Ohio, 5–7, 9, 11, 12, 16, 86, 148
Kling, Herman, 174

## L

Landon, Chas., 173
Lansaw, Emma M., 174
Larsen, Anna C., 174
Larsen, Dorathia, 174
Larsen, Maria, 174
Larsen/Nielson, Lauritz Alma, 164

Larson, Ane Marie, 162
Larson, Anna Christine, 159
Larson, Lars P., 162
Larsson, Lissa, 159
Larsson, Sjelan, 159
Law, William, 13–14
Lawrence, Henry, 98
Lee, John D., 32
Lett, Chas, 173
Litson, Richard, 144, 179
Lowry, Abner, 120, 125–26, 128, 148, 149, 154, 157–59, 160–67, 171, 172, 175
Lukesh, Jean A., 76
Lund, Niels L., 97
Lunn, John, 135–36
Lybbert, Anthonette Olsen, 111
Lyman, Amasa, 19

## M

Madsen, Haming, 174
Madsen, Karen Pedersen, 164
Madsen, Maria, 174
Madsen, Marie, 174
Majors, Alexander, 52–53, 54, 55
Markham, Stephen, 14
Marks, William, 13

marriage
    polygamy, 11–12, 13, 15, 77, 134, 185
    weddings, 92–93, 136–37

Marriott, Ann Gregory, 132–33, 135, 142–43, 150, 155
Martensen, Rasmus, 159
Matisen, Julian, 174
Maughen, Peter, 121

Maxon, John H., 40
McBride, Heber Robert, 182–84
McCann, D. J., 105
McCarthy, Emma, 44
McClellan, William E., 15, 147–48
*McClellan* (ship), 94
McDonald, Thomas E., 42
McFarland, John, 43
McLennan, William, 40
*Mexicana* (ship), 100–1
Mexican American War, 18
Mikkelsen, Christiane Margrethe, 76
Milden, K., 179
*Millennial Star* (newspaper), 134, 140, 167
Miller, Isaac, 43
Millspaw, Daniel, 55
Milspaugh, Daniel, 56
Missouri, 6, 7–9
Mitchell, John, 103
*Monarch of the Sea* (ship), 67, 81, 87, 90
Moore, Earl, 44
Mormon Battalion, 18–19, 25, 26, 70, 115, 169–70
Mormon-Carson Emigrant Trail, 18
Moroni (angel), 3, 4
Morrison, Frederick C., 59
mortality. *See* deaths
Mortensen, Johanne, 174
Morton, Nancy Jane Fletcher, 83–84
Mountain Meadows' Massacre (1857), 32–33
Murdock, Gideon, 81–82
Murdock, John R., 8, 70–75

## N

N., Nicholai, 174
Naisbitt, Catherine Hagell, 104, 116

Nash, Isaac, 69–70

Native Americans
    Battle Creek Massacre, 129
    blamed for Mountain Meadows' Massacre, 33
    nonviolent encounters with, 61, 129–30, 151–52, 155, 165
    threat of, 22, 74, 86
    violent encounters with, 83–84, 109–10, 150, 154–55, 164

Nauvoo, Illinois
    evacuation from, 15–18
    gathering in, 10–13

*Nauvoo Expositor* (newspaper), 13–14
Nebeker, Peter, 120, 124, 128–29, 146, 149, 157, 171–72

Nebraska City, NT
    economic concerns, 51–52
    as rival of Wyoming, NT, 40, 41, 49

Nebraska City Cut-off Trail
    creation of, 52–54
    freighting on, 54–55, 59–64
    road ranches, 55–56
    and steam wagon experiment, 56–59
    *See also* down and back church trains; independent wagon trains

Neeley, Ed, 44
Neilson, Sven, 110
Nelsen, Hannah, 174
Nicholson, John, 136
Nielsen, August, 163
Nielsen, Inger, 174
Nielsen, Marie C., 174

Nielsen, Nickoli, 174
Nielsen, Nikolai, 174
Nielsen, Severin, 174
Nielsen, Sven P., 174
Nielson, Andrew Christian, 67–68, 88, 148
Nielson, Ane Marie, 163
Nielson, Inger, 174
Nielson, John, 148, 161
Nielson, Karen Christine, 163
Nielson, Peter A., 102–3, 110
Nielson, Sven P., 174
Nielson/Larsen, Lauritz Alma, 164
Noon, Adolphus H., 112
Nuckolls, Stephen F., 40–41

O

ocean travel, 67–68, 78–79, 90, 100–3, 132–37, 158–59
Ohio, 4–6
Ohlson, Nils, 160
Olsen, Else Marie, 164
Olsen, Fred, 174
Olsen, Jens, 174
Osborn, David L., 59
outfitting stations, proposal for, 33–36. *See also* Wyoming, Nebraska Territory
Overton, Mr., 105
Oxbow Trail, 51, 52, 53, 54

P

Pardee, William E., 40
Patterson, A. P., 98
Peacock, Fillis, 174
Peacock, Martha, 174
Peacock, Sis, 174
Pederson, Erasmus, 159

Pederson, Lars, 105–6
Perpetual Emigration Fund (PEF), 29–30, 177
Peter (apostle), 5
Peteren, Ane Marie, 164
Peteren, Antomine, 174
Petersen, Christine M., 174
Petersen, Joseph C., 174
Petersen, Marie, 174
Petersen, Peter, 163
Petersen, Sine, 163
Peterson, Jen C., 110
Peterson, Parley Pratt, 163
photographic accounts, 143–44, 184–85
Pickett, John Warren, 129–30
Pixton, Robert, 112
Platte River, 23, 46, 47, 52, 116, 117, 130, 131, 133, 143, 146, 149-150, 153, 154, 164, 165, 172, 178, 182, 184
Plum Creek Massacre (8 August 1864), 83–84
Polk, James K., 27
polygamy, 11–12, 13, 77 *See also* Marriage
Pratt, Orson, 19, 23–24, 140
Pratt, Parley P., 27, 28
Preston, William B., 75–79
Pritchard, Hannah, 84–85

## Q

Quorum of the Twelve Apostles, 15–16, 22–23

## R

rail travel, 68, 137–38, 159–60
Raleigh, A. H., 123–24
ranches, 55–56
Rasmussen, Hans Peter, 163
Rasmussen, Johanne M., 174
Rasmussen, Karen Anderson, 162–63

Rasmussen, Maren Jorgensen, 163
Rasmussen, Niels, 161–62
Rasmussen, Rebekka, 163
Rassumussen, Johan M., 174
Rawlins, Joseph S., 81–83, 120, 123, 146–47, 149, 157, 188
Reed, John A., 57
Reed, Roland, 55
Reinwand, Louis, 186
relief and rescue trains, 111–12, 117–18, 152, 154, 165, 166, 170–76, 182–84
Relief Society, 20
Reorganized Church of Jesus Christ of Latter-day Saints (RLDS), 16, 181–82
Rich, Charles C., 124–25
Richards, Mary Haskin Parker, 21
Richards, Willard, 14, 19, 27
Ricks, Joel, 169
Ricks, Thomas, 120, 121, 128–29, 142–44, 151, 184
Rigdon, Sidney, 5, 6, 7, 15
Ringquist, Carl Peder, 160
riverboats, 11, 36–37, 39, 104, 127, 137–38
road ranches, 55–56
Robb, F. W., 44
Roberts, Brigham H., 144–45, 151–52, 154, 185
Rogers, A., 42–43
Rolfe, Deforest P., 60–61
Romney, Miles P., 108, 111
Roskelley, Mary Roberts, 68
Rover, Charles, 97
Ruopp, Anna Marie, 92–93
Russell, Majors and Waddell Freighting Company, 51–53, 54–55
Russell, William Hepburn, 52
Ryan, Matt, 63

## S

*St. Mark* (ship), 133

Salt Lake Valley and Utah Territory
    arrival of pioneers in, 155–56
    debates on migration to, 21–23
    early planting efforts, 24–25
    funding for migration to, 29–30
    growth of, 26–29
    traveling to. *See* down and back church trains; independent wagon trains; ocean travel
    vanguard wagon train, 23–25, 178–79

Sandersen, Johannes Alma, 164
Sanderson, Niels Jacob, 163
Savage, Charles, 143–44, 153–54, 184–85
Schettler, Peter, 49
Scott, Andrew, 120, 125, 146–47, 153, 157, 172–73
Second Great Awakening, 2
Sedgwick, Richard, 187
Sharp, Joseph, 89
Sharp and Spencer Freight Train, 88–89
Sharpe, Brigham, 173
Shearman, W. H., 102
Sheldon, A. E., 50

sickness
    cholera epidemic, 127–28, 138, 154, 157–66
    mountain fever, 24, 171
    during ocean travel, 67, 78–79, 158–59
    during wagon train journeys, 71–73, 88, 91, 96, 107, 109–10, 161–64
    *See also* deaths

Sims, Elizabeth McDermott, 100–1

Sims, George, 101, 104, 116–17
Sitton, Isaac, 94
Slade, Desla, 94–96
Smith, Emma, 14, 16, 70
Smith, George Albert, 19, 32
Smith, Hyrum, 13–15, 86
Smith, Jesse N., 96
Smith, John, 66, 86–89

Smith, Joseph
    angelic visions, 3–4
    establishment of church organization, 4–5
    imprisonment, 10, 14
    leadership in Illinois, 10–13
    leadership in Ohio, 5–7
    martyrdom, 13–15
    publications about, 185
    relationship with Murdock, 70
    religious upbringing, 1–3

Smith, Joseph, III, 16
Smith, Lucy Mack, 9
Smith, Silas E., 59
Snow, Erastus, 24
Snow, Warren S., 68, 91, 93–96
soldiers, 18–19, 69, 82, 107, 108–09, 150
Sorensen, Anna, 160
South African pioneers, 67, 100–1
South Pass, 23–24
Spencer, Claudius V., 98
Stannard, J. W. P., 86
steamboats, 11, 36–37, 39, 104, 127, 137–38
steam wagon experiment, 56–59
Stenhouse, T. B. H., 187–88
Stevens, Lawkin K., 179

Stone, John E., 174
Strang, James, 15
Street, Mr., 105
*Susan Pardew* (ship), 67
Swenson, John, 102, 110

**T**

Taylor, Charles B., 106, 112
Taylor, John, 14, 185
Taylor, Thomas, 99, 105, 111–12, 113, 115, 116, 117–18, 138, 171, 182
telegraph communication, 128, 147, 163–66
Thatcher, Moses, 128–29
Thompson, Anne C., 174
Thompson, Anne Maria Kershaw, 116
Thompson, Daniel, 120, 123, 128, 146, 149
Thompson, William J., 55
Thomsen, Anne Christensen, 174
Thomsen, Soren, 97
toll roads, 174–75

transportation methods
  freight wagon trains, 65–67, 88–89, 92, 96–98, 105
  ocean travel, 67–68, 78–79, 90, 100–3, 132–37, 158–59
  rail travel, 68, 137–38, 159–60
  riverboats, 11, 36–37, 39, 104, 127, 137–38
  steam wagon experiment, 56–59
  *See also* down and back church trains; independent wagon trains

Tullidge, Edward, 179

**U**

Underwood, William, 103
Utah Territory. *See* Salt Lake Valley and Utah Territory

Utah War (1857-1858), 31–32, 43, 51–52

## V

Voigt, H., 179

## W

Waddell, William Bradford, 52

wagon trains
    freight wagon trains, 65–67, 88–89, 92, 96–98, 105
    relief and rescue trains, 111–12, 117–18, 152, 154, 165, 166, 170–76, 182–84
    vanguard trek west, 23–24, 178–79
    *See also* down and back church trains; independent wagon trains

Wagstaff, Mary, 146
Walker, Henson, 106–7, 112–15, 117
Walker Brothers (retail firm), 92
Warneck, Johan Gustaf, 160
Warnick, Anders Gustaf, 163
Warnick, Anders Peter, 161
Warnick, Anna Helena, 159
Warnick, Charles P., 136-37, 140–41
Warren, William S., 83–86
Wasatch Mountains, 24
weddings, during travel, 92–93, 136–37
Wells, Daniel H., 37, 45, 170-71
Wells, N. P., 179
White, Hugh, 10
White, Samuel, 120, 121–22, 142, 144, 150, 151-52, 178
Whitmer, David, 4, 15, 185
Whitmer, Peter, Sr., 4
Wight, Lyman, 15
Willes, William S. S., 115–17, 118, 182

Winberg, Anders W., 108

Winter Quarters
    establishment of, 17, 19–20
    return trips to, 25–26

women's roles, 20–21
Wixsom, Justin, 146
W. Jennings (retail firm), 92
Woodruff, Wilford, 19
Wooley, John, 73
Woolley, Henry, 118
W. S. Godbe (retail firm), 92, 98, 105

Wyoming, Nebraska Territory
    arrival of pioneers in, 71–72, 76–77, 79, 97–98, 103–6
    cemetery in, 43–44
    establishment of, 39–41
    geography and climate, 38–39
    immigration administration in, 45, 47–50
    life in, 42–43, 44–45
    selected as outfitting station, 36, 45–47

*The Wyoming Post* (newspaper), 42–43
*The Wyoming Telescope* (newspaper), 42

## Y

Yard, Charles, 103

Young, Brigham
    on church train system, 120
    on Colorado River emigration, 37
    correspondence with Hinckley, 171–72
    correspondence with Joseph W. Young, 48–49, 87
    correspondence with Smith, 10

> correspondence with wagon train captains, 111–12, 116, 128, 163–66
>
> establishes Winter Quarters, 19–20
>
> freight sent to, 70, 75–76, 82, 97
>
> Hinckley as guard for, 170
>
> McClellan's suit against, 148
>
> and Mountain Meadows' Massacre, 32-33
>
> ordains John Smith, 87
>
> organization of Illinois evacuation, 16, 18–19
>
> organization of relief trains, 111, 154
>
> on PEF, 30
>
> preference for Salt Lake Valley over California, 24, 28
>
> proposal and plans for outfitting stations, 33–34, 45, 46
>
> in Quorum of the Twelve Apostles, 15–16
>
> relationship with government, 26–27, 31
>
> return trips to Winter Quarters, 25, 26
>
> revelation on western migration, 22–23
>
> support for Taylor, 137
>
> on vanguard trek, 23–24

Young, Joseph A., 45, 46–47

Young, Joseph W.
> as immigration agent, 45–49, 68–69, 86, 87
>
> ministers wedding, 93
>
> organization of freight, 94, 96
>
> overview of contributions, 179–80
>
> as wagon train captain, 34

Young, Lorenzo Dow, 179-80

## Z

Zollinger, Jacob, 142–43, 150-51

# ABOUT THE AUTHOR

Erick Wadsworth took his love of history to new heights when he wrote the history for the company that he worked for; *Franklin Building Supply: 40 Years and Counting*, was published in 2016. He enrolled at Brigham Young University (BYU) in 1969, taking a sabbatical until he reentered BYU's online program in 2004, graduating in 2010. He went on to earn his Masters of History at the University of Nebraska at Kearney (UNK). His thesis earned the "Outstanding Thesis Award" for 2013 – 2014 from the College of Natural and Social Sciences. While attending UNK, Erick was accepted into Phi Alpha Theta. He presented at three regional conferences and one national conference while attending UNK. Erick is retired from business, but stays busy by working at the Family History Center, researching American history, traveling, and spending time with his beautiful wife, 8 children and 26 grandchildren.

www.ingramcontent.com/pod-product-compliance
Lightning Source LLC
Chambersburg PA
CBHW030306080526
44584CB00012B/462